Sue

An excellent companion on the slopes

Valery

I was very fortunate that twelve years ago, during a career break, I had the opportunity to travel the world as a tour manager.

This career break became permanent and I abandoned the security of the legal profession for a more precarious but exciting career in travel. Legal textbooks were exchanged for travel guides and books on animals and flowers.

Ambition to visit every country in the world was soon replaced by a growing desire to return to my favourite destination, Madonna di Campiglio, in the Italian Dolomites. Each time I returned I learnt more about the place and the people.

Spirit of the Dolomites

Valery Collins

SPIRIT OF THE DOLOMITES

Vanguard Press

VANGUARD PAPERBACK

© Copyright 2008
Valery Collins

The right of Valery Collins to be identified as author of this work has been asserted by her in accordance with the Copyright, Designs and Patents Act 1988.

All Rights Reserved

No reproduction, copy or transmission of this publication may be made without written permission.
No paragraph of this publication may be reproduced, copied or transmitted save with the written permission of the publisher, or in accordance with the provisions of the Copyright Act 1956 (as amended).

Any person who commits any unauthorised act in relation to this publication may be liable to criminal prosecution and civil claims for damages.

A CIP catalogue record for this title is available from the British Library.

ISBN 978 184386 445 5

*Vanguard Press is an imprint of
Pegasus Elliot MacKenzie Publishers Ltd.*
www.pegasuspublishers.com

Photography by Valery Collins
Illustrations by Andrea Viviani

First Published in 2008

**Vanguard Press
Sheraton House Castle Park
Cambridge England**

Printed & Bound in Great Britain

Disclaimer

During the past twelve years as a tour leader I have shared many happy and funny memories with the lovely people I have met and reminiscences in this book are my version of events but I have changed the names to protect the 'innocent'.

Dedication

This book is dedicated to the many friends I have made in Madonna di Campiglio and in particular to the Lorenzetti family and all the staff, past and present at the Hotel Lorenzetti who have always extended such a warm welcome to me.

Acknowledgements

I would like to express my thanks to the Lorenzetti family, the staff of the Hotel Lorenzetti and my friends in the area who have embraced this project with enthusiasm, helped me with my research, the translation of documents and allowed me to use their names in the telling of my story.

I am most grateful to Simon Hedger for his advice and encouragement while I was working on this book.

Chapter One – A Year Out

"He is on his way," a disembodied voice rasped down the telephone.

"But you said that ten minutes ago," I whispered. I was terrified; it was all going so horribly wrong. Already the phone was silent and immune to interrogation. As I slowly replaced the receiver the room was suddenly awash with bright light. At last, it had arrived. Heaving a huge sigh of relief I left the house and raced down the driveway. There was indeed a car parked outside but a slowly flashing blue light suggested it was anything but a taxi. The driver was peering suspiciously at my new, rigid suitcase standing in solitary splendour on the pavement.

"Don't blow it up," I panted, a feeble attempt at a joke I knew but at three o'clock in the morning my brain was racing towards the next possible disaster on this black night. I was asked, very matter-of-factly, just why a suitcase had been apparently abandoned by the roadside, who I was, where did I live and why was I hanging around on a street corner in the early hours? Naturally I was able to answer all the questions but my agitated state and constant squinting at my watch did not help my cause. I explained that I was waiting for a taxi to pick me up and take me to the city centre bus station to catch a National Express Coach to the airport. Finally they believed me and with a warning never to leave my suitcase unattended again they drove off into the night. Immediately I cursed myself for not asking them for a lift! I really was getting desperate and did not dare go back into the house to call the taxi company yet again. I slumped down on my suitcase head in hands. It seemed my adventure was over before it had begun. Around me the leaves of my garden shrubbery waved gently in the breeze, reflecting the sulphur yellow of the street lights stretching towards the junction to my left. Occasionally there was a flash of white light as a car turned right from the main road just beyond but they never made the second turn into my street. My heart was pounding. Time was running out.

I was aroused from my stupor by the sound of an engine changing gear to turn into my road. Finally my taxi had arrived but by now we had only five minutes to get into the town centre, a journey that normally takes fifteen minutes. My suitcase loaded in the boot I leapt into the back of the car and told the taxi driver that he would have to move quickly if he wanted to avoid driving all the way to Leicester to connect with the coach there. I had done my homework on taxis that failed to turn up and discovered that there was actually a law that obliged a taxi that is late to take you to your destination should the delay cause one to miss some form of public transport.

We roared off down the road, my heart was in my mouth as we approached the first of many sets of traffic lights. If this one was green the rest should be green and we might just make it. It was green and we sailed through, the next one was amber but I yelled at the driver to keep going. Fortunately he did as he was told and we ran the gamut of lights successfully and the bus station soon loomed into sight. We were supposed to follow a circuitous one way system to get to the bays but I could see my bus and it was already pulling out so I told the taxi driver to enter by the exit knowing he was unlikely to meet any traffic at that hour and to stop in front of the departing coach. Amazingly, he did as I asked and even parked in the path of the departing vehicle. I suspected he was actually enjoying the 'chase' now.

Scrambling out of the taxi I ran to the coach and explained to the bemused driver and his assistant that I had a ticket for that bus and that my taxi had been late. They were very understanding and my suitcase was soon safely stowed below and we were on our way. Relieved I slumped down into the first empty seat I came to and stared out into the darkness. That was some close shave! If I had missed the bus, the only one that could get me to Gatwick in time for my flight then surely I would have lost the best job I had ever had.

Eight months of my one year career break had passed by already in a flurry of trips and adventures and this morning I was embarking on my first skiing trip as a tour leader. It was six years since I last skied and having spent the week skiing around muddy patches and down narrow strips of snow precariously passing skiers being dragged up the mountain on a lift, I had doubted I would ever ski again. Nevertheless I had agreed to do this trip, as ski lessons were included for everyone so it would be a chance to restore my confidence. Musing on this possibility I gazed out of the window watching the suburbs of Nottingham go by. As a true traveller I even enjoyed my bus journeys to the airport. It was not long before I drifted off to sleep and I never did get the cup of tea the cheery attendant had promised me after my scramble to catch the bus. I rectified this omission at Gatwick then refreshed and revived I donned my smart red blazer, pinned on my badge and made my way to the seating area in front of Dixons' where I was due to make contact with my fellow travellers.

Red blazers were very fashionable then, not only were they the uniform for a large company whose employees worked in the airport but I had seen several passengers around the departure lounge similarly attired including a lady seated at our meeting point. As I scanned the area for members of my group I saw a person approach her and then immediately back away with the temerity of someone who has just encountered a snarling dog. I suspected the lady concerned had already been approached by strangers enquiring if she was their tour leader. Hastily I made a detour to waylay the retreating passenger and check the label on her hand luggage. Yes, one of my group. I called out to her and introduced myself. Clearly she was relieved to see me and I was also glad to see her. This was one of the aspects of the job I had found most difficult when I started, meeting clients at the airport. I usually arrived at least two hours before necessary, spent more money than I had in the Duty Free shops and then went to the meeting place much earlier than indicated on our itinerary.

We were a large group, thirty of us in total, and I had been concerned about my ability to deal with so many people. Despite the assurances of my colleagues that all I had to do was get them to the resort then the hotel manager, who we will call Mario, would take over I had still been riddled with doubts. Fortunately I had been well primed by fellow tour leaders and was able to answer most of the questions that were fired at me on this my first acquaintance with the group. The first hurdle was remembering their names. It was relatively easy when they arrived one at a time and introductions were being made each time a new person joined us. I had tried various memory techniques including visualising something that would remind me of their name but this meant I stared at a face for so long trying to bring to mind a suitable object that the person under scrutiny must have thought I was very strange. I finally employed the technique of repeating the name over and over again in my mind while watching for newcomers. Of course when several people arrived together it descended to a name ticking exercise.

It was soon time to make our way to the Boarding Gate and I herded them all in the right direction confidently dealing with questions that were constantly being asked. I could describe the hotel and the ski area as though I had already spent several weeks there. But Mario, who would be organising the programme for us? Now that was another matter and even chatting to the people who were returning for a second visit had not enlightened me. I would just have to wait and see.

After the scramble to collect cases and boot bags at Verona airport we emerged into the arrivals area and I quickly spotted our bus driver holding our company sign aloft. Clearly he was used to our groups and although he did not speak any English he was soon leading us to the bus, bizarrely bronze in colour, and was expertly stacking cases, boot bags and skis in the cavernous storage area while we clambered aboard the scenic cruiser. Once everyone had settled down we departed and I decided to walk down the bus to check that everyone was comfortable. Bad decision. There are several sharp bends between the airport and the motorway and my composure was soon rattled by the need to grab hold of seat backs to avoid being pitched face first onto the floor of the aisle. Scuttling back to my seat at the front of the bus I opted for the safer but more formal technique of imparting information using the microphone. There was not much to say really, transfer of two hours, passports for hotel check in, ski hire and then the Information Meeting at which we would be presented with the programme for the week. I could then settle down to enjoy the scenery and the anticipation of three weeks skiing in the Dolomites.

My first day nerves evaporated as I gazed through the coach window. I had heard that the snow was good this year and was relishing the thought of swishing down the slopes again. I had just spotted the sign announcing we had entered the small mountain village that was our base for the week, when our driver executed a rather alarming two point turn, the end of the bus hanging over precipitous edge during this manoeuvre, and then began to reverse slowly up a narrow road. Craning my neck I could see above me a white building with *Albergo* emblazoned on the wall. We had arrived and I was about to meet the infamous Mario. One naturally conjured up an image in the mind about the appearance of such a well known personality and I expected to be greeted by a tall, dark, slim gentleman who spoke heavily accented English. As I descended from the bus I was surprised when I was welcomed by a stocky gentleman with a round rugged face, light coloured hair and intense pale eyes. I sensed that the group were immediately captivated by this alluring personality.

We were all greeted enthusiastically and, after sorting out our various pieces of luggage, we were shown to the reception area. This was at the top of two short flights of stairs and it took a while to get everyone and their bags up there. Meanwhile Mario had skipped up the stairs and started the check in process. Passports and lift pass photos were collected, keys were distributed and greetings exchanged with old friends. All I had to do was assist those struggling to get their cases up the stairs. At least there was a lift from the reception area to the rooms but as it could only take one person with one suitcase at a time it was a slow process.

Finally it was my turn and I was given my key and made my way to my first floor room at the back of the hotel. While waiting I had had time to appreciate the fabulous views from the front of the hotel over the town of Trento sprawling along the floor of the valley below us. Needless to say the window of my very small twin room looked out on a grassy bank and a stack of logs. The room was simple but homely, the bright orange and black bedspreads a startling splash of colour against the pale walls. A pine wardrobe, a desk and a nice picture on the wall completed the furnishings. Tipping the contents of my case onto one of the narrow single beds I quickly divested myself of my formal travelling clothes and dressed in ski gear ready to make the short walk to the ski hire shop in the centre of the village. We had been encouraged to get ready then make our way downstairs to meet Mario as soon as possible.

On my arrival downstairs Mario immediately set off down the road with the first group leaving me to round up the stragglers and follow his brief instructions concerning the whereabouts of the ski hire shop. I was slightly concerned that I might not be able to find it on my own but I need not have worried, the village had just one main street and the hire shop was so small people were queuing outside so I only had to follow the sound of chattering voices. As soon as I arrived Mario relinquished the list of ski and boot numbers that he had been filling in and was gone.

Once I had completed my list it was my turn to be fitted with skis. Since I last skied technology had moved on a lot and I was offered a pair of carving skis which just about made it to my chin. Used to having skis that continued at least six inches above the top of my head I was a bit suspicious that maybe these were the only skis left in the tiny shop. However, much gesturing on the part of the owner indicated that these skis were the best so I accepted them graciously. As I was gathering up skis, boots and poles in preparation for my walk back to the hotel, a bottle and three glasses were produced from under the counter and Mrs Ski Hire appeared from upstairs where she had been dispensing the boots. The bottle contained a clear liquid and it was proffered to me so that I could read the label. *Grappa*. I had no idea what it was so when a small measure was poured out and given to me I had a quick sniff. Wow! It smelt like something I would use to clean stubborn stains.

My new friends raised their glasses and, with a cheerful "*salute*", they downed the colourless liquid in one gulp. I was clearly expected to do the same. Smiling weakly I raised my glass, whispered "cheers" and poured it straight down my throat. There was a sudden searing but almost immediately after that a warm glow radiated through my entire body. A smile spread across my face. Elated by their success my companions produced a second bottle from below the counter. A whole plant floated in the pale yellow liquid contained in this bottle. Our glasses were re-charged and raised to a chorus of "*salute*" then emptied in one go. This flavour was slightly different but still accompanied by the same sensations as before although now my knees had started to feel decidedly wobbly. Time to go. I thanked my new friends who tried to persuade me to have another glass with them. I declined, fearful that I may not be able to stagger back up the hill to the hotel if I imbibed any more of this potent liquid. By the time I and my skis had made it back to the boot room the place was deserted and hastily dumping my skis I clambered up the stairs to reception to collect my key. Mario was there and I gave him the list and then escaped to my room. As I never normally drank spirits two small glasses of *grappa*, at 40 per cent proof, had had quite a dramatic effect. I was glad that I had at least an hour before we were all due to meet for our Welcome Drink.

Just before the appointed time I made my way downstairs. In the gloom of the half light I could see shapes slumped in the large comfy leather chairs. Occasionally a groan was heard as someone struggled to extricate themselves from the depths of the plump upholstery. An open wood fire flickered in the centre of the room enticing people to perch on the stone hearth or rock gently in the cane rocking chairs placed nearby. The huge television screen was blissfully grey and quiet in the corner and the only noise to be heard was the soft murmur of voices as the early arrivals got to know each other. I had just joined one of the groups gathered around a low coffee table when the lights went up and Mario appeared wheeling a trolley of drinks before him. He was followed by a very attractive, slim, dark girl who was introduced to us all. This was his wife, Lucia, who also spoke excellent English. Lucia was in charge of the kitchen and decided the menu each day. Sociable and good fun she mixed well with my groups.

We sipped our drinks and made polite conversation. As usual this first social gathering of a new group was subdued but I knew that by this time tomorrow they would be acting like old friends. Lucia, I noticed had slipped away almost immediately after the introductions had been made. She re-appeared to announce that dinner was ready and indicated that we should follow her. A very short distance beyond reception we were shown into the dining room a brightly lit large square room. Through the large picture windows along one side of the room we could see the twinkling lights of Trento far below us. Square wooden tables were surrounded by square wooden chairs and each one be-decked with red and white table cloths. At the far end, tables had been joined together to form three long rectangles. These were to be our tables for the week. We took our places and while waiting for our first course to arrive I continued my scrutiny of our surroundings.

Pictures marched in a row with military precision across one of the walls coming to an abrupt halt at the start of the closed room divider. Behind this was a second dining area the same size as the one in which we were now seated. Shelves, open units, glass fronted units and drawers lined the remaining walls housing glasses, cutlery and bottles of wine. Music blared out from the radio and noisy radiators belted out heat. All very simple and functional. Before our first course arrived, Flavia, the waitress appeared with the ubiquitous trolley which this time transported quarter litre carafes of red and white wine. Once we had all made our choice of wine we were invited to help ourselves to salad or soup from the buffet laid out on two tables at the other end of the room.

After much scraping of chairs and jostling for position around the tables we finally began to eat, ravenous after a long day travelling and surviving on airline food. The next course, copious amounts of pasta, was served at the table. Unsure whether or not this was the main course some of us went for second helpings and were then unable to finish the meat course which arrived soon after. A small dessert completed the meal after which we returned to the bar to be informed of the programme for the week.

On our return we found the television had been activated and was running a video showing the group that had been here the previous week. This video, accompanied by a droll commentary from Mario was hilarious and a good icebreaker. We watched the groups having ski lessons, Mario always seemed to be around when someone fell over. Interspersed with the skiing were glimpses of the afternoon activities. Snow shoe walking featured in one clip and showed a colleague of mine stumbling through the snow cursing as she tried to mobilise the tennis rackets attached to her feet to keep up with the group ahead. A notoriously heavy smoker we could hear her gasping for breath. I decided to be wary of the camera during the week ahead but I was soon to discover that this was easier said than done!

"*Allora*", Mario attracted our attention in order to begin his presentation of our programme of the week. His dry and very English sense of humour soon had us all roaring with laughter as we were introduced to the various activities planned for the days ahead. We were given copies of the programme for the week and our host described the events in store for us. His delivery was enhanced by his emphatic pronunciation of the English language, *mustt, hadd*. I looked forward to the days ahead although I did wonder what my role would be as there had been no mention so far of any duties I would be expected to fulfil.

Finally we were encouraged to relax and enjoy the slower pace of life in the mountains although "in slowing down maybe you sleep through breakfast, naturally you will miss breakfast but this way you will gain two hours' sleep." This statement, delivered with his deadpan expression evoked more chuckles. As the meeting drew to a close those not intent on an early night gathered around the small bar, some perched on high wooden stools to continue their acquaintance with this charismatic personality. While amusing them with anecdotes of the antics of previous groups he carefully avoided precise answers to specific questions about the activities we would be experiencing during the week ahead. Mario thrived on the element of surprise, it made good video footage and also allowed him to build up the drama by leaving explanations to the last minute. Did he have a great sense of theatre or was he a realist who knew that our groups would not pay attention to instructions until it became absolutely necessary? I was never sure but looking around the bar I could see that already they were all under his spell. I slipped away and climbed up the stairs to my little room.

I was up very early the next morning and had a stroll along the main road through the village to orientate myself. This took five minutes during which I established the whereabouts of the two lifts to the ski area above us, the only village shop, two bars, and a surprisingly large Information Centre. On my return I discovered several members of the group loitering in the bar area waiting for the dining room to open so that we could have breakfast. We chatted about the day ahead. Several of us had not skied for a few years and were anxiously discussing whether or not we would remember how to do it. Reminiscing about past experiences we were all trying to decide the level of our respective skills and I began to worry that I would be far worse than anyone else and an embarrassment to my role as their tour leader.

We heard the scraping as the heavy door was opened announcing that breakfast was served so we made our way into the dining room. At every place was a warm croissant and baskets of fresh bread rolls punctuated the tablecloth at regular intervals. One croissant and one bread roll each supplemented by slices of cheese and ham from the buffet accompanied by either tea or coffee. This simple but adequate breakfast was soon eaten and we then gathered at the main entrance by which time I was getting quite nervous about the 'test' we were about to undertake to grade us for lessons and listened with sympathy to others expressing a similar fear. I hoped that I would not fall over or otherwise disgrace myself.

Mario had gone on ahead and I had been given instructions to send everyone to the bottom of the nearest lift, just fifty metres beyond the garden of the hotel along a rocky path. They were to be sent up to join him in small groups so I was running around counting them as they left and then going back into the hotel to chase up the tardy ones. Having finally rounded them all up I was the last to leave the hotel. As I stepped out of the door one of the group, Debs, having shouldered her skis in readiness to walk up the path, swung round to talk to the person next to her and I was smacked across the face by the end of the skis. Almost immediately I found myself plunging forward into a pile of soft snow by the roadside and being held there for a few minutes. This was the result of the initiative of another member of the group in order to stem the flow of blood from the resulting cut on my face. It succeeded but I had no time to return to the hotel to check the damage in a mirror and had to content myself with dabbing at the area with a paper handkerchief to check if the bleeding really had stopped. Concerned bystanders had assessed the damage for me and seemed to relish the idea that I would have a real shiner.

Drama over I set off with the last few along the path. Debs, the perpetrator of my misfortune could be heard muttering darkly that I had walked into her skis and was therefore entirely to blame. Tempted to point out that standing in a doorway swinging a pair of skis around was not the most sensible thing to do I managed to refrain from comment; one of the hardest things about my job is having to keep quiet in order not to offend or annoy the client.

Earlier in the morning I had examined the rather unusual ski lift that was to convey us to the ski area but I was none the wiser concerning the method for loading skier and skis into the metal contraption that resembled a stall for an animal. Indeed, I was not surprised to learn later that previous groups had christened it the bucket lift. Mario was there to furnish an explanation and demonstration. Two people were to travel up together and in between buckets had to take their place one in front of the other on the two white lines marked on the ground. Skis were handed to a lift attendant and loaded into the bucket as it completed the loop prior to starting the ascent. The first passenger then had to leap on board and shuffle as far forward as possible. The second passenger had to be quick to get on board behind the first so that the confining gate could be slammed shut by a second lift attendant who often had to run some distance behind it before the occupants had moved forward sufficiently to allow him to corral them inside.

Mario, having already taken some footage of failed attempts to get on this lift now announced that he would ride up the mountain ahead of us in order to catch our attempts to dismount at the top. He re-iterated instructions to dismount backwards as he was swept upwards. Our attempts to get on the lift had us convulsed with laughter. The lift attendants did their best to co-ordinate our clumsy efforts but the end result was that buckets trundled off with just two pairs of skis, only one person aboard, or two people and no skis.

Finally all the people and all the skis were on their way. The ride up was wonderful, giving us our first real chance to enjoy the spectacle of the majestic mountains around us. Below we could hear the swish of skis as people descended the slopes through the trees. As the journey took at least twenty minutes I and my companion forgot our instructions regarding the dismount. I had also forgotten that the skis would be the responsibility of the lift attendant. The entire group were gathered by the exit and Mario was poised with his camera when I unwittingly turned round to step forward out of my bucket as soon as I was liberated by the lift attendant. We had shuffled around on board in order to lay claim to our respective pairs of skis. I heard shouts of turn round and leave your skis but the dismount was suddenly upon us and I stepped out and immediately fell forwards. Fortunately the lift attendant was ready and he caught me before I hit the deck. My skis and poles clattered to the ground around me. These had to be kicked to one side as the next bucket was already nearly upon us. Bright red with embarrassment I gathered up my equipment and trailed after the departing group. Mario, I soon discovered was not one for sympathy and understanding and I suspected he was finding this rookie tour leader rather exasperating.

After a quick tour of the ski area including the *pizzeria* where we were to meet for lunch it was time to make our way to ski school. A large crowd had gathered outside the small wooden building that housed this institution and people were being directed to the top of the blue run where instructors were telling them to put their skis on and then wait until everyone else was ready. We then followed the ski instructors a short way down the slope before stopping again and being organised in lines to take the dreaded 'test'. We were not the only people taking the lessons and it soon became clear that we would not necessarily be in classes with other members of the group. I managed to evade public assessment by persuading the ski instructors to allocate me a class based on composition rather than standard and selected my own level – easy.

Once we were sorted into groups we set off with our respective instructors to begin the lesson. I was with seven other people from the group and our instructor was Primo. He was grey haired, short and lean and a cheeky grin was constantly breaking out across his face as he charmingly misused the English language. Most of the time we tolerated his mistakes, as generally we could understand what he was trying to say. However, on the occasion when he told me to screw my knees into the mountain I felt I should offer an explanation of the meaning of the word in English. Clearly delighted at the result of this faux pas when we finished the lesson Primo shouted after me not to forget to practise screwing in my room that evening!

We all gathered together for lunch; a *pizza* and a beer at a bargain price was on offer and hugely enjoyed as we were all hungry after the morning's exertions. And there was more to come. Each afternoon a different optional activity was offered and today it was cross-country skiing. Only eight people had opted for this diversion, the rest preferring to practise their downhill skiing. Mario took us to the cross-country ski centre at Viote in his minibus and then disappeared. I had already discovered that he had a penchant for short, unexplained absences but guessed that as he was running both the holiday and the hotel he really was trying very hard to be in two places at once. Unsure what was supposed to happen next we trudged across the car park and made our way to a small wooden building that Mario had indicated as the place where we could get our boots and skis. There was no one around but as soon as we entered the hire shop two men appeared and quickly organised boots and skis for us all. The flimsy boots and thin skis looked impossible to control and I began to doubt my ability to master this new skill. I was not alone, we all sat outside in the sun casting doubtful looks at our equipment and predicting disasters ahead. It seemed a shame to waste such a beautiful afternoon and as we could see people speeding around a track just across the road we decided to go and try it ourselves before the lesson started.

We soon found a place where we could get on to the track. Having briefly experimented with this activity on a trip to Lapland I knew that the idea was to get the skis into the parallel tracks in the snow and then propel oneself along. It all looked very easy. First we had to attach the skis and it took some time to insert the metal clip on the front of the boots into the holder on the skis. I had forgotten how narrow the skis were and we all found it quite difficult to keep our balance, as there was a tendency for the boot to slip off the narrow surface of the skis. It was not long before the first person went down and as we had all been standing close to each other this created a skittle effect and soon several of us were spread-eagled on the snow with no idea how to get up. The length of the skis and the poles hampered rather than helped our clumsy attempts to regain the upright position. Assistance from those still on their feet was also not very effective as they were distracted by their laughter at our predicament. Eventually we decided the only solution was to remove the skis. As the technique for this is to push the pointed end of the pole into a small indent on the binding just in front of the boot it was quite difficult to manoeuvre oneself into the correct position to achieve this. It was some time before we were back on our feet and our skis had been re-attached.

Still no sign of an instructor or Mario. The track in front of us was empty and tempting. I explained that there were two sets of tracks, inner and outer, and that the tracks used depended on the direction you were going. Then I suggested that we make our way to the top of the slight incline we could see just ahead of us and then cross over to the other track and make our way back. Warning bells should have sounded when I voiced my suggestion at the use of the phrase "up that hill". However they did not and as I had been elected the leader I got myself in position, one ski in each track and pushing off with one of my poles slid the opposite ski forward and I was soon shuffling up the incline, my companions wobbling along behind me. We had covered about one hundred metres when it was time to re-trace our steps. We lifted our skis out of the tracks and waddled across to the track opposite. It was then I realised that the journey back was all downhill and I could not remember having covered this technique before.

My companions were asking me how to apply the brakes at the bottom. I suggested a snowplough but we soon realised that this was extremely difficult on the long narrow skis as they kept tipping right over when we experimented while stationary. Surveying the lie of the land I decided that the circuit flattened out sufficiently at the bottom for the gentle slope below us not to be a problem. One of our number having bravely offered to test this theory, stepped into the narrow tracks and pushed off. We watched in admiration as he trundled downhill. It looked so easy that I decided to follow suit without waiting to see what happened when he got to the bottom. I quickly picked up speed and was soon catching up with Jerry who was now rapidly slowing down in front of me whereas my speed seemed to be increasing rather then decreasing. Suddenly Jerry was sprawled on the track in front of me. I had to veer out of the tracks and realising that I was now heading at speed towards a tarmac road threw myself to the ground. I went down with a thump and was just catching my breath when I heard a warning shout from behind and looking round could already see the alarmed expression on the face of the next skier who was now hurtling towards me. Lifting my legs to get the skis clear of the ground I rolled over and had just managed to get everything out of her way when she crash landed just inches away from me. The others had wisely remained at the top of the slope to watch the result of our efforts and rather than add to the heap of humanity below removed their skis and walked down to us. We were still gasping with laughter and marvelling at the fact we had actually managed to miss each other when they reached us and began to untangle us and help us to our feet.

An angry shout brought the hilarity to an abrupt halt and Mario could be seen striding towards us, his face like thunder. We waited, subdued and anxious, like naughty children. I was not sure what crime we had committed. Maybe there had been complaints about our antics from the experienced skiers on the course. I stood nervously as Mario and the instructor, who I could now see running along behind him, approached us. By the time Mario reached us he had regained his composure and introduced us to his breathless companion who was to teach us the basics of cross-country skiing. Our instructor could speak enough English to take us through the technique and after the introductions we set off behind him. I noticed with relief that we went in the opposite direction where there was no sign of any inclines. Mario trotted along beside us, video camera at the ready but nobody obliged by falling over or even gave the appearance that this was a possibility. We were all concentrating hard and trying to behave like model pupils. In fact we all did very well and were soon whizzing along the track having mastered the technique of sliding and poling with opposite leg and arm. No interesting video footage which I realised was probably the cause of Mario's earlier loss of equanimity.

Having conquered the flat section we were introduced to the skill of skiing downhill. I was rather sceptical about this and glad that I would be the last to go. I expected that this exercise would produce a lot of interesting footage for the video. In fact with one exception, Jerry, we all negotiated the slope without any problem and when Jerry went down Mario had been talking to the instructor so he missed it! Soon it was time for the lesson to end, the equipment was returned and we were our way back to Vason to meet up with the downhill skiers and then make our way back to the hotel with them. Mario was very quiet and grumpy all the way back and clearly not amused as we discussed our antics on the cross-country piste prior to his arrival. As we clambered out of the van he took the opportunity to tell me that in future I should make sure that we waited for his arrival before we started an activity otherwise he missed the best opportunities for 'funny things' to video. Chastened, I joined the others in the bar where they were pondering over a mouth-watering selection of home made cakes and ordering *vin brulèes*, the Italian version of mulled wine. Relaxed and happy, our first day on the slopes was concluded by skiing all the way down to our village.

Later, after dinner we assembled in the games room for our first taste of Mario's evening entertainment programme. Most of this room was filled with a snooker table and we were squashed around the edge of it. On the table were two snooker balls, the white and a red. The object of the exercise it seemed was to hit the red ball with the white ball while the former was still in motion and from any position around the table provided that position was obtained by travelling there in a clockwise direction. The explanation was hilarious and it was difficult to concentrate for laughing. We were allowed a trial run with Mario bellowing instructions at us but inevitably people forgot to continue in the same direction and reversed into those behind. As we still did know each other very well there were lots of polite apologies and excuse mes. It was a different matter when the game was for real and there were shouts to get out of the way as people tore around the table chasing first the white ball and then a good position to roll it against the red ball. The air was punctuated with shouts of *outt* as Mario refereed us ruthlessly. Those who had failed in their mission to strike the red ball were clustered at one end cheering the others on. Each game became more intense and more frantic as the competitive streaks surfaced. Finally, exhausted, we returned to the bar to end the evening with a quiet drink.

Next morning quite a few people were up early and away to practise before lessons began at eleven. As I had to make sure everyone arrived at their lessons in time this was not a possibility for me unless everyone went out early which was highly unlikely. There was always at least one person who would not leave the hotel until the last possible moment or would sleep through their alarm. I also had to stay until everyone was united with the right pair of skis. Despite the fact that each ski was inscribed with a number and there was a list of numbers and owners in the boot room, nevertheless at least once during the week somebody went off with the wrong skis. Generally this was easily solved by exchanging the skis at the sister shop at the ski area.

On one memorable occasion when this occurred the lady concerned, Madge, was not prepared to carry anybody else's skis anywhere. As a compromise I suggested we just take them to the local ski hire shop and change them there. Although this alternative was deemed acceptable Madge still refused to carry the skis so I had to accompany her. Madge also refused to wear her ski boots to walk this short distance which meant we would have to return to the hotel before we could go skiing. For some perverse reason Madge then changed her flat snow boots for a pair of very high heels and tottered off down the road. Petite and pretty, never a hair out of place, Madge was someone who never set foot outside the door unless 'properly' attired. I trailed behind, a pair of skis over my shoulder and a not very happy expression on my face. We could so easily have been skiing by now! Sighing heavily I plodded along trying to keep a neutral expression on my face. I sincerely hoped that the ski hire shop would be open as generally they restricted their opening hours to arrival and departure days. Despite trying to explain all this to my client she was adamant we tried there first. I suspected that she thought I should order the perpetrator of this heinous crime to return with the original skis which, I was informed, had been specially selected and she doubted we would find another pair that was suitable. Knowing who the perpetrator was I doubted there would even be an apology and I was sure she had already changed the skis and would be racing up and down preparing herself to be the best and fastest in class today. Debs was a complete contrast to the lady trailing in my wake. Tall, athletic, not a trace of make up on her slightly tanned face she would have viewed her 'mistake' taking the wrong skis as a minor irritation, nothing more.

These dark thoughts occupied me until we arrived at the hire shop. Fortunately the proprietor was outside opening up so we were able to organise another pair of skis. I had had the presence of mind to bring the list with me so that I could point out the problem by referring to the number on the list and the number on the skis. Finally Madge found a pair of skis that she was prepared to try but I was left in no doubt that she did not think they would work as well as the others and if they did not it would be my fault and I would have to retrieve the originals for her. I raced back to the hotel hampered by the skis. By the time Madge had returned I was ready to leave. Tempted though I was to leave her to follow on her own I decided this would not be a good move but thought the fact I was standing outside ready to go may encourage her to get a move on. It did not. I had to wait for a long time and eventually she emerged and we made our way along the path to the bucket lift. By now I was struggling to be polite so when we got to the lift and she started to express doubts about the two of us being able to get on the thing safely, I gallantly suggested that she go first on her own and I follow, also on my own. I needed the space! That was the time I decided to employ the twenty minutes doing exercises to strengthen my legs and spent most of the journey squatting, my back pressed against the metal cage. I was really proud that I managed to hold this position for such a long time but when I came to dismount discovered that my legs would not function properly and I staggered off into the arms of the waiting lift attendant. For the rest of the week I had trouble walking, so painful were my thigh muscles. And I had no one to blame but myself!

By the time we reached the ski area all the groups but one had already started their lessons. As my group had known that I might be late, it was no surprise they were not waiting for me. I was left with two options, join Madge's group or ski on my own. As it was a good opportunity to ski with some other people in my party I chose the former and we set off. Madge was still full of righteous indignation and I spent the entire morning re-living the dreadful thing that had happened to her and the fact that it had ruined her day, and probably her holiday.

Our last ski lesson that week was something of a surprise to us all. When we arrived at the meeting point the whole area was a hive of animated activity. Ski instructors were racing around handing out bibs with numbers and communicating with each other on two-way radios even though it would have been easier to shout. There was a general air of excitement and expectation among the pupils who were all chattering to each other and not listening to their instructors who then got very agitated. With a sense of foreboding and having also spotted some red and blue slalom poles below me as we ascended in the lift this morning it dawned on me that today was *The Slalom Race*. As racing had never been my strong point I began concocting reasons in my head as to why I did not need to take part.

Our group was one of the first to go and Primo was making a list of names in large capital letters and checking that he had the correct spelling. This was my chance. "Primo, the tour leader does not usually compete in the race as it would be too embarrassing were she to win a medal." Primo countered this by saying it would be interesting to get a time for me and compare it with the others. This was said in a manner that did not invite further discussion and we were soon following him in snake formation. When we arrived at the start of the slalom course we were lined up and the first one was told to take their place at the gate. "Three, two, one" and he was off. Style a bit ragged but all poles negotiated successfully and from the right side. There was no time to applaud as the next contender was on his way before the first one had finished. I shuffled to the back of the line and resolved to somehow delay my start as due to an inability to control my speed I suspected I could finish ahead of at least two people who had set off before me.

My heart was thudding and my mouth was dry. It was ridiculous as I was not even in the competition for a medal but when one is naturally competitive it makes no difference, the desire to win is always there. As a child I was driven to making cakes and hand sewing soft toys just to be 'best' at school handicraft events. Needless to say as an adult I never cooked or sewed unless it really could not be avoided. Just two more to go and it would be my turn. Suddenly I was there 'in the blocks' and had just pushed off when the starter grabbed my jacket jerking me to a standstill half way through the gate. Trouble on the course below, the previous racer had fallen and I had to wait while the pole was replaced and he got himself off the course. Now everybody would be looking up and watching me, not the time to fall or miss a gate. I decided to ski the course with elegance and control, as my time was irrelevant. I set off and negotiated the first two poles quite stylishly, my speed was picking up but I was managing to turn quite well by keeping in the tracks of those who had gone before me. I was nearly there and could see the finish ahead of me and hear the encouragement of the rest of the group. Allowing my speed to pick up I flew through the finish, past everyone watching and then braked and turned so I was facing uphill. Lifting my poles above my head in triumph I had forgotten that I had my back facing down the slope. Shaking my arms jubilantly my skis took off again and I was away, backwards and totally out of control. Veering off towards the side of the piste I had barely time to collect my wits when I slammed into something firm but yielding and was thrown forward landing flat on my face in the snow.

There was silence all around me but then, when everyone realised I was all right, a babble of voices and some laughter broke out as they hunted around for a camera in order to record my predicament before helping me up. Mario had been notable by his absence this morning and I was very grateful that he had not been there to record my spectacular finish.

And so the pattern had been established. Lessons in the morning and optional activities in the afternoon. Dinner in the evening involved somewhat rustic cuisine, plenty of it and very welcome after a full day's activities. With thirty people to look after that first week it was hard work but also very enjoyable. Sleep was essential but not easy as my room was immediately above the bar and every night after the last drinker had abandoned their bar stool Mario would pull all the tables and chairs back into position before retiring to bed in the early hours of the morning. Once the noise had abated I then had the sagging mattress to deal with. So bad was the sag in my mattress I suspected that anyone sleeping in the second bed and looking across the room would be unable to see me. I had tried this second bed but inevitably it was rock hard. My compromise was to push the beds together to make space to place the first mattress on the floor and I slept there. As it meant I had to replace the mattress on the bed each morning this also reduced my sleep time. Both problems were solved the following week when I asked Mario if I could have a room at the other end of the hotel over the restaurant. He agreed and the following two weeks I had peaceful nights and plenty of sleep.

It was sad saying goodbye to the first group but with only thirty minutes between getting them checked in for their homebound flight and making my way to arrivals to meet the new group I did not have time to dwell on this. The next group was much smaller, just nine of us in total and I looked forward to a slower pace this week. Also, by now I was familiar with the resort, the hotel and mine host Mario. Indeed the week did follow pretty much the same pattern but due to bad weather two optional activities had to take place on the same day, cross-country skiing and snowboarding. Mario put me in charge of the snowboarding. I had just gathered my charges together, three of them, when Mario appeared with a video camera and I had a thirty-second lesson on how to use it. I had never used a video camera before and I was apprehensive as I made my way to the nursery slope where the lesson was to take place. Fabrizio was the instructor: a lean, tanned Italian with long dark hair that he normally wore in a ponytail. The two females in the class were very impressed but Frank, our only male in the group, was only interested in his teaching skills, simply wanting to get on with the lesson and impatient with the simpering and preening.

Videoing on the nursery slope was easy as it was very short and I could stand at the bottom and film everything that was happening. Then Fabrizio declared he was so pleased with their progress that he thought they could try snowboarding down the blue run. Off we went, the three snowboarders dragging their boards behind them and me trying to shuffle along on my skis and not drop the video camera. This was altogether a different matter as not only did I have to move with my subjects but they were soon scattered all over a wide area. First I turned my attention to Frank, typically macho and over confident he strapped his board on and set off across the snow in a lovely wide turn that just went on and on. Clearly he had forgotten how to turn the opposite way and continued beyond the edge of the piste. I finally lost sight of him as he disappeared into the trees on the horizon. My concern for our hero vanished at the sight in front of me. Both girls had fallen over and neither could get themselves up again so I was presented with two bottoms about six feet apart. Confident with the camera I started to practise my zoom technique so that I could capture them conversing from this rather unique position. Their predicament continued for some time as they struggled to push themselves upright.

Looking up to see where Fabrizio had gone I caught sight of Frank emerging from the trees disconsolately dragging his snowboard behind him. My sniggers became great guffaws of laughter and I kept telling myself to shut up, as I was concerned about shaking the camera and getting out of focus footage. I also suspected the video camera may be recording sound as well. The girls were now pleading for mercy and assistance in righting themselves so I let the precious camera dangle around my neck and went to help them up. It was not easy, me on skis and them on snowboards but finally we got there. When Frank joined us I remarked on the absence of Fabrizio and was informed that he had another lesson and had left while I was concentrating on my video skills. We were to continue down the run to a bar and wait there for Mario who would collect us in the hotel minibus. Camera at the ready I skied down a short distance and invited them to snowboard towards me trying to capture all three on one screen. Within seconds the screen was empty as Frank veered off out of sight again and the girls collapsed in a heap at my feet. More laughter from me. At this point they all decided that enough was enough as the struggle to get up was taking its toll. Snowboards were removed and the journey completed on foot. The resulting footage was amazingly good in the circumstances and my snorts, sniggers and self-admonitions become part of the final production. At the viewing the audience were reduced to helpless laughter and even Mario had to suppress a smile.

As it was a lovely sunny day we sat enjoying a *vin brulèe* on the terrace while awaiting our transportation. One became two and two became three. It was very pleasant sitting there chatting and time passed quickly until the shadow of Mario was looming above us. As we had to take the boards back to the hire shop he suggested that we return to Vason where he had left the others, collect some toboggans and use those to return to the hotel. We agreed, our sense of adventure fuelled by alcohol. Soon we were equipped with a toboggan each and joined the others who were waiting for us in a bar. As they had just ordered *vin brulèes* it seemed churlish not to join them. Later that evening, during dinner, I began to develop a serious headache, a hangover! If only I could follow the lead of my two afternoon companions who had slipped quietly away to bed. But I was required to make up numbers for the billiard game and spent the rest of the evening chasing round a snooker table, head thumping, wishing I could go and lie down in a darkened room.

One of the highlights every week at this house party was the toboggan race. Everyone would meet in the bar after the lifts closed for the day and have a *vin brulèe* while waiting for the slopes to empty. Dutch courage was also a consideration as the contraptions we were about to hurtle down the mountain on resembled large plastic trays with a shallow rim around them. There were two brakes but these did not look very effective. Once the all clear had been given we made our way to a flat area of snow where Mario demonstrated the technique to us and showed us how to use the brakes to stop and to steer. Then we were off, tearing down a blue run. Speed did not matter here as the slope soon descended into a big dip and insufficient speed was rewarded by a long walk to the summit. At the top we were lined up and then offered a slug of *grappa* from the bottle Mario produced from his rucksack. Mario himself was on skis and skied backwards while recording our attempts to master the art of tobogganing. It was not easy as too violent an application of one brake to steer the contraptions usually resulted in it tipping over or veering off piste. One was supposed to keep one's feet within the confines of the shallow rim. But this was virtually impossible due to the small space available for a pair of feet, the uncomfortable position of having one's knees up around one's chin and the fact that every time the toboggan hit a bump the feet escaped and flailed around until the toboggan was either halted or upturned. My first experience was really scary as I never felt in control of my conveyance. However, it was thrilling flying across the white, glistening snow in the half light of dusk.

By the third week I was becoming more expert and decided to risk taking my camera with me to get some group pictures. It was a very cold day and by the time we had gathered for our descent the snow was already glistening with ice. I soon discovered that in these conditions the toboggans were very difficult to control and from my place at the back I watched the others veering all over the place as they struggled to control pace and direction. The race was a shambles as some people were not able to stop at the starting 'line' and just continued all the way to the bottom. Mario was chasing after them trying to get them back but finally gave up and led the rest of us down to the bottom exhorting us to go slowly.

I waited until the last ones were down the steepest part and then set off. Almost immediately I hit a patch of ice and my toboggan was away, skimming at great speed over the unyielding surface. Hauling furiously on both brakes I tried to slow it down. Then I hit a bump in the snow and I was flying through the air. When I hit the ground my feet were thrown out of their resting place. My main concern was for my camera, a recent purchase and quite expensive. It was slung across my chest in a padded rucksack but the jolt had freed the rucksack which was now swinging wildly in front of me. Clamping down the rucksack with one hand I tried to brake and steer with the other hand. Impossible, and with two legs and one arm stuck straight out I felt as though I was in free fall mode. By now I was lying flat across the toboggan and hurtling towards the group all standing chatting at the bottom. One final attempt to check my speed sent me into a perfect 360 degree spin. Amazingly I stayed in contact with the plastic beneath me and could feel myself slowing down at last. Finally I slid to a halt and looking up from my prone position found I was perfectly framed in Mario's video. Giggling weakly with relief I gathered myself together and picked up my toboggan ready to walk back to the hotel. The group were really impressed with my performance and demanding lessons in 360 turns. If only they knew that had been my first, and would be my last.

My final week here was also the first week that we participated in the torchlight descent, previous groups having declined the offer after discovering that they had to ski down with flaming torches and no ski poles. I had been uncertain whether I was missing a treat or had been spared a disaster. As we had some willing participants it seemed I had no choice. Mario had briefed us the evening before and had exhorted us not to wear gloves, the theory being that if the flames did start to lick up your arms you would immediately feel the heat on your bare hands and drop the torch before your ski suit caught fire. This activity was open to all skiers in the resort and most of them seemed to have gathered together that evening. We were issued with long torches made of wax and hessian and then began the slow process of lighting them all. Mario took this opportunity to give us a lesson in the technique of keeping the flame going without spattering yourself with flecks of molten wax. It seemed the torch had to be held so that the wind blew the flame away from the body but at the same time it had to be turned regularly to prevent it burning unevenly and the flames licking up one side. This was possible while stationary but once we started skiing down the slope there were other considerations such as remaining upright and not colliding with the person in front of you.

I was lucky as I was placed immediately behind the first ski instructor with the rest of my group behind me. Setting off into the blackness of the night it felt a bit scary as I was not sure if I would be able to see sufficiently well to make good turns. I had heard that skiing in the dark makes you 'feel' the snow beneath you but doubted the truth of this, as I had to feel through the thick sole of a ski boot and the ski. Extraordinarily you can feel the terrain and I had soon found my rhythm and was happily traversing down the mountain behind our leader. Only the sound of our skis swishing across the snow could be heard. I suppose it should have struck me as strange that I could not hear anything behind me when in theory I was being followed by fifty other skiers but in practice I was completely immersed in this magical experience.

Finally it did occur to the instructor that it was too quiet behind him and that he should stop and investigate. He stopped, I stopped. We listened. Nothing. Looking back all we could see was the eerie glow of white snow under a dark sky and the black shapes of trees in the distance. Not a skier in sight. Unsure what to do we continued to scan the empty horizon until a speck of light appeared and soon revealed itself as Mario's torch bobbing around as he skied frantically towards us, video still at the ready. I was expecting to be told off again for ruining his film but he was not at all cross as it seemed we had missed all the fun. The lady immediately behind me had nearly managed to set herself alight as, concentrating on her skiing she had neglected her torch. Intense heat in her hand and gloves had finally convinced her that it would be a good idea to drop the torch but in order to do so she had stopped suddenly and the skiers behind her had been forced to break ranks and either ski round her or stop. The resulting chaos had compelled the order for everyone to stop so that they could regroup and start again. It was not long before we could see a line of dancing lights heading towards us. Re-joining them at the head of the procession we then all made our way down the mountain stopping for a welcome *vin brulèe* at the bar near the bottom, lighting our way to the door by sticking the still burning torches upright in the snow. We all agreed it was a wonderful experience including the lady who had set herself on fire but fortunately a full investigation revealed that the only damage was a melted trim on her ski gloves.

All too soon my time in the Dolomites was over but on one of my many solitary journeys up the mountain in the bucket lift I had made a decision. I was not going to pursue a career in the legal profession I was going to become a full time tour leader and travel the world.

Lago di Malghette

Pietro welcomes guests to the Hotel Lorenzetti

Day breaks over the Brenta Dolomites

Cascata Nardis in the Val Genova

A Red Run on Pradalago

Chapter Two – First Acquaintance

Never again I told myself firmly as I snuggled down into my distinctive red ski jacket at the very front of the bus. Even if the company begged me and paid me double, I would not return here. I gave the driver the thumbs up and the bus slid silently out of the deserted hotel car park. The road home stretched before us, welcoming and empty. The past week lay behind me wrapped in the history of the hotel whose grey morning face watched our departure without a flicker of interest. Inside I knew preparations would already have started for the more important new arrivals today.

Most of the group had retreated to the back of the coach and I could sense that many were already dozing. Those who were talking did so in hushed tones, respecting the early hour and their slumbering companions. No doubt they were discussing the events of the morning.

Peter had been very late this morning. Peter had been late every morning this week but this time it had jeopardised our flight home.

Aware of this possibility I had called Peter fifteen minutes after we had all been aroused from sleep by our wake up call. He had answered but in a manner that suggested getting out of bed was far from his thoughts. I rang again after another fifteen minutes had elapsed, by which time everyone else was huddled over their first cup of coffee in the dimly lit breakfast room. Same response, he would be there on time but again it sounded as though it came from the depths of his duvet.

Sighing heavily I returned to the reception area to check off the cases that Marino, the night porter, was heaving along the short passage from the lift and stacking around one of the plush settees. Soon every case was accounted for – with one exception. As I called Peter for the third time I could see through the glass of the main entrance door that our bus had arrived and was reversing into the car park, skilfully avoiding the cars that some guests had abandoned there last night.

"Peter, the bus is here and we are starting to load the cases, can you bring yours down now please?"

"Okay, okay, I'll be there," he said in a voice that implied he had no intention of moving just yet. I went downstairs to the ski and boot room to check that everything was packed up and ready to be carried out to the bus and found Peter's belongings were still scattered all over the place. Time was passing quickly and there was now very little to spare for poor conditions and busy roads. I gritted my teeth and began to collect his skis, poles and boots together – but I also needed to be upstairs checking all the suitcases were loaded on the bus.

Dragging all the gear up the metal steps I dumped it in the car park and then organised the porter to carry all the suitcases to the bus. A further phone call to Peter was met with the same response but I was desperate by now and told him that if he did not appear within five minutes we would be gone. I also mentioned that his ski gear was still unpacked but was now in the car park and would have to be loaded as it was. This did produce a response, a yelp that indicated his concern at the thought of his precious skis and bright yellow racing boots strewn over the dusty tarmac outside.

Impatient murmurings from the lobby led me to suggest to the waiting group that they get on the bus, as I was sure Peter would not be much longer. This was the signal for the majority to disappear for a last visit to the toilet before commencing our three-hour journey. Clearly the feeling was that I should have gone up to Peter's room and prised him out of his bed. Now that the bus was loaded, I had sent Marino upstairs and told him to keep knocking on Peter's door until he produced his case, well both his cases in fact. This guy did not travel light and had arrived with two holdalls stuffed with designer clothes including at least three fancy jackets. His extensive wardrobe had put the ladies to shame and had led to much discussion about the background of this fascinating character. Peter revealed very little about himself and had never disclosed what he did for a living. Somebody reported during the week that he had claimed to 'chase storms' but had not explained what happened when he caught them! Certainly his sleek appearance reminiscent of a greyhound at the peak of fitness, suggested he chased something. I had dismissed this as a flight of fancy and an indication that he did not wish to discuss his work. My own theory was that he could be a lottery winner.

I was now becoming seriously worried and retreated to a far corner of the car park to pace up and down. The group were all inside the bus and were, I was sure, pontificating loudly about how I should be dealing with the situation. Our driver, Aldo, was leaning against the bus puffing unconcernedly on a cigarette. No doubt he had seen it all before. I began to review my options. Storm up to his room and drag him and his belongings down to the bus. Call my boss in London for advice – not very wise at six on a Sunday morning. I looked at my watch again, we were now running thirty minutes late and, although not in danger of actually missing the flight should there be any problems on the road it could become a close run thing. I decided I would wait a further five minutes and if Peter was not on the bus by then I would call his room and tell him we were leaving and he would have to follow us down the mountain in a taxi.

My decision made, I jumped on the bus and informed the group of my intentions and reassured them that we still had plenty of time to get to the airport and check in for our flight but maybe not enough time to stop for a coffee and toilet break on the way. My announcement was greeted with silence and resignation. I descended and began pacing again. My heart was pounding at the thought of confronting this reluctant client with the news we were leaving without him. It would not look good in my report and no doubt would result in a serious complaint from the person concerned. But, what else could I do? I had to consider the well-being of the group.

As I marched determinedly back into the hotel I was relieved to see Marino staggering towards me clutching one partially packed holdall. Brushing past me he continued through the door and handed his burden to the coach driver who shoved it unceremoniously into the bus. Glancing at his watch and then at me Aldo conveyed that even he was now becoming anxious regarding our late departure. I just spread my hands and shrugged my shoulders, my Italian version of "I am doing my best".

I was about to throw skis, boots and bags separately into the bus when our hero himself appeared, his second bag over his shoulder. This bag was hastily dropped as he propelled himself across the car park to beseech me not to throw his second ski into the boot after the first ski. He began to gather up his remaining belongings which he then insisted on packing properly, the rest of the group bemused spectators through the bus windows.

Peter's usual arrogance evaporated when he fell flat on his face mounting the steps into the bus. This was the result of an aside to me concerning a complaint to the company about the morning's events to which I had responded that I would look forward to reading it! His startled backward glance had led to him missing his footing and sprawling into the aisle. Not one expression of sympathy or concern was heard and the bus driver had started the engine and was moving away before he was even back on his feet. I sat back feeling the tension draining out of me. Finally the nightmare was nearly over. It had all started so well too.

* * *

As the coach swung round the last hairpin bend it was suddenly there in front of us, a beautiful four-storey dark wooden building, imposing against a backdrop of stark white peaks. One could be forgiven for thinking we had crossed the border into Austria so reminiscent was it of a typical chalet of that country, every balcony bedecked with branches of spruce and the whole building outlined with white lights. Despite the apparent orderliness there was also an air of cosiness. As the smiling receptionist flung open the main door I saw the light and sensed the warmth that would soon envelop us. I pulled my jacket tightly around me and picked my way carefully across the tarmac, shimmering icily in the glow from the surrounding windows. I shouted a warning to the descending clients. We were ushered into the building and told that our luggage would be looked after. Reception was a beautifully decorated area with its carved wood panelling, space enhancing mirrors, comfortable chairs, tasteful pictures and harmonising ornaments all interspersed with lovely flowers. One had the feeling of being welcomed into a private home. I was looking forward to my week here in the best hotel that we featured in our brochure.

I handed over my rooming list and was rewarded with a blank look from Monica, the receptionist and a muttered "*che disastro*". Monica did not speak any English and I did not speak any Italian but she was able to convey to me that their list had one fewer name than my list. My heart skipped a beat. Was I going to be accommodated in another hotel or bed and breakfast? This would be hugely inconvenient particularly in an unfamiliar resort. Barbara, the daughter of the owner was summoned as she spoke excellent English. Long discussions ensued which I assumed related to the late booking.

In fact the last booking had only been made this morning as I had been informed by the client herself when she arrived at the airport an hour before the flight left. It seemed she only decided to come on the holiday at the very last minute and had called the company who had called the hotel and the airline and set the whole thing up in time for Tina to grab all her belongings and do her packing in a taxi on the way to the airport. British Airways then managed to lose this carefully packed bag and Tina spent the next morning treating herself to a brand new set of items 'essential' for skiing. I had not been convinced that the airline would settle a bill of such wanton extravagance but once I had pointed out that the 'usual' compensation was a T-shirt and a tooth brush duly distributed at the airport I decided to say no more other than offering the loan of some of my own clothes. I never did find out if Tina succeeded in her claim against the airline but the lady had such an air of confidence that it led one to believe she could succeed at everything. Tina also spoke Italian so was able to join in the discussion regarding the deficit of a single room while I was well and truly side-lined, feeling miserably useless.

Finally it transpired that the hotel were aware of the very late booking but were not aware of an earlier booking with the result that we were one room short for the first and last nights. This meant that I would have to share a room with Tina on these two nights. Tina was offered a reduction for the inconvenience and I was given a lecture about the lack of communication regarding bookings taken after the 'release' date. As a relative newcomer to the travel industry, I had not been aware that unsold rooms were taken back by the hotel three weeks before the group were due to arrive. Any bookings made during that period had to be confirmed directly by telephone.

Thoroughly chastened I turned my attention to the distribution of room keys, the collection of passports and the delivery of suitcases. Thanks to the helpfulness and efficiency of all the staff reception was soon empty of people and luggage and owners were in their rooms settling in. I dutifully sank into a comfortable settee for a while in case there should be any immediate problems. I doubted that there could be as my first impression of the Hotel Lorenzetti was very favourable and I was sure that the bedrooms would be as beautifully furnished as the reception area.

How mistaken can you be? Within minutes the telephone was bouncing off its rest in reception. It was answered and immediately held out towards me. Peter was not happy with his room; it was too small, he wanted a room with a larger bed! Barbara was summoned again and explanations made. The room planner, a large sheet of cardboard with a pocket for each room number was produced and owner, daughter and il Direttore pored over it for a long time, moving slips of paper from one pocket to another before arriving at a solution. Peter could have a larger room for six nights but would have to move back to the smaller room on the seventh night. Peter, notable for his absence, was informed of this solution by telephone and agreed. The porter was then dispatched to help him move his considerable belongings which included the biggest boot bag I had ever seen.

Problem solved I returned to my seat and began to prepare for the Information Meeting that would take place that evening before dinner. However, it was not long before, already glimpsed through the archway from reception, I could no longer resist the lure of the welcoming, wood panelled bar with its dusky pink high backed chairs and gleaming bottles reflected in the mirror behind them. The barman, resplendent in his black jacket and matching bow tie, greeted me warmly. Tempted by the smell of mulling wine from a large silver tureen in front of me I was soon settled in a corner enjoying the restful ambience and sipping the comforting liquid.

Snow drifted down outside and through the windows I could see into the restaurant across the building. How inviting it looked with tables laden with gleaming cutlery and sparkling glassware. Sandro, the charismatic maître d' came into the bar to tell me that our Welcome Drink would be served at seven thirty. Because we had arrived too late in the day to deal with all the incidents of skiing such as hiring equipment and getting ski passes my first 'official' duty would be hosting the Welcome Drink.

Re-appearing in the bar later that evening, complete with name badge, I was greeted enthusiastically by the barman, Giacomo who led me round to the far side of the bar and showed me where our Welcome Drink would be served. Glassware glistened on one small table, neatly arranged in triangles of champagne flutes and small wineglasses. Jugs of colourful cocktails and fruit juice also adorned the table. One jug contained dry sparkling white wine, or prosecco, mixed with a fruit cordial and another, a non-alcoholic mixture of fruit juices. Glass bowls full of crisps, nuts and olives were tastefully arranged on the tables where we would be sitting and I was told that the warm snacks would be served as soon as the group arrived.

I accepted a glass of prosecco and took my place on one of the seats in the circle of chairs that had been arranged for us. Next to me was a small grand piano, its black polished surface reflecting the subdued lighting from the lamps strategically placed on the windowsills and occasional tables. The only other source of light came from the discreet strip lights above the paintings on the walls. Suddenly the door behind me burst open and a blast of cold air whistled through it. A man staggered into the bar with three large musical instruments, still in their cases, stowed them under the piano, hailed the barman cheerfully and then disappeared into the black night as suddenly as he had arrived in the mellow bar.

"Stefano," said Giacomo nodding at the pile of instruments as though that was sufficient explanation. "*Il musicista,*" he added. The arrival of other hotel guests prevented any further explanation.

Accepting a refill, well it had been a stressful arrival, I sat back to enjoy some peace and quiet before being bombarded by questions from my clients. I think it was at this point, as I sat there revelling in the comfort of this pleasant bar that I realised that I had not seen the town and I had no idea where it was! Leaping to my feet I ran out into reception and asked for a map of the area. I had to resort to gestures as the only person on reception who spoke English had now gone home!

I managed to make myself understood and quickly studied the map so that I could tell the group which direction the town was in and assure them that the hotel ran a regular shuttle bus to the bottom of the main ski lifts. I also realised that although I knew the ski hire shop and lift pass office were in town I did not know exactly where to find them. Reports from my predecessors had been scanty and I was struck by the realisation that I had not seen any details regarding a local agent. In the absence of anyone to take control it was all down to me and right now I had no idea where I was. I grabbed all the leaflets I could find in reception and returned to the bar to study them in the hope that I could glean all the required information.

The early arrival of the first member of my group interrupted my frantic researching. Now I had to concentrate on remembering the ingredients of the different drinks in the jugs and offering snacks. As my knowledge of the resort was so scant I tried to direct the conversation along the more general lines of "Where do you come from, what do you do for a living." More people started to arrive so I was soon too busy making introductions and handing out drinks to answer any questions.

As promised the warm snacks, platefuls of mini *pizze* with mouth-watering toppings of tomato and mushroom or tomato and spinach, were passed amongst us. These delicacies were very much appreciated and quickly devoured. More irresistible savouries appeared, mini filled croissants and small, breadcrumb covered balls of an olive and sausage meat mix. These too soon disappeared. By now everyone was present so I did a quick introductory talk and handed out the leaflets I had harvested earlier.

It was a relief when Sandro arrived, upright and dapper in his black ensemble, menu always at the ready under his arm, and escorted us towards the dining room. Individual menus had also been placed precisely at each place setting on top of the neatly folded linen serviette. This elegant dining room was also, I discovered later, a well-established and very popular restaurant in the town. As I had been in there earlier to check where our tables would be and to confirm numbers with Sandro I could confidently lead the group straight to them and invite them to sit down.

There was a general chorus of appreciation regarding our sumptuous surroundings and the splendid view of the mountains outside now glowing eerily in the moonlight. My extensive research may not have established the whereabouts of the hotel in relation to essential services such as ski hire shops and lift pass offices but I had unearthed some fascinating legends one of which was immediately brought to mind by the shadowy night panorama before me.

Gazing at these amazing pinnacles of beauty stark against the grey translucent night sky I recalled the legend of the first mountain climber in this area, the son of the King of Ladinia. This prince was convinced that he could climb the pale crags above his valley and reach the moon that he could see after sunset, just above the peaks, tantalisingly near and yet so far. One day the prince decided he just had to try and climb up to this enticing orb. He set off along a path through the woods, climbed up the rocky ledges and traversed the scree to the small terraces protected by the crags. He climbed higher and higher making his way along the shadows and up the clear rays that linked the rocks to the moon. Finally he arrived on the moon, a mysterious pale and glowing disk. There he found a castle and in the castle a beautiful young girl. He immediately fell in love with her and his love was returned but they were never destined to live together because neither could live in the other's land. The prince did bring his beloved to earth to live among the beautiful high mountains but after a few weeks of happiness she began to pine for the paleness and flatness of the moon. So the prince followed his love back to the moon but the quiet, shadowy whiteness made him long for the life, colour, sun and wind of his own planet. The lovers exchanged flowers. White edelweiss for her so that she might find among the alpine meadows the pallor that she yearned for and for him a red rhododendron so that on the pale distant moon he could recall the fiery red of his mountains at sunset. But all to no avail, they were always destined to live apart.

My reverie was interrupted by Sandro asking, probably for the third time, what I would like to eat. Fortunately Sandro spoke good English but he always spoke it in dulcet tones, a strange contrast to the crisp, confident orders he rattled out to the waiters in his mother tongue, yet very endearing. The menu required more attention than I had been able to give it. So many choices and unusual combinations and all accompanied by a light chardonnay, or a pleasant cabernet, the house wines that were served in jugs on the table. When the strawberry flavoured dessert wine and small, sweet biscuits were offered as a finale to our excellent meal I had to decline. I had also had to admit defeat earlier when invited to make a selection from the well-stocked cheese trolley – another evening maybe. The dinner was so extravagant that I suspected it might be a special welcome feast and that the next evening we would be presented with the usual ski fare, good, plain cooking.

During dinner I had been aware of the owner, Signora Silvana, a very petite, attractive lady dressed totally in black gliding gracefully from table to table and engaging the occupants in several minutes' conversation. At some tables the occupants would rise to greet this daintily elegant lady enthusiastically and they would talk for much longer with animation and affection. Seated at the far end of the restaurant I was able to watch her progress with interest and the awareness that she spoke to every single guest. Suspecting that it would soon be our turn I began to hope that she spoke some English and to curse myself yet again for not even knowing how to say good evening in Italian.

Fortunately I was not the only person who had been watching her progress among the diners and as she approached our tables Sandro materialised beside me and whispered that she was the "Signora", the owner of the hotel. Introductions were made with Sandro as interpreter and we were all individually welcomed with a warm handshake and a lovely smile. I then accompanied the Signora to our second table and made the introductions in English. Tina had assumed the role of head of this table and soon took over conversing easily in Italian and translating for the rest of the table. I crept back to my place feeling utterly inept yet again. As I slid into my seat my napkin fell to the floor. Before I could bend down to pick it up it had been retrieved by one of the waiters and whisked away. Within a few seconds the waiter had reappeared with a fresh napkin neatly folded on a plate which he offered to me. I was impressed by such prompt and courteous service, unique in my experience so far as a tour leader.

After dinner we moved through to the bar and settled ourselves around the small wooden tables. Almost immediately the bar man was there asking if we would like to order any drinks but in such a manner that one felt to decline would not be taken amiss. Stefano, the musician that evening, was in full flow but playing at a volume that did not intrude on our conversation. His repertoire was extensive and he switched easily between the five wind instruments that were strewn around him, accompanying himself with backing tapes that I subsequently learned he recorded himself. Regular guests came over to him to chat and make requests and the whole atmosphere was very informal and relaxing.

Finally, replete and exhausted we said our goodnights and made our way to our rooms. This was the moment I had been dreading as I had not shared a room with anyone but my ex partner since my childhood. The room I was sharing was long and narrow with two beds head to toe. Tina had already settled herself in the bed by the window, as she would remain in this room for a week while I migrated to another one for five nights before returning here for the last night. In view of this I had not bothered to unpack and just pulled the items I needed out of my case and hastily prepared for bed.

Very early next morning I crept out of my bed as soon as my alarm, discreetly placed under my pillow, buzzed in my ear. I dressed quickly in the darkness and crept upstairs. Around me the hotel slumbered deeply and when I made my way through reception all I could see was a tiny pinprick of light through the glass partition that separated this area from the breakfast room. Discovering that the door that gave direct access into this room was blocked on the far side by one of the tables laden with the breakfast buffet and obstructed on my side by a decorative, old wooden spinning wheel I retraced my steps down a passageway and found another entrance. Light streamed out of the service area and I could hear someone clattering about behind the partially closed door. I stood there hesitantly, taking in my surroundings.

One side of this room was lined with food starting with a lovely display of home made cakes neatly sliced and a cake server placed invitingly under one piece on each of the plates. Above the cakes were baskets of fresh bread rolls, croissants and freshly sliced brown bread. No toaster, the usual centre piece of a breakfast buffet, I noticed but was informed later that if anyone wanted toast it would be prepared and brought to them. Beyond the cakes were several glass bowls of fresh fruit peeled and sliced so that guests could choose their own combination of fruits and also the option of a freshly prepared fruit salad. On a shelf behind the fruit were more baskets, a variety of shapes, containing sweet and savoury biscuits.

Next in line was a selection of cold hams and cheese all neatly arranged on pristine white plates under a large protective container. Clearly this was local, regional fare and very tempting. Freshly boiled eggs nestled in a small covered basket just beyond the cold cuts. As I was marvelling at the choice a waiter appeared from the service area and escorted me along the rest of the buffet, revealing pots of cereals, large bowls crammed with flavoured and natural yoghurts and a variety of fruit juices and mineral waters. He then told me that the bacon and scrambled eggs would arrive later. I was invited to sit down and asked what I would like to drink.

Giuseppe, my breakfast buffet guide, was able to speak some English so we could communicate quite easily. He was a charming young man, diffident yet efficient and a radiant smile that occasionally spread across an otherwise serious countenance. The impeccable service of the restaurant yesterday evening was reflected in the more informal breakfast room, tea and coffee being served in individual jugs brought to the table with a fresh cup for each person. Only the saucers were already placed on the tables.

I had just settled down with a jug of hot coffee and one of hot, frothy milk when the first members of my group started to drift into the breakfast room. Giuseppe was there to welcome them and show them to a table before taking orders for tea, coffee, hot chocolate indeed anything that might be required. Just as the breakfast room began to get very busy Sandro appeared like an actor responding to a cue and began to orchestrate the service. He still found time to chat to me and I got my first glimpse of his outrageous humour. I had become aware of some agitation on the part of Giuseppe and the junior waiter who was now assisting him but had not worked out the reason for this. My group were still appearing individually and joining those already seated. Some ate quickly and left, some lingered over second and third cups of coffee just chatting. Italian guests arrived, sat down, ordered an espresso, selected a cake or croissant and within a few minutes had finished and gone. As soon as a table became empty the condiments were put to one side and the top tablecloth was removed and a freshly laundered one replaced it. New covers were placed on the still well defined fold marks and the next guests were seated immediately. Any attempt to change tablecloths on our tables were thwarted by the continual ebb and flow of my clients who, finding an empty place without a setting would wander off and help themselves to a cover from another table.

I sensed Giuseppe's frustration at not being able to fulfil his role properly and I could see the anxious glances he kept throwing at Sandro. Sandro simply shrugged and continued with his tasks but he did find time to inform me of the reason for Giuseppe's discomfort. "The Italians they eat and go, the English they have breakfast, they have lunch and then they go," was the gospel according to Sandro.

The minutes raced by and soon it would be time to meet the group and head for the slopes. I had checked that everyone was up before I hurried back to my room to don bulky ski gear and pack my pockets with essentials such as goggles, hat, sunglasses and sun cream. I then headed for the ski room and crammed my feet into stiff, unwieldy ski boots before clumping up the metal steps into the car park where the others were beginning to gather. I knew that the hotel ran a regular shuttle bus to the resort, just five minutes' drive down the road but had failed to appreciate the complicated mechanics of getting twenty people to the same place at the same time when only one ten seater vehicle was available. Did I go with the first group or the second group? If I went with the first group could I rely on someone to make sure everyone was on the bus for the second run?

Inevitably there were anguished shouts of "don't go without me" as people announced their intention to return to their rooms for forgotten items. Finally I decided to send the first ten into town and tell them to wait for the rest of us. I asked Goran, the Croatian shuttle bus driver to take them to the lift pass office at the bottom of the cable car and stressed several times that they should wait there until the rest of us arrived. It was like trying to control a herd of stampeding cattle – the race to the slopes was on and no one wanted to wait for anyone else!

My head was spinning and my mind struggling to cope with all the questions and anxieties being thrown at me. I escaped into the relative peace of the reception area to find Barbara standing serenely behind the desk. She rapidly explained the quickest route from the lift ticket office to the ski hire shop and Goran was requested to return to the ski hire shop to collect us as soon as the first ten people were ready to go skiing. Fortunately I had studied the piste map and knew where I wanted to take them skiing this morning – a nice easy blue run with a coffee bar near the top of it. So I was able to explain which lift we would all be taking to the top of the mountain. Having removed my boots to re-enter the hotel I now raced back out of the hotel in my socks (it would be sacrilege to walk on the luxurious carpets in ski boots) just in time to see the shuttle bus, crammed with eager clients, pulling out onto the road. There had been no opportunity to do a head count before the bus had roared off down the road so I made the assumption they had been sensible enough to get ten on board before departing.

Wrong and wasn't my boss always saying we should never assume anything with our clients? I had just gathered the remaining ten people together when an eleventh literally fell out of the main entrance clutching all her ski gear except her salopettes which were, fortunately, on her legs. She had lost track of time and suddenly realised she might be late. We all waited patiently while she dressed herself despite my gentle hints that maybe this could be done while queuing for lift passes or waiting to hire skis. I was fascinated by the procedure taking place in front of me – everything was done so meticulously and in a certain order. Even the gloves had to be pulled on and the strings of her Laplander hat tied under her chin. Finally she was ready and we could set off. Although, of course, the next problem was that the bus could only 'legally' take ten people.

Goran had disappeared leaving the bus doors open so I packed the remaining ten into the vehicle and then waited at the back of the bus hoping to persuade him to let me ride in the small space behind the last row of seats. When he returned he was clearly not happy with my solution but he could see my state of agitation as the minutes ticked by, and my imagination embraced the vision of clients wandering around the town with no idea what to do. Finally he relented and I scrambled into the back. This was not easy as he had clearly collected supplies during one of his sorties to the slopes and I had to step carefully over boxes of groceries and then arrange myself on the shiny metal hub of the wheel. Ski boots do not lend themselves to such manoeuvres and I became very embarrassed by my clumsy shufflings in the back accompanied by a chorus of "are you all right" from the people in front and some half hearted offers to swap places from the gallants in the group.

Fortunately it was a very short journey and I did not have to cling on for long. We were soon spilling out onto the busy main street and, to my great relief the advance party were waiting there. People look so different in their ski gear and I had been dreading not being able to identify my clients in the general melee of the first day of a skiing week. I decided to start by hiring skis as we had been deposited right by the ski hire shop so we all trooped into the shop and joined the long queue. My heart sank, we would be there for a ages and I could see impatient faces looking at me obviously expecting me to perform some miracle. More and more Italians were crowding into the shop and queue-jumping outrageously. Clearly there was nothing I could do, we would just have to be patient but I had realised that this would be a good opportunity to do a quick reconnoitre of the town so muttering to those nearest to me that I was going to see if there was a less busy alternative elsewhere, I escaped outside. Right in front of me was the Tourist Information Office and

I scuttled in there to find out where to purchase our lift passes. I was overjoyed to discover that they spoke excellent English and were able to pinpoint exactly on my map where everything was and to advise which was the best of the two available ski passes to buy.

I then raced off to the ski school office to discuss lessons. This was not so easy as they seemed to have only one instructor who spoke English but we finally established that they could organise group lessons every day just for my people. However, those interested would have to go and pay first so that they had in their possession a ticket to give to the instructor at the start of the lesson. Exasperated I agreed to send all interested parties to pay their dues before we made our way to the slopes. We had agreed that eleven o'clock would be a good time to start the lesson and the hour hand on my watch was already creeping menacingly towards ten.

Armed with all necessary information, I thought, I tore back to the ski hire shop and burst in amongst them red faced and out of breath, so much for appearing calm and collected, I was now in panic mode. The shop was still full of people milling around, trying on boots, discussing the merits of downhill skis and carving skis. As soon as I appeared I was greeted by a chorus of questions concerning the best skis to use. My advice was to ask the assistants but unfortunately none of the assistants spoke much English. However they did understand 'carvers' and I was able to persuade most people that it would be better to go for this option as these were the skis of the future and much easier to use than the longer alpine skis.

The next problem was paying for the skis and this had to be done before anyone was allowed out of the shop. Generally in Italy a document such as a passport had to be left as security. Having told the group to leave their passports locked up in the safety deposit boxes in the hotel I had, for once, followed my own advice, and that was where my passport was as well. Finally it was agreed that I could leave my credit card as surety for the whole group and I handed it over somewhat reluctantly. I was right to be concerned because when I returned to retrieve it on our last day it had been lost. Finally after much jumping up and down and gesticulating on my part it turned up under the till. I subsequently discovered that my predecessors had left shop loyalty cards with them as surety and vowed to do the same should I ever be faced with the same situation again.

At this point Tina suddenly appeared having taken herself on a shopping spree. She was now dressed in brand new ski apparel and carrying her other clothes in a plastic carrier bag. I was so glad to see her and did not mind at all when she marched straight to the head of the queue to organise her ski and boot hire as I took the opportunity to suggest that maybe she could translate for the others while I established who wanted to take lessons that morning. Trying to talk to them as a group was impossible and after a few attempts yelling at the top of my voice to get their attention I had to go round with a list and ask each individual if they wanted to take group lessons every morning. During this task I discovered that I had a complete beginner in the group! Although our brochure stated quite clearly that the holiday was not suitable for complete beginners nevertheless there was one with me now and it had to be dealt with.

Back in the ski school office I was able to relate my problem to them and was mightily relieved when told that if I took her to the ski school office as soon as she had her boots and skis they would take her to the nursery slopes in their bus where she would join a lesson for beginners. I returned to the ski hire shop and collected my client, now kitted out, and accompanied her back to the ski school office where I left her to fend for herself with promises to make my way to the nursery slopes to meet her for lunch. This turned out to be a rash and stupid promise but I had not realised that the teaching area was separated from the main ski slopes and difficult to access without motorised transport.

Back to the ski hire to collect the others, now waiting disconsolately outside and they were definitely not impressed when I told them that ski lessons had to be paid for now. Off they went and at last I had time to hire myself a pair of skis and ask the shop to call the hotel for the shuttle bus. We had precisely twenty-five minutes to get to the ski school meeting point, would we make it in time for the lesson?

Finally we were all assembled but still a long way from the slopes and still without lift passes. What a relief when the white minibus emblazoned with the name Hotel Lorenzetti slid to a halt beside us. The first ten were loaded up and given instructions to buy their lift pass as soon as they got to the bottom of the cabin lift. Tina was dispatched with them to ensure this operation went smoothly and they were all advised to buy the area ski pass rather than the local ski pass. I hopped from one foot to the other as the bus roared off up the road even though I had been assured that the journey would only take two minutes and that Goran would be back in no time for the rest of us.

By now the queues for lift passes had abated and when I arrived with the second group most people had purchased their pass and were on their way up the mountain. I was the last to purchase my lift pass and hurrying through the turnstile just managed to squeeze into a cabin with several other members of the group. Feeling an enormous sense of relief I discreetly checked my watch, just ten minutes to go, and then, tipping back on my heels attempted to rest my backside against the small ledge that ran round the interior of the cabin. Unfortunately, being short with a low slung bottom, a fact most of my boyfriends have quickly pointed out, I missed and my boots started to slide across the wet, slippery floor. There was nowhere else to go and I slid gracefully down until I was lying full length across the floor gazing up at a circle of anxious faces.

Scrambling unceremoniously to my feet I looked down in horror at my mud streaked ski suit. I had been so proud of my predominantly white all-in-one suit with brilliant flashes of yellow. Not generally a flamboyant dresser I had surprised myself by purchasing this symbol of confidence or maybe it was the ten-pound price ticket that was the main attraction? Whatever my motivation, it was now a very be-draggled figure that crept out of the cabin and tried to stamp its authority on the waiting group. I pointed to the building a short distance down the slope in front of us and told the group that this was where the ski instructor would meet us. I watched them all set off while making furtive attempts to clean the mud off my suit with a well used and totally ineffective paper handkerchief. Ski resort mud always seems to be blackened by oil that stubbornly resists any attempts to remove it.

It was with a great sense of relief that I waved goodbye to the departing ski class and could now take refuge in the toilet of the nearby Rifugio Viviani, a restaurant and bar, and attempt to repair some of the damage done to my ski suit. Ten minutes and a roll of soggy toilet paper later I had to concede defeat and crept out of my hiding place to join the rest of the group now gathering for a coffee here in the bar section of the *rifugio*. Pushing my way through the melee of skiers that seemed to have appeared from nowhere I struggled to the bar to order a much needed coffee only to be re-directed to the cash desk where I first had to purchase a ticket which would then be exchanged for a drink. The length of the queue at the till was prohibitive so, heaving a sigh of exasperation, I decided to go without otherwise the group would be getting impatient. Finding the group was not an easy task amongst all those skiers. Aware that I may not recognise the group when they exchanged their evening finery for all enveloping ski suits I had tried to memorise some of the colours. Suddenly I caught sight of a very bright yellow all-in-one suit, the one that Peter had been wearing at breakfast this morning. Edging around the crowded space I eventually squeezed into a space at their table.

Most people, having had their first fix on the slopes were now relaxed and happy and were studying the piste map to decide where to ski between now and lunchtime. Only Peter and his new best friend Jack were straining at the leash and they were loudly discussing a tour of the blacks before the lunch break. I had decided, to make everything easier, that we should meet in the restaurant section of the Rifugio Viviani and suggested this to them. My suggestion was carefully weighed up and finally agreed to when I pointed out that I had to go and meet Clare at the nursery slopes and somehow get her to the restaurant – at least this restaurant was conveniently close to a cabin lift. There was a flurry of zipping up jackets and donning of hats and gloves and suddenly I was on my own.

Pulling out a now very crumpled piste map I spread it on the table in front of me and began to plan my route to the nursery slopes. It looked very simple on paper. Down to the bottom of the blue run, across the road, up a cabin lift and then follow the blue from the top of that cabin lift to the nursery slopes. I had taken the precaution of suggesting to Clare that she wait for me at Bar Piccolo, a meeting place recommended by the ski school, in case I was late.

Why don't they indicate flat parts of blue runs on the piste map? I cursed under my breath as I used my poles to propel my skis along a very flat stretch of a blue run. Already I was hot and out of breath. I thought I had given myself plenty of time to tackle two blue runs and one cabin lift but of course, had been totally unaware that one of the blue runs had a very long flat section. Those familiar with the run had known exactly what was round the bend and had launched themselves straight down the run, crouching like demented downhill racers and shouting warnings at me as I innocently traversed from side to side enjoying what had started as a very pleasant tree lined run. Now it had become a nightmare. I was so busy trying to get up speed on this impossible terrain that I was taken completely by surprise when I emerged from the trees into a large car park! This was not part of the plan and now I had no idea where I was. After some frantic map reading I realised where I had gone wrong, clearly I had been poling so energetically, head down and stubbly arms flailing like pistons that I had completely missed the turning I should have token. I weighed up my options. Skis off and walk across the car park, back up the cabin lift and follow the correct route down the blue or some uphill trekking to re-trace my steps along the blue run?

Neither solution had any appeal for me but I could not simply abandon Clare to a solitary lunch. I decided to pursue the second option and began to retrace my steps proceeding against the flow like an ungainly cross-country skier, the top of my all-in-one suit gaped open and my pockets were stuffed with discarded hat and gloves to try and cool myself down. Just before I reached the junction of the two runs I glimpsed a path through the trees at the end of which I could see the drag lift of the nursery slope. Ski tracks through the snow indicated that this short cut had been employed by others before me so without a second thought I launched myself off the piste expecting to glide down the path and swoop onto the beginners slope below.

A competent but not a great skier I soon discovered that my technique was not good enough for deep snow and following narrowing tracks and as soon as I deviated from the tracks my skis disappeared from view and I pitched head first into at least one metre of soft snow! I tried to stand up but it was impossible. The more I struggled the deeper my skis buried themselves. There was no way I was going to ski out of this predicament so I had to find a way of extricating myself without losing my skis in the fluffy depths. I could not shake the snow off them as it was too heavy so I began to scrape it away until I could manoeuvre the skis and shuffle back into the tracks made by my predecessor. Aware that too much speed would precipitate me into virgin snow again I adopted an ungainly snowplough position and very carefully slithered down towards the slope. I was becoming uncomfortably wet as the open top of my suit had allowed snow to invade its depths and it was now melting and seeping everywhere even filling my pockets and boots. It was not a great way to discover that fashionable ski suits lack any sort of defence against wet snow. My discomfort was considerable but more was to come.

At the end of the path I did not find, as expected, a flat junction with the nursery slope but instead I was presented with a steep drop of about two metres. Although I was glad my progress had been slow enough to stop and view this obstacle I was unsure how to tackle it and rattling down at speed may have been the best solution. As it was, aware of my earlier adventures in deep snow I was reluctant to risk another snow bath. There was only one thing for it, the skis were removed and I had to descend in my ski boots. Ski boots were not designed for hill walking and I made slow progress, sitting down suddenly several times when the boots took off by themselves. Finally I made it to the bottom and heaving a sigh of relief shuffled into the queue for the ski lift. I was nearly there, once at the top of the drag lift I could ski down to the meeting place. I hoped that Clare had waited as I was now at least half an hour late.

"Non è valido," the lift attendant announced smugly when the turnstile remained stubbornly shut despite my presenting the card reader with a lift pass that was supposed to take me everywhere. He pointed to a small wooden hut next to the bar that was my objective indicating that I should buy a ticket there and then propelled me unceremoniously out of the queue as a large ski class had just arrived and their ski instructor was already pushing the first ones through the turnstile – well, under it actually and the lift attendant had probably seen my eyes light up at the thought of following their example. It does very occasionally pay to be short.

Ejected from the lift queue I had no alternative but to walk up the nursery slope. Shouldering my skis again I began to plod uphill. I was sure Clare would have gone by now but could not take the risk of her maybe still being there. I was also sure that if she was still there she would be really fed up so I began to think of plausible excuses for my tardy arrival, hoping that she had not been watching my progress from the bar.

Deep in thought I was suddenly aroused by shouts and laughter and looking up saw a vision of buttercup yellow. Peter was sprawled in a chair outside the bar, Jack and Clare sitting next to him. Smoke spiralled up from their cigarettes and their faces were split with huge grins so I knew immediately that they had been watching me and clearly enjoying the fun. But how had they got there I asked them. Steve, I discovered during the next few days, had an instinct for finding people on the slopes and was also very good at finding his way around. Initially very evasive I subsequently discovered that they had got themselves totally lost and had called the hotel requesting the shuttle bus to take them to the nursery slopes. This discovery was made on my return to the hotel when I was given a copy of the shuttle bus timetable and the route and it was pointed out to me that the nursery slopes were not on the route of the shuttle. If my clients called them to request a lift to the nursery slopes this meant other guests at legitimate stops would have to wait longer and the whole timetable would go to pot much to Goran's chagrin. I felt suitably chastened, even more so when I discovered that ski school organised a service from the nursery slopes before and after the group lessons.

By now it was far too late to entertain any thought of joining the rest of the group for lunch so I had a large slab of nearly warm pizza while suffering the merciless teasing of my colleagues. Peter and Jack soon bid us a hasty farewell and set off to find more black runs leaving me to ski with Clare on the nursery slopes but as Clare was getting very tired we soon decided to quit the slopes and returned to the hotel.

What a relief it was to remove my sodden ski boots, peel off my damp jacket and finally gain the privacy of my own room. The room was delightful. It had a large double bed and a beautiful light green, hand painted wooden wardrobe. No time to linger and enjoy the peace however as most of the group had now returned from the slopes and it was time to socialise over a glass of mulled red wine.

As I approached the bar I could hear people chattering and on entering was quite taken aback by the sight before me – the whole of one corner was occupied not only with people but a good scattering of jackets, gloves and hats reminiscent of a stall at a jumble sale. Fearfully I glanced at the immaculate barman expecting a look of disapproval but it was not there. His countenance was as serene as ever and he was busily fulfilling orders for large beers and glasses of mulled wine. Each order was accompanied with small dishes of savoury snacks. Some people had ordered pots of tea and were presented with a small plate of tiny biscuits, freshly baked each day in the hotel kitchen. It was such a warm, relaxed atmosphere that I felt the tension seeping out of my body and was glad I had not bothered to do more that pull on a pair of cords.

On joining the group I soon discovered that news of my abortive attempts to ski to the nursery slopes had been widely broadcast and I had to deal with a lot of teasing. But at least our first day of skiing seemed to have been a success and it was not long before people began to drift off to their rooms to change for dinner.

"I am glad you are early as I wanted to speak to you privately," my spirits sank as private conversations with clients generally indicated trouble on the horizon. I steered the speaker to a table in the corner abandoning all hopes of having a quiet drink on my own while working out the programme for tomorrow. "Is there a problem?" I asked.

"Well I am not one to complain but …" This phrase always strikes terror into my very being as one knows instinctively that this is a serial moaner and the prospects for a trouble free week suddenly diminished. The problem it seemed, related to ski school and although the group were all about the same standard one of their number had a tendency to 'freeze' at the top of a steep slope. In the past I had endured a few such moments myself not having a great head for heights so I could sympathise with the subject of our discussion. Now that I was working as a tour leader I was not 'allowed' to indulge in any such weaknesses myself. My suggestion that I join the group tomorrow in order to be on hand to resolve any problems was readily accepted.

By now the rest of the group had assembled in the bar and I quickly went through the programme for tomorrow before leading them into the restaurant. I was once more in awe at the elegance of the dining area and delighted to be presented with an extensive and different menu. Accepting a glass of white wine I took a small sip, sank back in my chair and looked forward to a pleasant evening. And indeed it was as the conversation ebbed and flowed around me. The only hiccup was the smoker versus non-smoker issue, often a problem with our groups. Smokers were requested not to smoke until the meal was finished and usually they respected this request. Those who needed to smoke during a meal would absent themselves in order to indulge. We had two dedicated smokers in this group, Peter being one of them, and his interpretation of our 'request' was that it was okay to smoke provided the people either side of him were not actually eating. I could feel the friction this was creating as people cleared their throats loudly, exchanged looks and generally found ways of expressing their disapproval without actually voicing their opinions to the persons concerned. Aware of the storm clouds gathering I decided to deal with the matter after dinner by taking the culprits to one side and appealing to their better nature. There was none!

The second morning started badly with the non-appearance of Peter at breakfast. This meant calling his room to check he was okay and also to tell him where the group would be skiing. His response was less than gracious and basically informed me that he did not want to be called in the mornings. Then the ski school bus failed to appear – according to Clare – but according to the ski school it had been there but Clare had not. I had to employ all my charm to persuade Goran to make a detour to the nursery slopes and deliver

Clare to her instructor. By now I was running late and scurrying to and fro with armfuls of ski gear causing a raised eyebrow from the immaculate receptionist watching my antics with interest. I never seemed to be able to achieve the cool, detached and efficient air of my colleagues.

I had missed the start of the lesson but I was confident I could catch up with them. As the ski instructor was wearing a very distinctive jacket I soon spotted him on the piste below me surrounded by a very disconsolate group all gazing back up the slope. Unfortunately I had already skied past the object of their interest on my way to join them. There was a problem and it was well above them sitting in the snow removing skis and boots. As I skidded to a halt by the side of the instructor a huge expression of relief traversed his bearded features. "He must stay with you, we continue," he said indicating the pupil stranded on the piste and with a cheerful "*andiamo*" to the remainder of the class he swooped off down the run. His pupils grinned sheepishly as they gathered together poles and gloves and followed his lead soon vanishing into the swirl of skiers. Surprisingly, the lady I thought had been left behind was amongst them and had skied off confidently.

Scanning the slopes above me I could make out the hunched figure on the ground and knew that I would have to clamber back up the slope to deal with the problem. I started to herringbone, a technique for climbing up a mountain on skis by splaying the skis out and walking with the edges turned inwards to prevent them sliding down the hill. It was exhausting when practised for long periods of time and my legs already ached after being subjected to hours of snowploughing yesterday! After a few metres I was breathless, hot, tired and fed up. Muttering to myself I removed my skis and balancing them on my shoulder continued my marathon ascent on foot.

Stopping to rest for a while I was able to establish the identity of my objective. It was Don who could ski quite well but he had spent a long time in the boot room yesterday evening adjusting his boots which he said had caused him some problems during the day. Clearly his efforts had not been rewarded and he was still sitting in the snow, both boots had been removed and he was in the process of putting his socks back on. An explanation was never offered concerning why it had also been necessary to remove this item of clothing.

"More problems with the boots?" I greeted him with as much sympathy as I could muster through my gasps for breath. A long explanation was supplied, not much different from the one I had heard yesterday but I listened patiently. There had been no suggestion that we re-joined the group so I had all morning to deal with the problem. The boots had been bought at great expense in London and had been moulded to fit his feet. Despite the fact they had caused problems yesterday and he had been told by the instructor to hire a pair to use during the remainder of the week (this was news to me) he had persisted with them. He was furious when he discovered that the rest of the group had carried on without waiting for him. Tactfully I pointed out that the others wanted to get on with the lesson but that I was sure that if we could get the boot problem solved this morning he could rejoin them tomorrow. Rashly I promised to get him a discount for the lesson he was not getting this morning.

Finally the boots were back in place and we set off down the mountain. One thing I had begun to appreciate about Madonna di Campiglio was the fact that all the lifts were inter-connecting and it was possible to ski down into the centre of town and then get back into the ski area via a drag lift. Proudly displaying my new knowledge of the area we made our way, slowly, down into the town. I managed to explain the problem to the assistant in the ski hire shop but Don himself was still not convinced there was a problem and when he was offered a pair of hire boots to try on he waved them aside. After all he had not paid over three hundred pounds to not wear a pair of boots. He suggested that I ask the assistant to 'fit' his own boots for him and I conveyed this message by mime and gestures. A shy, retiring person by nature I had initially found this aspect of my role very difficult and I found myself blushing profusely. Determined not to resort to repeating myself slowly and loudly in English over and over again I finally managed to convince the assistant that this was what my client wanted. Shrugging the hire boots aside adjustments were made until Don declared that the boots were comfortable and we set off back to the slopes. I suspected I had not made a friend of the puzzled assistant who watched us walk back across the small *piazza* in front of the shop, a resigned expression on his face.

When we re-joined the group for lunch I was not surprised to see the exasperated expressions of Don's group when he announced that the problem had been solved and he had not had to change his boots. In fact the problem had not been solved and I endured an afternoon of boot removing and excuses. A solution was found the next morning when the ski instructor simply refused to allow Don to join his class unless he changed his boots. So it was back to the hire shop for us. I wished I dare go to a different hire shop but as the one we used belonged to the hotel I decided this would not be a wise move and I suffered the triumphant demeanour of the assistant as he fitted Don with a pair of hire boots.

I continued to stumble through the week clinging to the thought that the nightmare would last only seven days. The smokers resolutely refused to stop smoking between courses and the division within the group became wider. When we met for drinks in the bar before dinner the non-smoking group always sat by the entrance to the restaurant and would actually stand up and block the way to the others while I was talking to them about the programme for the next day. As soon as I finished talking they would race into the dining area and commandeer a table on a 'by invitation only' basis.

Needless to say I was never invited to join them and dined with the smokers every evening.

Clare progressed well with her skiing and was soon promoted from the nursery slopes to the main skiing area which meant she could join us for lunch everyday. Don decided not to continue in ski school having been advised by one of his fellow pupils that he would be better off skiing with me every day. At least the boot problem had been solved so our progress was much quicker but how I longed to get away and explore further than the blue run we spent the whole week conquering. At the end of the week Don requested the promised 'refund' so I made my way to the ski school office hoping that there would be someone there to interpret for me. Fortunately there was someone who understood what I wanted but there was no comprehension of the problem. From their point of view Don had paid for lessons and he had chosen not to continue. But, as I pointed out, he had been ejected from the class by the ski instructor. The debate continued for some time and, although I could see their point, I had to represent my client who had been adamant that a refund was due. I was not one to crumple up in a weepy heap when not getting my way but my frustration was mounting and I was rapidly reaching the end of my tether. At the sight of my distress and no doubt alarmed at the thought of dealing with a sobbing female, the ski school director suddenly caved in. With an exasperated *"basta!"* (enough) he reached into the drawer in front of him and produced a handful of cash which he slapped on the counter between us.

My hard won victory now seemed very hollow and for some reason, instead of gathering up the cash and retreating with as much dignity as I could muster, I angrily pushed it back towards him and rushed out of the office. I walked back to the hotel to give myself time to calm down and decide what to do when confronted by Don who would no doubt expect a full refund! A partial refund out of my own money in the hope that he would be satisfied was my conclusion. After all, the director did have a point when he said that

Don himself had chosen not to continue with the lessons and had only actually been barred from one lesson. But abandoned during another I mused... But not really abandoned because he had been left in my care and also had not taken the advice of his instructor to change his boots. All too soon the brightly lit outline of our hotel loomed up in front of me and I pulled myself together ready to partake in the après ski gathering I was sure I would find in the bar.

* * *

I was jolted out of my reverie by a request from one of the group for the air conditioning in the coach to be turned on. We had completed our descent into the valley where the temperature was much warmer. Soon we would be speeding along the motorway towards the airport and the nightmare would be over. I told myself again this was definitely an experience not to be repeated. It had been so unexpectedly bad and not at all like my first experience of working as a tour leader on a ski holiday in the Dolomites. Never, ever again I told myself firmly.

Chapter Three – Summer Sojourn

Hooves clattered hollowly on the paved street and the people around me craned their heads forward, jostling for position, tense with expectation. Cheering broke out as first two horses and then a carriage came into view and made its way towards us, stopping just a few feet away. A footman rushed to open the door and lower the step. There was a rustle of crinoline as a beautiful lady stepped daintily down from the interior followed by her splendidly attired escort. Arm in arm they made their way slowly down the cobbled street acknowledging the populace with a casual wave. The first courtiers of the great Emperor Franz Josef had arrived in this, their summer retreat. This handsome couple then waited to be introduced by the master of ceremonies before making their way past the uniformed orchestra and taking their places alongside two empty thrones on the stage.

More courtiers followed some in carriages, some on horseback and some strolling arm in arm along the main thoroughfare. The orchestra started playing and the strains of Strauss waltzes floated in the background. The courtiers began to dance and the stage became a whirl of colours; the pastels of wide, flouncing skirts and the primary colours of jackets secured across the shoulders of the male escorts – hussars or dragoons maybe. The master of ceremonies, having completed his introductions began his narrative explaining the connection between this remote ski resort, high in the Dolomites and the mighty Austro-Hungarian Empire. Scandal had preceded the establishment of Madonna di Campiglio as a favourite summer haunt of the nobility of the Hapsburg court in Vienna. Rumours abounded that Franz Josef Oesterreicher who built the first modern hotel in the town, Grand Hotel Des Alpes where the court presided, was an illegitimate son of the Emperor Franz Josef himself. Further, it was suggested that the purchase of the necessary land was 'arranged' to ensure that this son had a beautiful place to live well away from the malicious gossips of the Viennese Court.

As the strains of the last waltz faded away the courtiers lined up each side of the still empty thrones ready to welcome the most famous of guests at this ball, none other than Franz Josef himself and his beautiful wife, Elisabeth of Wittelsbach, nicknamed "Sissi". Sissi, born in Bavaria, a region of woods and forests, had suddenly found herself 'imprisoned' by the trappings of the Hapsburg court when she was married at a very young age to Franz Joseph, Emperor of Austria. It is recorded that she suffered bad health and only found her release when sent away from the court to recover. Thereafter, this rebellious and sensitive spirit began to travel, always in search of inspiration. An accomplished rider and lover of nature she was also reputedly one of the most beautiful women in Europe and she took great care of her figure and her magnificent long hair. Sissi visited Madonna di Campiglio briefly in the summer of 1889 at which time the town was already popular as a holiday resort with the nobles and wealthy bourgeois of Europe who came to hunt and enjoy the incredible scenery.

It seems that Sissi vowed she would return to enjoy the pure air and amazing landscapes which this poetic lady found charming and peaceful. Indeed the imperial couple did return six years later in 1895 and resided for a month in the Hofer Hall in the Grand Hotel Des Alpes. Their arrival has been re-enacted in summer pageants and the elegant balls have been replicated during the famous Hapsburg Carnival, a week of splendid events held in February and featuring the Emperor's Great Ball. Anyone could attend this event, provided they were in costume. Local beauties competed to play the part of Sissi and open the dance flanked by two rows of Hussars and Dragoons, accompanied by the unforgettable waltzes composed by Strauss and his son who had provided the official music for this elegant era.

This pageant was a wonderful way to end my first summer working in Madonna di Campiglio. Yes, despite my resolve never to return to this place again, I was back! When our summer schedules were being discussed I had approached my turn with trepidation. Gripping the edge of the desk in front of me I leaned forward to learn my fate. Would it be Australia at last? My heart was pounding and I realised I was holding my breath. Madonna di Campiglio. I exhaled in a rush with a squeak of anguish. I dare not refuse, as it was my job to go where I was sent, but I was not looking forward to spending several weeks in the place where I had been such a disaster the previous winter.

When I arrived with the first group at the hotel I received a very warm welcome from all the staff. I was amazed that they even remembered me! I had forgotten just how beautiful and welcoming the reception area was, arrangements of fresh flowers reflected the care and attention to detail lavished on the hotel by the owner Signora Silvana and one really felt that she was welcoming guests into her own home. During the next few weeks I saw her many times coming back from an early morning walk with a large bunch of wild flowers that would then be arranged in small vases and appeared later on the dining tables. Exotic plants and flower arrangements decorated the reception and bar areas and there was always a beautiful collection of orchids positioned on the windowsills in the bar framing the wonderful view of the mountains from the picture windows.

I approached the first week of my summer sojourn in Madonna di Campiglio with all the energy of an enthusiastic ignoramus. Having discovered during my rather sketchy Information Meeting the first evening that I had a 'know-all' in the group (nearly every group has one) and determined not to be outwitted I got up at six o'clock the following morning and walked into town along one of four possible routes, a road parallel to the main road that was quiet and without traffic thundering by. I then strolled back along the route through the woods following the *Giro di Campiglio*, a wonderful experience. The flora on this beautiful path was festooned with dew-encrusted cobwebs shimmering in the pale early morning sunshine filtering through the trees. I was back in time to beat the early risers into breakfast and ready to outline the plan for our first day. We would walk into the town, have some free time exploring and then go up to the top of Spinale in the cabin lift for lunch. I had given everyone a map of the walking area the previous evening and I was able to point out our proposed excursion on the map – it all looked so easy! I was even able to counter our know-all's assertion that the fourth route, through the wood and over the stream below the hotel was a better route by announcing that as there had been a lot of heavy rain recently it would be too wet. I am sure that Neil's determination to tell me everything there was to know about the holiday emanated from the best of intentions but I would have much preferred that he did it in private. Public corrections made me feel very vulnerable. However, once I reverted to seeking his help when occasion demanded I saw another side of this skinny, professorial character and he subsequently proved to be a useful ally.

We set off into town making our way down the quieter 'low' road past row upon row of empty, shuttered apartments, too early in the season for most of the occupants. After crossing the stream and stopping to appreciate the small lake where fishing competitions were a regular occurrence through the summer, we arrived in the centre of town and paused in the main square, Piazza Righi, so that I could point out places of interest such as the local supermarket, the Tourist Information Office and the best place to get a pizza, the Ristorante Belvedere. I suggested we meet up in an hour and walk to the Spinale cabin lift to ascend the mountain and have lunch in the restaurant at the summit.

Many of us did not get beyond that square preferring to sit under a large sun umbrella outside the popular Suisse Bar enjoying a coffee and people watching. It seemed that the day was going really well and I was lulled into a false sense of security. Then, after marvelling at the views and taking some photos at the top of the Spinale cabin lift we made our way to the restaurant to find that it was closed. Never mind, we could descend in the cabin lift and have a *pizza* at the Belvedere *pizzeria*. We re-traced our steps to the cabin lift. Also closed. I had not considered the possibility that the ubiquitous siesta would affect our conveyance up and down the mountain. It would re-open in an hour so we had to decide whether to sit and wait or walk to the restaurant we could see in the distance. I had no idea how long the walk would take but at least we would feel that lunch was getting closer. As there was an overwhelming majority in favour of walking we set off along a path that seemed to take us in the right direction.

We were all captivated by the mass of wild flowers that carpeted the ground on either side of the path. Brilliant yellows, bright oranges and regal purples interspersed with pure white occupied our foreground and the wonderful panorama of the Brenta Dolomites made a perfect background. Our objective was clearly in sight ahead of us and we strolled happily along until our path swung to the right whereas our restaurant was to the left. Naively I decided to strike out across country. At first everything was fine and we ambled across a grassy meadow keeping an eagle eye open for the occasional cow pat. In the distance we could hear the tinny clanging of the bells of the perpetrators. It was blissful, we all agreed that lunch could wait. We gambolled down a gentle slope to find our progress abruptly halted by a shrub-encrusted precipice. Casting my eyes wildly around I spotted a narrow track heading in the right direction and calling out gaily to the group that 'this is the way" we set off. The path petered out and we were surrounded by a sea of green beyond which the restaurant was tantalisingly close. There must be a way down. I would hate to have to re-trace my steps. Frantically I scanned the impenetrable shrubbery and finally decided to force my way through. Feeling my way gingerly I told the group to form a single file behind me and we descended slowly. Only once did I encounter a hidden hollow and pitched forward into the greenery. Fortunately most of the group had a sense of humour and were able to see the funny side of our adventure when we were safely seated inside the restaurant ordering our food.

The next day I felt I was on reasonably safe ground as it was our first included half-day walk and we would be in the care of our local guide. We all assembled in the lobby at the appointed time and Nereo was introduced to us. Small in stature with white hair and weather-beaten face this was truly a man of the mountains, quiet and self-assured. *"Non parlo inglese"* he announced proudly. I was a bit alarmed to discover that he did not speak a word of English but having mastered the two hundred and fifty words necessary to get by in Italian I was sure we would manage. I knew that he had always been the local guide for our groups so I was ready to fall into place at the back of the group as the backmarker and follow his lead. Our first walk began at the far end of the town and Goran took us to the starting point in the hotel shuttle bus. We began by walking straight up a ski run. It was not long before we were all puffing and panting and begging for a rest but Nereo just plodded slowly along. I could disguise my own discomfort by pleading that as backmarker I had to stay behind everyone else! When we did stop we turned back to admire the views on the other side of the valley including the stark grey plateau of the Passo del Grostè accessed by the Grostè cabin lift. Unanimously we chorused our opinion that the panorama spread below and around us merited the effort of climbing up to this vantage point.

The following week when I had a regular visitor to Madonna di Campiglio in the group he told everyone the first evening that the walk started with a very steep ascent and the next morning when we assembled for the walk there were only three of us – Nereo, me and Rod the regular. However, things do change and Rod was not aware that after my first experience of the steep ascent I had investigated an alternative path and we now started on a level track through the woods emerging half way up the steep ascent which was within everybody's capabilities. Nereo waited patiently while I summoned up more support for the walk and we set off with nearly a full complement.

After the open green sward of the ski run we followed a lovely path through the woods that was strewn with tree roots and rocks. In places it was dappled with sunshine where the beams had penetrated the ceiling of leaves and branches above us. Rivulets of water gurgled down to the valley floor taking the quickest route through the trees and sometimes splashing across our path. Where some trees had been felled we emerged into a clearing, a slash of green grass on the wooded slope. We were right above the town which we could see in the valley below at the bottom of the steeply descending swathe of grass. Cow bells clanged in the distance and insects droned around us. Nereo was not one for pointing out photo opportunities so I told the group to stop and take pictures if they wanted to and we could then catch up with our guide who would eventually stop and patiently wait for us. After an hour strolling along enjoying this wonderful woodland way with occasional bursts of greenery spangled with multi-coloured wild flowers we emerged from the trees. And were amazed to see Lago di Nambino spread out before us, its green glossy water that reflected the green of the enclosing tree clad slopes, shimmering in the sunshine. Occasionally there was a small silver flash, and crystal drops glittered as a fish flipped out of the water causing ever widening circles to appear on the calm surface. We walked around the lake to the welcoming Rifugio Lago Nambino: a beautiful wooden structure built from local larch that grew in abundance on the slopes around the town. It had not taken me long to realise that the Italians had a real talent for ensuring that a welcoming *rifugio* was placed at strategic points on the network of paths that criss-crossed the mountains. These varied from quite basic wooden refuges to lovely rustic restaurants but they all offered food and shelter and some had rooms for guests seeking true solitude or trekking across the mountains.

Adults, children and dogs were sprawled on the small pebbly beach or relaxed in the chairs outside the *rifugio* which housed both a snack bar and a restaurant. Others enjoyed their refreshment at the tables and benches in the shade of the trees. There was a rotund wooden snack bar to ease the rush at busy times, a bowling alley and a large stone tank housing beautifully speckled trout. These lovely fish floated lazily in the clear water of their enclosure, moving as one large black shadow with an occasional ripple as a fin broke the surface. It must be coffee time I thought and indeed Nereo indicated we would have a break here, and then disappeared inside for beer and a *panino* (filled roll). It was so tranquil by the lake we were happy to relax and enjoy the calming scenery around us – some people were scanning the slopes with binoculars and when an eagle was spotted there was a clamour to have a turn with them in order to see a clear image of this regal bird.

The calmness of the water belied the legend that once the lake was home to a monster, initially considered harmless as it browsed on the little fish on the bottom of the lake and the algae in the water. Occasionally, when no one was around, it would emerge from the water and graze on grass around the shore. One day the creature emerged from the water and slaughtered two sheep, a calf and the shepherdess tending them causing great consternation in the region. No one had the courage to go near the lake to find out what had happened until two hunters from Val di Sole, the next valley, offered to seek justice for the shepherdess for a substantial reward of course.

So, one Sunday morning everyone from the town, the parish priest at the head of the procession, made their way to Lago Nambino. They all stopped and waited at the base of the last ascent while the two hunters continued alone. As they neared the lake the elder hunter told his younger companion to wait while he went ahead to see what was happening. When he arrived by the lakeside, heart in his mouth, he found a huge creature as big as a large bull, scales still damp from the water, curled up on a large slab of stone, its muzzle hidden between two powerful front legs. The hunter put his gun to his shoulder, took aim and fired. There was no movement from the beast and all that could be seen was a gush of blood from its throat. The hunter exclaimed with glee that he had succeeded and would now receive a fortune. But when the crowd finally made their way to the lakeside they did not, as expected, find the hunter holding his trophy aloft but instead he was lying on the ground in a faint a short distance from the slain beast. His young companion urged the crowd to stay back for he had realised immediately that the vile smelling gases emanating from the body of the beast had poisoned his friend causing him to pass out. Keeping his distance from the dead beast he managed to drag his friend away and he was laid across the back of a donkey and taken to the hospital in Madonna di Campiglio.

A few hours later when the air around the beast had returned to normal another surprise occurred. When they turned the body of the beast over in order to move it, the corpse burst into flames and from between its powerful back legs emerged a large white egg, the egg of a dragoness. The parish priest exclaimed that this was the cause of the unexpected madness of the beast, the imminent birth of another such creature and that the shepherdess had paid with her life for this new life. The priest took custody of the egg. Great celebrations were held in the weeks that followed and both the egg and the skin of the beast were displayed on the wall of the church. The hunter recovered and he and his companion claimed the reward that had been promised to them.

While the group were enjoying a coffee I wandered along the shore of the lake and came across a choir, out walking together, but now, seated on the ground, they were singing and their audience was joining in. It was magical and I stayed and listened for a while before going to tell the group so that we could all enjoy this impromptu concert until it was time to leave. We followed another rocky track through the woods and then emerged onto a road where Nereo indicated that we could have lunch at the Rifugio Patascoss ahead of us or we could continue down the road to another *rifugio*, a distance of about two kilometres. Everyone was happy to carry on and we followed the road through beautiful woodland, the grassy slopes on either side encrusted with the startling colours of wild flowers and in particular orderly rows of pale lilac hemp and bright yellow patches of ragwort. We ate at Malga Ritorto which was both a restaurant and a summer farm. We had encountered some cows ambling along the road towards their barn at the malga and we had watched in amusement as several frustrated drivers had been forced to get out of their vehicles to persuade recalcitrant beasts to move to the side.

Nereo was astonished by the request of the group to eat at the tables outside. But then Nereo was permanently amused by the antics of my groups. When we stopped for coffee (white wine or beer for Nereo whatever the time of day) or lunch he recounted our adventures to the locals and in particular his amazement that English people could walk and talk incessantly not even pausing when the path became too narrow for two people to walk abreast. Indeed on one occasion Rod actually fell off the path and Nereo had to rescue him! He was particularly amused when one lady, complete with walking poles and map strung round her neck fell over one of her poles while walking and consulting the map at the same time. Luckily only her pride was dented. He guffawed with laughter when I showed him my purple trophies after falling flat on my face when I tripped over the walking pole of the lady in front of me – a combination of my taking a step forward to hear what she was saying and the lady stopping to emphasise the point she was making, walking pole trailing behind her. On one of our walks Nereo found a porcini mushroom which he wrapped lovingly in his handkerchief and stowed in his rucksack. He managed to convey to the group that this was a real treat: *"gustoso"*, and it would be dried before being used for cooking. We often encountered locals with baskets searching for porcini which they would then sell to restaurants and hotels in the area to be made into delicious pastas and risottos.

Perched on a ridge above the valley the views from this *rifugio* were stunning, in front of us the peaks of the Brentas and behind us the peak of Palon. A popular place for picnics the grass was strewn with small groups of people, families and friends, enjoying a meal al fresco. Bizarrely, on this occasion a large group of nuns all clothed in black habits and white headdresses stood demurely in a circle throwing a ball from one to the other. The stage seemed set for the Sound of Music and some of my group felt compelled to break into song. Lots of photographs were taken before the sisters clambered back into their bus giggling shyly.

Large timber tables with sturdy wooden benches outside the building were crowded with people enjoying the traditional cuisine and two young waitresses passed to and fro holding aloft plates of steaming polenta with a variety of accompaniments such as goulash, melted cheese, spicy sausage and sauerkraut. Some people I noticed had retreated inside to the welcoming atmosphere of red and white check clad tables and shiny wooden chairs and I was happy to join them.

Nereo had already disappeared inside and ate on his own but he did re-appear to check that we were okay and to ask if anyone wanted to return to the hotel in the shuttle bus or did they prefer to walk back. Most opted to return to the hotel on foot and after the shuttle bus had been ordered for those who had decided to go back and wallow on sun beds on the sun terrace of the hotel, the rest of us set off after our guide. After an hour walking down a very pleasant path through the woods we were soon at Panorama, a popular viewpoint, from where it was not far to our hotel. A lovely day, one without incident and I looked forward to the second walk with Nereo. The following day I hoped would also pass without incident as were spending the day on Lake Garda, the first of our optional full day excursions.

After dinner that evening Stefano was playing in the bar and the group loved him. He was a great musician and switched easily between several instruments including the trombone, trumpet and keyboard. At first we sat and applauded politely after each rendition but then we started to sing along and Stefano came alive and turned to play in our direction. My feet were tapping and before long I was on the floor and pushing tables and chairs out of the way so that we could dance to the music. It was a great night and one that has been repeated with nearly every group that has stayed there. What I hoped never to repeat was the occasion when two girls decided, as a joke, to dance round their handbags which they placed right in the centre of the floor and one of them tripped over the bags and spent the next few weeks on crutches recovering from torn ligaments.

Setting off early the next morning in our hired coach we meandered down the mountain on our way to the northern shores of Lake Garda, the biggest lake in Italy. During our journey we criss-crossed the River Sarca on its journey from its source in Madonna di Campiglio into the lake at Torbole. Volume and speed of traffic could be an issue on these days out, particularly as road works burst out like flowers in spring as soon as the winter snows receded. Gradually this main thoroughfare to Trento or Lake Garda was being widened and straightened and the numerous small towns were being by-passed. As we wended our way along the valley floor Arco Castle stood proudly above us on a natural rock summit guarded by sentinels of cypresses that marched up the slope from the town. This imposing castle housed the Arco family between the twelfth and sixteenth centuries when they were finally enticed down from the heights to more convenient accommodation in the town. Our first stop was Riva del Garda a pretty, elegant resort that stretched along the lakeside and was memorable for the pastel coloured buildings that surrounded the Apponale Tower on the waterfront. From the top of this tower the lake stretched out ahead of us, the green clad slopes of the magnificent Dolomite Mountains plunged straight into the glacial blue waters. While recording these fabulous views we kept our distance from the large bell that still chimed the quarter hour.

A gentle stroll along the waterfront was rewarded by the sight of many welcoming tables and chairs shaded by sun umbrellas, a chance to idle away some time chatting over a welcome cappuccino or maybe an early morning cocktail. Such was the enthusiasm of the waiters all vying for custom that we found ourselves seated and ordering before making a conscious decision to do so. Some lingered there appreciating the spectacle before them but the ardent shoppers in the group were keen to take advantage of the many bargains in leather goods available.

Just beyond our coffee stop was the fortress, the Rocca of Riva, originally Roman and built by the inhabitants in 1124 to defend their city. Built on the lake itself, it has been enlarged and altered over the years and is accessed across a drawbridge. At the foot of Monte Rocchetta behind the ferry port was the impressive Hydroelectric

Power Station Ponale which was opened in 1926 by the famous Italian poet Gabriele D'Annunzio. Designed by local architect Giancarlo, it was the first project to exploit the Ledro-Garda waters using the 500-metre drop between the two lakes in adjoining valleys. On the west side of Riva, high above the town is the Bastione, a Venetian fortress of 1505, originally established in 1450 it was rebuilt by the Venetians as a round shape to avoid gun shots and was now one of the symbols of modern Riva.

It did not seem long until we had to join the scramble to board the ferry to Malcesine and we were soon chugging sedately across the vast expanse of water. First stop Torbole where brave windsurfers flirted outrageously with the wake of our vessel, often being rewarded with a warning toot from the bridge. Our ferry then made its way back across the water to Limone where the majority of the passengers disembarked and we could spread ourselves out ready to enjoy the last half hour of our journey. As we approached Malcesine, the Castle Scaligero, built from the stone malus silex from which the name of the town was derived, quietly observed our arrival from its vantage point above the town. It was certainly worth ascending the narrow cobble stoned streets to enjoy the views from there but first stop, lunch. We soon left the milling crowds on the lakeside and plunged down the shaded back alleys arriving, after a few twists and turns, in a small courtyard bounded on one side by the lake and on the other by a row of three restaurants. A friendly waiter emerged from the depths of *La Pace*, the middle restaurant, greeted my group and started arranging tables for them in the shade of the outside canopy. Relaxed and content we drank in the georama laid out before us, not to mention a carafe or two of the local wine which slipped down nicely with my favourite dish, *spaghetti alle vongole*. Some livelier members of the party decided to grab a slice of *pizza* and make their way to the cable car in the hope that long queues would not thwart their desire to ascend to the top of Monte Baldo in the large revolving cable car.

Back at the ferry most people appeared laden with carrier bags full of irresistible bargains gleaned from the many sales that seem to be permanently in full swing here. We joined the queue for the ferry and a much more sedate embarkation. This time we travelled on the massive vehicle ferry although there were no vehicles aboard. Sun loungers were lined up on the top deck and most people raced up the narrow steps to take full advantage of this sun bathing opportunity. Despite my jocular warnings about not relaxing too much and falling asleep inevitably there was the occasion when that is exactly what happened. As usual I had waited until everyone was off the ferry but this time although I had not seen one of our group his companions were certain he had disembarked ahead of them. The ferry was already on the move but I remained where I was watching the ferry recede into the distance, half expecting to see someone on deck frantically waving – nothing. As I finally turned away my mobile started vibrating in my pocket. It was Ian to tell me that he was still on the ferry having dozed off and then, aware that he did not have time to get down to ground level to disembark had decided to remain where he was and soak up a few more rays. Now, of course, it had occurred to him that he was heading back to Riva del Garda but the bus was meeting us at Limone! Every group was instructed to keep the hotel phone number with them and to call the hotel if any problems arose wherever they were so this call had been re-routed via the hotel switchboard (nice to know my system worked). The problem was easily solved and we were re-united an hour later when our bus drove back through Riva del Garda.

Once, while waiting for the ferry from Malcesine to Limone one of the group was missing – people did tend to get carried away in the shops and appeared as the ferry approached the jetty but this time the ferry was already disgorging its passenger and still there was no sign. Then I caught sight of a distraught figure emerging from one of the side streets and racing towards the ferry, her hair was soaking wet and plastered to her face – indeed so was her shirt! As she ran towards us I realised she was my missing person and waited on the gangplank to make sure the ferry did not leave without her. Today it was the steamboat that operated as a ferry on the lake. A beautiful reminder of times gone by and on board strategically placed glass panels allowed passengers to watch the wheels churning.

As soon as my lady was on board I could satisfy my curiosity about her sodden state and inquired if she had been swimming. I was rewarded with a scathing glance and the response that she had deliberately gone into the water fully clothed. In fact she had been reading by the waterside and when she leant forwards to look down into the water her sunglasses had slipped off her head and drifted down to the bottom of the lake. So clean and clear was the water that she thought she could reach down and rescue her glasses but in fact her hand went down and down and then she overbalanced and almost toppled into the water. By now her head and shoulders were immersed in the water but fortunately help was at hand and a gentleman came to her rescue, pulling her back onto dry land. She did at least have the presence of mind to hang on to the sunglasses and then to make her way straight to the ferry having realised that time had passed more quickly than expected. Clucking sympathetically I suggested we hang the wet shirt out to dry while we were on the ferry – her skimpy sun top underneath would also benefit from a good airing. By the time we arrived in Limone her clothes and humour were restored and she was ready to explore this enchanting little place.

Although Limone does mean lemon this is not generally considered to be the derivation of the name of this fascinating lakeside town but rather from the Latin word '*limes*' meaning border, as the village was situated on the former Italian-Austrian border. Strolling through the narrow, winding cobble streets overlooked by rows of olive trees on the terraces above, one could imagine its origin as a simple fishing village. Then during the fifteenth century Limone developed into the most northerly centre for the cultivation of citrus fruits and it was during this period that the world famous Limonaia or lemon groves were constructed. Distinctive high stone walls protected the trees from the cold winds and the huge columns in the groves supported the wooden rafters of a cover used in winter to create a greenhouse effect. However, it was a struggle as earth to grow the trees had to be imported from the southern part of the lake to supplement the impoverished soil in the area. An impressive irrigation system was devised to water the trees. During the nineteenth century, while part of the Hapsburg Empire, Limone was producing an impressive list of products such as magnesia, paper, quicklime and silkworms. Sadly due to its position on the border, right in the middle of the combat zone, Limone was completely evacuated during the First World War and when the inhabitants returned after the war nothing remained of their former prosperity. They began again as fishermen and olive growers hampered by their isolated position as the village was accessible only by water or over difficult mountain paths. Limone was not connected directly with the next villages until 1932 following the construction of the renowned Western Gardesena Road, still used today. The opening of this road heralded the arrival of tourism in the area which transformed this poor fishing village into one of the most prosperous centres on the lake. Olives were still grown there and, pressed cold inside a stone mill, these well-nurtured, hand-picked fruits produced a pure, high quality oil, delicious when dribbled over a piece of fresh white bread.

We all met in the coach park at Limone at half past four to make our way back to the hotel, a journey of one hour and a half but as most people dozed in the bus it passed quite quickly. For the first fifteen minutes we drove along the lake side through the tunnels that penetrated the hard rock of the mountains, glimpsing the water through the regular natural windows hollowed out of the rock. A last opportunity to savour the unique vista of mountains shelving into the waters of the lake. And to watch the numerous yachts and wind surfing boards scudding across the water taking advantage of the wind that blows across the lake every single day of the year.

The following day we renewed our acquaintance with Nereo, our walking guide. Some people approached this, our second walk with some trepidation as our Know All had warned of steep ascents up the side of the waterfall. I had encouraged them to come on the basis that they could turn back and retrace their steps at this point and we could still all meet up for lunch in the same *rifugio*. We departed from the hotel and joined the Giro di Campiglio just across the bridge and made our way through the wood, across another road and then back into the woods. This path went right down into the bottom of the valley where we crossed the stream again on a wooden bridge reminiscent of the rickety rackety bridge where the trolls lived. One could even imagine a troll jumping out from one of the caves around you or lurking under one of the massive overhangs of the dolomite stone on either side of the water.

The path then crossed one of the many small rivulets that crept slowly down the slopes to join the stream. According to one of the local guides all rivers and streams in Madonna di Campiglio were referred to as the 'Sarca' and certainly from this network of small rivers and streams one main river finally emerged and flowed down the mountain eventually entering Lake Garda. We followed a lovely leaf strewn path through spaciously placed deciduous trees that allowed the sunlight to stream through and dapple the ground around us. It was possible to see the valley floor at the bottom of the sloping bank to our right and occasionally one was rewarded with the chestnut flash of *capriolo* (roe deer) scampering down the slopes and vanishing into the trees. Not too many roots to negotiate so one's feet could wander as freely as one's thoughts with impunity. From the silence in front of me I suspected that I was not the only one occupied with my own thoughts. During our first walk everyone had chatted animatedly the whole time but now that the group had got to know each other we walked along in companionable silence.

We heard the thunder of tons of water crashing down from a great height long before we could see the rush of water sparkling through the trees and then it was right there before us, le Cascate di Vallesinella di Mezzo, a breathtaking sight. There was plenty of time to contemplate this marvel of nature as this was also our coffee stop and we reconvened at the little *rifugio* above us before continuing on our way to the second waterfall, le Cascate Alte di Vallesinella. Rod the regular had left much earlier than the rest of us and had arranged to meet us here when we stopped for coffee. When we left there was still no sign of him so we split up and I took an alternative route, straight up a gravel road rather than the more gentle zigzag that climbed up the side of the waterfall in case he was on that road. Rod was famous for getting lost. I waited for a while but he did not appear. While waiting I recalled that two days earlier Rod had volunteered to show some people a short route back to the hotel along the path through the woods. As he walked he had been so deep in conversation that he had taken the wrong path and they had retraced their steps back to Malga Ritorto, the lunch venue! Rod became aware of his mistake when he caught sight of the *rifugio* through the trees and immediately did a complete about turn to avoid the realisation they had walked a complete circle. Meanwhile I was fretting at the hotel because we had completed the longer walk and they were at least an hour overdue.

I rejoined the group at the point where our two paths met and we continued on our way towards le Cascate Alte. We did not see Rod again until we all met for dinner that evening as he had indeed got lost, very lost. Despite persistent questioning during our evening meal I never really established exactly where Rod got to that day. I suspect Rod had no idea where he had been either!

On our way we passed the Rifugio Vallesinella where we would return for lunch later, and traversed a large car park, the starting place for serious walks in the mountains above us. We passed an Information Point which signified that we had just entered the Parco Natural Adamello Brenta. Madonna di Campiglio is an island in the 618 square kilometres of this extensive park in the western area of Trentino. Created in 1967 the park included 39 municipalities and a diverse environment as the height of the terrain varied from 400 metres to 3,500 metres and covered woods, pastures, grasslands, rocky areas and glaciers. The flora and fauna were among the richest in Europe and included the brown bear which was the subject of a local conservation programme. Park authorities organise transport and events to maximise enjoyment of this amazing area. One initiative was the regular shuttle bus that ran between the centre of Madonna di Campiglio and the car park at Vallesinella. This was a big improvement as previously cars could go in both directions along this narrow road and would often come to a halt with two or three cars trying to pass each other. On one occasion while walking back down this road there was a complete impasse as a nervous lady driver did not dare manoeuvre her car too close to the edge of a precipice, so a gallant gentleman jumped out of his car and moved it for her allowing the other cars to get past safely. The new system dramatically limited the traffic on this hitherto busy road and the cars that did drive along the road had to follow the *navetta* (shuttle bus) thus preventing traffic jams.

    Back in the woods we made our way along a wide path through the trees occasionally catching glimpses of the river gurgling and splashing beside us. One last steep climb, round a sharp bend of craggy rocks and we found ourselves gazing up at le Cascate Alte. This final ascent sometimes represented the last straw for novice walkers in my groups and I often had to encourage them to take the last few steps in order to enjoy the spectacular view of the second waterfall rather than simply turn back and retrace their steps to the lunch spot. At this point the water rushed down past us and sometimes spilled on to the path convincing some that we were already by the waterfall.

Now we had alternative paths available and we could either walk up the side of the waterfall on a well-constructed path guarded by fences where the mountain descended suddenly to the valley, or to re-trace our steps to the *rifugio*. Generally the majority chose the first option. The first time I did this walk even I was in fear and trembling at the thought of clambering up the side of the waterfall having listened to the dire warnings of our Know All. Fortunately, unbeknown to him since his last visit here the path had been improved and fencing had been erected on the side of the steep drop. I was glad I had waited to see just how difficult the path was before expressing any opinion to the group and we all successfully conquered the climb without any problem. Half way up the clear water gushed past us and Nereo indicated that the water was good to drink so I filled my small plastic water bottle to try it. It was wonderful, icy cold and very refreshing.

At the top of the waterfall, which we had climbed amazingly quickly we caught our breath in a wonderful mountain meadow from which there was a fantastic view of the stark grey peaks above the tree line. *"Che bella vista"*, Nereo summed it up in one short phrase and an expansive gesture with his hand. No wonder this was one of the most popular paths in the area. Once we had reached the summit we generally took a group photograph and everyone usually gathered around a large mossy rock. On one such occasion unbeknown to me happily snapping away on fifteen different cameras they were actually perched on a wasps nest and as soon as I had finished they all leapt up and scattered in all directions. I have often wondered about the facial expressions in that particular photograph.

Our path continued through the meadow and then around the contours of the mountain before plunging down to the Rifugio Vallesinella. It was a lovely path with stunning views across the valley and banks thickly carpeted with flowers on either side. On future walks I was tempted to dawdle along at the back and risk incurring Nereo's serious displeasure. But there was a time I became totally engrossed in deep conversation with a member of the group. We kept stopping to admire the flowers on our way and especially the extraordinary displays of lilac coloured hemp whose leaves were being munched into intricate lacework by an army of caterpillars. It seemed one could actually hear the chomping of hundreds of tiny jaws and see the patterns forming instantly on the broad leaves.

Our objective now was lunch and we were soon seated outside the Rifugio Vallesinella under a large awning protecting us from the strong sunlight and enjoying a house speciality, the delicious *pasta delle delizie di bosco*. This dish generally comprised tagliatelle in a sauce of tiny mushrooms, tomato and cream with a hint of something it was difficult to identify. I had to forgo this treat on one occasion when, having just placed my order, a client announced that she had left her camera at the top when we had taken the group picture. I cancelled my order and then went inside to find Nereo and tell him I was going to walk back up to the top to look for the camera. He indicated that it would no longer be there as there were so many *stranieri* walking in the area it had probably been picked up already. If a local found it then it would be handed in to the *carabinieri*. Nevertheless I decided to take a chance and in the hope that it had not been discovered yet. I went back along the path we had just descended, asking people I met on the way if they had seen the camera at the top. My Italian had been improving with each new situation I had had to deal with. No one had seen it and a thorough search at the top was not successful. I walked back down, reported back to my client and said I would ring the *carabinieri* as soon as we got back. I was not without hope as earlier this season a client had dropped a wallet in the centre of town and it had been taken to the *carabinieri* and later re-claimed by the owner, the contents still in tact.

After lunch the group split up some returning to the hotel and some walking back down the road. Nereo never joined us on this walk preferring to ride back in the hotel shuttle bus as he did not like walking down the road and he considered the other option, a narrow path that clung to the side of the mountain, a dangerous alternative. Ultimately I investigated this possibility and found it to be a delightful path as it did take one high above the town but I could see why Nereo was wary of taking a large group along this barely distinguishable leaf strewn track.

Trento, originally settled by the Romans when it was called *Tridentum*, was next on the programme. This name was derived from the fact that the original settlement was surrounded by three hills or 'teeth'. I was eager to explore this lovely town again as I knew that over the last few years the many historic buildings in Trento had been lovingly restored and the town boasted many beautiful frescoes. We left our bus at the Castello di Buonconsiglio, a fascinating building constructed over three separate periods, which was reflected in the diverse architecture. This castle was once the home of the Prince Bishops who wielded both temporal and religious power in the area between 1027 and 1796 when Napoleon conquered the area. The region was later assigned to the Hapsburg Empire in 1813 and the Austrians took possession of the castle. Strolling along the Via Antonio Manci we retraced the steps of the Prince Bishops between their splendid residence and their private church, the Cathedral, where they worshipped. The importance of this route was reflected in the magnificence of the buildings that lined the street. As Trento was strategically positioned on the main route from Northern Europe to Southern Europe through the Brenner Pass and it was acceptable to both Italians and Germans it was selected as the meeting place for the Council of Trent. Bestowing such an honour on this small city led to a flurry of building, grand renaissance residences in the town itself and also on the outskirts so that the members of the Council could retreat from the heat at night time.

Due to pestilence, plagues and floods the Council, an attempt to rectify the differences between Catholic and Protestant teaching, lasted from 1545 to 1563. Subsequently, when the railway was built in 1850 the course of the river, the River Adige, was changed and the advent of the railway dramatically reduced the traffic on the river. Via Manci was still punctuated with narrow alleys that once led down to jetties on the waterside but now emerged onto Via Torre Verde that was built along the old river course. On our way we passed the arcades of Mancini Suffragio; originally built of wood it was here that the German merchants sold the goods they had brought down the river. Just down this road we could see the medieval Torre Verde Green built to defend the port on the river and where ships loaded with goods had to pay the tolls imposed by the Prince Bishops.

Our route took us past the Tourist Information Office and we called in to collect maps of the city before we continued on our way to the main square, Piazza Duomo. As Thursday was market day a short coffee break was followed by a meander through the numerous stalls that straggled along three streets and spilled into the Piazza Duomo adding bustle and colour to this lovely square. We sipped our coffee overlooked by the tower, the oldest building in the *piazza*. This tall, narrow stone tower was built in 1000 and was the first building in Trento to be constructed in stone. Originally a prison it has retained the small cell windows. The building next door, the Palazzo Vango, was built by the Prince Bishops who lived there until they moved to the castle. While enjoying our break we had time to admire the lovely frescoes on the buildings around us which were painted at the beginning of the sixteenth century. The Duomo was Romanesque style reflected by the wheel of fortune on the outside wall, typical of this architectural style. As the Duomo took 200 years to build, the outside and the inside reflected very different styles as it was finally completed during the Gothic era.

Later we made our way back to the Castello del Buonconsiglio to enjoy a wander around this fascinating building and explore the current exhibition housed within the many interesting rooms. The highlight of our tour was viewing the unique medieval painting, the Ciclo dei Mesi that decorated the interior of the Torre dell' Aquila. An audio guide provided some background history and a fascinating explanation of the content of the paintings and the techniques used in those days to produce such detailed representations of the daily life of that period. When we finally emerged into the bright sunlight again we discussed our experiences over a snack lunch under the cool shade of a large white sun umbrella outside the small café in the castle grounds.

Soon after leaving Trento we passed by the beautiful Lago di Toblino and stopped briefly at the Castello Toblino to enjoy a stroll along the lakeside. A small snack bar on the waterside offered a chance to enjoy the peace and tranquillity and to share some titbits with the ducks, drakes and moorhens that seemed to know when an opportunity to cadge some food had arrived as they suddenly appeared and bobbed expectantly in the water below us. Once a summer retreat for the Prince Bishops the castle above us was now a private restaurant. Lazing by the lake we could see a flock of blue herons flying to and from their nests in the trees across the water. We paused again on our journey back to Madonna di Campiglio to call in at the Cantini Pisoni, a vineyard where four generations of the Pisoni family have been producing wine since 1862.

Our tour began in a cave, once a refuge during World War II and now a cellar for the fermentation of *spumante* produced by the *metodo classico* and lined with high racks of bottles on both sides. The constant temperature of 13ºC was a welcome relief from the heat outside. Following the production line to its conclusion we saw bottles inverted in the wooden *pupitre* where Uncle Vittorio turned every single bottle every single day for thirty days until the dead yeast had all collected in the neck of the bottle. This 'plug' was then ready to be quick frozen and was expelled when the cap was prised off the bottle. Uncle Vittorio, a sprightly sixty year old, seemed to be the permanent 'guardian' of the vineyard as he was always around and I came to know him very well. He would tell me who, if anyone, was available to conduct our tour. On one occasion he took us round himself, assuming my Italian was good enough to translate his narrative. He spoke at such speed I found it almost impossible to follow what he said but I could remember a lot of information from previous visits and relied on that to explain to the group what they were seeing. However, I did understand his invitation *"prendite un po' di spumante?"* He could always be relied on to produce a bottle of *spumante* to taste.

By this stage of the tour we were surrounded by barique barrels in which genuine Vino Santo was fermenting naturally, an agreeable sweet wine and a good accompaniment to a strong cheese such as Gorgonzola. Next stop was the *grappa distilleria*, designed by Giuliano Pisoni, a structure of copper and aluminium, sparkling with cleanliness and bristling with dials it filled a large, lofty room, reminiscent of many a science fiction adventure. Finally we entered the small tasting room where we were offered the opportunity to try the *grappa*. Such a confusion of flavours it was difficult to decide which to taste first, the 'pure' *grappa* at 40 per cent proof or one of the many interesting flavours such as bilberry, green apple, rose, honey or mouth-watering chocolate, all a mere 20 per cent.

During our tasting Bruno, our bus driver, suddenly burst into the room an alarmed expression on his face and he indicated that I should return with him to the bus immediately. Mystified I followed him out to the small courtyard where we had parked. I clambered onto the bus and could immediately hear a strange whirring noise. Making my way down the bus I discovered that the noise was coming from a camera that had been left on one of the seats. I remembered that a lady in the group, while soaking her feet in the shallows of Lago Toblino had dropped her camera in the water. She had left it on the bus to dry out and when it did so it then started to noisily re-wind itself to the consternation of Bruno who had no idea what was going on! When we explained what had happened he was soon able to see the funny side of the situation and just roared with laughter. I suspected the contents of the tip envelope expressed the concern of the group regarding the fright he had received while recumbent in the coach waiting for our tour to finish.

Our last full day was imminent and we discussed the options over dinner the previous evening. Several people wanted to explore the next town down the mountain, Pinzolo, and as the small weekly market would be taking place in Carisolo, so close it was virtually part of the same town we decided to go there. Half the group on the local bus and the other half on foot. I was delighted to have the opportunity to explore the original road between the two towns as this road had been replaced by another road in the 1930s. Having waved goodbye to the group at the bus stop we made our way down a path from the hotel, past the new cemetery and on to the old road that descended down to the valley and then back up again emerging in the small village of Sant' Antonio di Mavignolo. It seemed churlish not to stop at the bar on the opposite side of the road and we sat in the sun enjoying a drink before setting off again. This time our route took us past a tiny old church and then a more modern place of worship as we continued our descent. We strolled along by the river and past the hydro-electric power station, a very pleasant, easy walk along a wide gravel path that finally led us onto the bridge that separated Carisolo from Pinzolo.

As the market was already packing up we continued into the town pausing briefly to appreciate the macabre painting of the Dance of Death that adorned the exterior of the church of St Viglio. This was the work of the Bascheni brothers and was completed in 1539. The brothers were responsible for many other wonderful works of art in this area. After admiring this masterpiece and investigating the interesting interior of the church we crossed the road and ascended the cabin lift to the mid station. Much fear and trepidation ensued at the sight of our second conveyance to Doss del Sabion at the summit, a four-man chair lift. Eventually, with much squealing and giggling everyone was on their way and we were soon re-united with the rest of the group in the restaurant at the top. From here we could enjoy a panorama that included views both up and down the valley and we could pick out the Hotel Lorenzetti at the entrance to Madonna di Campiglio that sprawled along the valley ahead of us. We could have stayed up there for hours but we had to descend and make our way back to the hotel, the group to do their packing and me to sort out my lists and confirm arrangements for the new arrivals.

As we parted company at the hotel entrance I noticed some mountain bikes parked outside and decided that it would be a good idea to use one of them to go into the town as I needed to do some shopping. Wobbling round the corner on the bike I was trying out for size I suddenly found myself in the middle of a flurry of fur, paws and furious barking. I managed not to fall off the bike and was relieved to see that the rope to which the dog was attached was at full stretch and it could not get any closer. I was also aware that despite the racket the tail was wagging furiously so I suspected it was all noise and no threat. Nevertheless, I retreated rapidly to the safety of the hotel car park. Despite having now stayed in the hotel for two full weeks I had been totally unaware that they had a dog on the premises. As I backed away the dog immediately calmed down and returned to the shadow of the building and once again curled up into a tight, tight ball.

Regaining my composure I paused before setting off down the main road. It was a beautiful summer afternoon and everything around me gave the appearance of slumbering under the azure sky. Bees droned lazily in the bright pink blossom of the creeping geraniums that adorned every balcony. Another perfect day. I felt content and at peace, an unusual feeling for me as I was constantly on the go. Gazing at the mountains above me, my mountains, I began to yearn for some free time alone in this beautiful place.

The Brenta Dolomites from the Hotel Lorenzetti

Le Cascate di Mezzo in winter

Last Run

Walking in the Brenta Dolomites

Reflecting in Style at the Hotel Lorenzetti

Lake Garda at Riva del Garda

Piazza Duomo, Trento

Delicious Dessert at the Hotel Lorenzetti

Chapter Four – Tabata

A brilliant white patch of snow, lingering after the spring melt, glistened in the afternoon sun that bathed the soft grey and pink peaks in warm light. The pale blue, cloudless sky and filigree haze made a perfect background for these splendid cathedrals of nature. Occasionally a metallic flash and a white trail indicated passing air traffic. For once I was glad not to be aboard one of them and on my way somewhere else. I was content to laze in a chair on the balcony gazing at the sharp turrets that towered above me. I wanted to imprint this picture on my mind forever.

This glorious view of the Dolomites, or, more precisely the Brenta Dolomites was the perfect backdrop for the Hotel Lorenzetti perched by the main road a kilometre down the mountain from the fashionable ski resort of Madonna di Campiglio. I was not the only one fascinated by this fabulous view as below me a constant stream of cars pulled into the car park and remained there for a few minutes while the occupants got out to marvel and take photographs. I had a whole week to take as many photographs as I liked, I was on holiday, my first holiday for five years.

Some days tiny white fluffy clouds scudded playfully around the peaks in a sea of electric blue like waves teasing rocky islands. When long fingers of mist wreathed the lower slopes the spires and steeples above had the appearance of a fairytale castle housing a princess awaiting her prince to scale the heights, an edelweiss plucked from the crags clutched in his hand to prove his love, devotion and courage. Other days these summits were obscured by thick grey clouds that occasionally parted to reveal dark, menacing peaks that would emerge later clad with fresh snow, whatever the season. This incredible landscape had drawn me back, like many others before me, to explore the numerous well kept and clearly defined paths that scaled the heights and meandered through the valleys.

I lingered over tea and some of the hotel's delicious *biscottini*, tiny sweet biscuits made daily in their kitchen. Through half closed eyes I watched Giacomo the barman threading his way smoothly between sun beds supporting sprawling bodies as he delivered trays of tea and cakes, cups of coffee and large glasses of cold beer with savoury nibbles. I wondered how he could remain so coolly efficient in his black jacket and black bow tie as he trotted up and down the stairs from the bar to the sun terrace below.

Being entirely on my own in a hotel was a completely new experience for me but I was not concerned as I had already made many friends among the staff, people who had worked here for many years and who always gave me a warm welcome. I was particularly glad that I would be able to renew my acquaintance with the delightful owner, Signora Silvana and try to converse in Italian as I had been practising several phrases that I could use for the occasion. I was aware that I would probably need Sandro, the maître d', to help me to understand the answers though. I glanced at my watch and decided it was time to change for dinner.

Later, as I made my way to the restaurant I caught sight of Giacomo who gave me a cheery wave and invited me to indulge in a prosecco that he knew was my favourite aperitif. I perched on one of the high leather covered bar stools and sipped my drink and munched a few crisps while we caught up on the news. Giacomo teased me by asking at what time he should prepare the Welcome Drink for the group. I responded laughingly that I was "*in vacance*". It was so good to be back! Giacomo was very slight in build and nearly always seemed to have dark circles around his eyes. Phenomenally he seemed able to work and sleep at the same time. And although he appeared to spend a lot of time propped up against the bar, usually at the opposite end to any clients who may be there, the bar was always spotless, he was always available when required and within a few hours of their arrival he would know the room numbers of everyone in my group. The only time he slipped up was when three men, in one of my groups, always drank together and the same person always ordered the drinks but gave different room numbers. When the bills were paid at the end of the week the gentleman whose bill was three times the amount he expected had a 'quiet word' with me. Not surprisingly the other two whose bills were zero, said nothing! Eventually the bill was divided equally between the three of them.

I was slightly nervous about my first meal alone in the hotel and approached the restaurant with a paperback clutched in my hand. I need not have worried. Sandro, who really did have eyes in the back of his head, was by my side instantly and led me to a table in the middle of the dining area. The other setting on this table for two was immediately removed and while this was happening Sandro continued to chat and to include the guests around me in the conversation with the result that every evening thereafter I was always given a friendly greeting when I went into dinner. Regulars returned here year after year and as Sandro conversed with them he would draw newcomers and single diners into the conversation creating a wonderful atmosphere of conviviality between the guests. I felt really at home and instead of burying my nose in a book found that I was happy to observe what was happening around me and I became fascinated by the performance that was dinner in the hotel.

By seven fifteen every evening the stage was set. Preparations had begun at eight o'clock that morning and had continued throughout the day every player in the drama taking a part, the two maître d's and several waiters all in their pristine white shirt sleeves going about their business following a well rehearsed routine. From the breakfast room, while enjoying the first meal of the day, it was possible to hear the chink of cutlery being polished and see the shadows of waiters gliding from task to task in the restaurant area. Fresh, discreet, pale cloths had been unfolded and spread carefully on table tops which soon shimmered with sparkling glassware and gleaming cutlery. Each piece of cutlery had been buffed before being laid precisely in its place, every glass had been polished and then set down with its companions in groups of three. Bundles of decorative twigs or small vases of fresh flowers and a single candle completed the setting. The dark pink upholstered chairs, each in its correct place, awaited their occupants.

Now, waiting in the wings were the key players of this daily show, Sandro and Paolo, who shared the role of maître d', each having their own areas of responsibility. Sandro was in charge of the waiters, supervising their work and their training. Paolo took care of the wine. Very different in character they worked well together and complemented each other. Sandro was neat and efficient in everything he did. His handsome Southern Italian dark appearance had caused a flutter in many a female heart. A true perfectionist, when Sandro served a coffee everything was placed conveniently in reach, he even took the top of the sugar basin and propped it against the side, the spoon inside turned in the direction of the drinker.

Paolo was leaner and taller: a chirpy personality who loved to clown around to the great amusement of the guests. Always cheerful he trotted around doing his job and occasionally displaying great flashes of humour as he would suddenly poke his head through an archway between the different sections of the restaurant and burst into an operatic aria. If a guest requested the appearance of someone from the kitchen more than likely it would be Paolo wearing a chef's hat on his head and carrying a wooden spoon in his hand, all set up by Sandro, to whom the request had been made. They make a good double act and between them managed to maintain a perfectly organised restaurant. Seasonal ebbs and flows meant that sometimes they had to wait on table as well as fulfilling their other roles as the number of waiters diminished in proportion to the reducing number of guests. Sandro would also occasionally appear behind the bar and, as with every task he undertakes, did an excellent job shedding his serious countenance and becoming charming and mischievous while entertaining the guests with his wicked sense of humour.

Supporting cast were the waiters in their white jackets but also wearing a black bow tie and when the restaurant was busy bit players were co-opted including the barman and a part time receptionist, Igor, a cheerful Croatian lad with black spiky hair, incongruous with his smart dark suit. Even after three years of trying, Igor, never managed to understand the table occupant numbering system and would appear at the end of a table with three plates in hand, dithering because he could not remember where each plate should be put. If the maître d' was not there to help out, and he usually spotted any hesitation on the part of his cast and was there to prompt them immediately, Igor returned to the service station, plates in hand, to consult the table plan. His youthful appearance and cheeky grin meant that the guests were generous in their forgiveness but not Sandro.

Sometimes a new waiter would try and get round the system altogether and would appear at the end of our table, plates in hand, and ask who had ordered that particular dish. This was a great opportunity for the more experienced waiters to play a trick and when asked how to say *"vitello"* (veal) in English would respond "beef". Needless to say this would result in puzzled expressions on the face of the recipient when presented with the wrong dish and I quickly learnt to check the translation. One day Giorgio, a trainee, frustrated by his inability to work out the correct places for the plates in his hand and the failure of the guests to hear his soft query, "beef?" above their animated conversation realised that as there was only one empty place it must belong to the occupant and he shouted "lady" at the top of his voice. Sandro was beside him in seconds, he was relieved of the plate which was placed neatly on the table and he was summoned to the kitchen. Sandro preceded him grandly flinging open the double doors that in those days guarded the entrance to the kitchen. A subdued Giorgio trailed along behind. A few minutes later Sandro made as grand an exit from the kitchen as he had an entrance and marched purposefully to the far end of the restaurant where he took up his favourite pose, leaning slightly against the wall, arms crossed over the large leather covered menu he also used to rest on when taking orders. Several minutes passed before a red-faced Giorgio crept out through the double doors and scuttled to the nearest service station to resume his duties.

During the lull before the real rush began the few people who arrived early had all the waiters dancing attendance on them. Every new arrival was greeted with a smile and shown to their place. In high season when the hotel was full of Italians some expressions would show immediately that the table was not to their liking. Ever alert to such nuances Sandro either changed the table immediately or promised a better one for the next evening. Everything was done with charm and a smile. So much pride was taken in their work that every plate had to be placed in front of each guest the right way round and should a new waiter fail to do so Sandro, always on the lookout, was soon there muttering "*gira, gira*" until the correct position was obtained. This position related to the decoration on the plates generally a carved piece of carrot. Condiments, bread and bread sticks were all in place but no black pepper as this was personally served by the waiters from large wooden pepper mills. There was friendly banter between guests and cast but it never overstepped the mark to become familiarity. Should a member of staff overstep the mark they would receive a warning and further infringements resulted in a wage packet and a ticket on the local bus to Trento, the nearest train station. Francesco, an agency barman suffered this fate when he found the lure of the microphone irresistible and would insist on giving a husky rendition of My Way, the first resulted in a warning, the second, a summons to see *il Direttore* after which he was never seen again. Of course it could have been the quality of his singing and not his general demeanour that was the culprit. Even his propensity for decorating cups of cappuccino with a heart drawn in *cacao* powder did not rescue him from this predicament.

Now the plot was unravelling in earnest and at the service stations instructions were given crisply but *sotto voce* so that the general calm of the restaurant remained undisturbed. Commands were rapped out as a series of numbers, table number then place number. Sandro attended each table to take the order that was then handed to a passing waiter, one copy to the kitchen, one to the service station. New waiters were plunged straight into this melee, often before anyone even knew their name. Not all of them survived as Sandro was a hard taskmaster and expected his own perfectionism to be reflected in the work of his colleagues and generally it was. Sometimes a waiter would only be seen for a few days and then vanished because not coming up to the mark was not tolerated here in this top class establishment. Now and again one knew that there was a sow's ear that would never become a silk purse but Sandro would soldier on even though it meant twice as much work for him.

Imperceptibly the pace quickened even more and the waiters wove smartly in and out of the three dining areas, avoiding each other and stray children, not rushing but moving quickly, always passing on the right. Failure to adhere to this rule resulted in Sandro muttering "*destra, destra*" to the miscreant. If my table was positioned near the sliding door entrance to the kitchen when the doors silently slid apart one could hear the clash of cutlery and shouting of orders and the frequent yells of "*VIA*" when dishes were ready to be collected. There was a time, one winter when the doors stubbornly refused to slide open at all. Paolo executed a great pantomime mime which alerted the guests to the problem and at the same time he was trying to force the reluctant sections apart. Waiters were racing outside, through the car park then back in through the main doors bearing plates of food until the '*techno*' who had been immediately summoned arrived and managed to prise the doors apart and then propped them open for the rest of the evening.

Of course the centrepiece and the perfect finishing touch of the entire performance was the superb food as fantastic gourmet meals were served every evening against a backdrop of the most incredible scenery that every diner could enjoy through the picture windows of the well appointed main restaurant. With huge central crystal chandeliers replicated by smaller versions set into the walls and strains of Strauss waltzes whirling in the background the setting was reminiscent of the days when the Hapsburgs came to town. The players in this the final scene were unseen, the chefs, who scuttled efficiently around the gleaming steel appliances out of sight, behind closed doors. All this was masterminded by *il Direttore* who organised and worked in the kitchen every day, an unheralded genius who slipped quietly between the kitchen and the office to perform his dual role.

After dinner I made my way in to the welcoming bar area and was immediately greeted by a cheery wave from Stefano, the multi-talented musician. Stefano, with his shaven head and permanent smile had an enthusiasm for his music that was infectious. This local music teacher who seemed to have taught the entire local population under the age of thirty, played in a local band and had a grand passion for British brass bands. When he actually went to hear brass bands live at the Albert Hall in London he was dancing around the bar with excitement. The diversity of his music meant that he could cater for all tastes but my favourite evenings were the ones when he played his repertoire of songs from the shows on his pianoforte. I would find myself a quiet corner and enjoy a last prosecco of the day as the melodies swirled around me.

Even though I had no place to go and no clients to organise I was still up very early the next morning. This was my favourite time of day and I loved to watch the hotel waking up from my balcony, now bedecked with pretty pink geraniums that always seemed to be in flower. I smiled as I recalled one evening earlier this summer when I thought it was raining and stepping out on to my balcony to investigate had received a soaking from the automated sprinkler system. First there was a succession of deliveries starting with brown paper sacks full of fresh rolls and bread, then boxes of dairy produce followed by large wheeled cages of laundry. Waiters and cooks strolled across the car park and disappeared through the side door into the kitchen. Each new entrant was acknowledged by the flick of the tail from a russet coloured dog stretched out on the warming tarmac of the car park. I remembered our brief encounter earlier this summer. Looking up I could see the tree clad slopes of the resort and the top of Monte Spinale. Birds twittered in the branches of the trees opposite and the stream gushed down the slope behind them. Although the room behind me was small it was comfortable and welcoming. All the rooms were different but this was one of my favourites as I could hear the stream rushing past the hotel, so soporific at night.

I returned to my room, my 'usual' room, and gazed appreciatively at the pleasing décor. Nothing had changed. Room thirty-five was a small double room on the first floor. On arrival I had immediately emptied my cases and stored them on the top of the small wardrobe to free enough floor space to walk around the small double bed. Most of the small desk in the corner was occupied by a large television which I rarely switched on as there never seemed to be time to watch it because there were so many things to do here. Below the television was a cupboard occupied by the mini bar. A small chair and two bedside tables adorned with pretty, brass based lamps completed the furnishings in the room. Patterns in restful colours of pale green and apricot on the bedspread, curtains and chair seat blended in pleasing harmony, all completed by a frieze of green leaves adorning the wall. The small bathroom also had a balcony door and a great power shower.

Size and style of every room varied as the hotel was not purpose built but full of character. Originally the building had been constructed in two separate blocks by Giovanni Lorenzetti and his uncle in 1985. Their business partnership stretched back over the years to the days when Giovanni, as a young boy, would collect wood from the local forest for use in his uncle's workshop. Giovanni had used his part as a bed and breakfast establishment but the other side remained empty. Five years later Giovanni bought this half from his uncle it and with the help of his lovely wife, Silvana, modified the building and opened the fabulous four star Hotel Lorenzetti to welcome their first guests in the winter season of 1990/1991.

The Hotel Lorenzetti was the jewel in the crown and the pinnacle of achievement by a local lad who had seized his chance when visitors flocked to the area to exploit the many opportunities for winter sports. Giovanni had left school early and by the age of fourteen was working in the ski hire section of Serafini Sport, a local shop. By the time he was sixteen he had accumulated enough experience to open his own ski hire business in the lobby of the Hotel Montanara. This business thrived and his hard work was rewarded by the establishment of his first shop, Barbara Sport, named after his second daughter for by now he had married Silvana Saudi, who had been working as a shop assistant in Olimpionico. They had two young daughters, Assunta and Barbara. Business flourished and expanded and other businesses were gradually established. Giovanni was a wonderful example to local inhabitants as he demonstrated how hard work could help this small mountain village develop into a popular resort both winter and summer. By the time the hotel was established three other shops had been set up. There were two branches of Lorenzetti Sport, one in Madonna di Campiglio and one in Pinzolo and the very exclusive Lorenzetti Chic, the former selling a wide range of sports goods and still hiring out skis and the latter fashion clothes including top designer labels. Unfortunately Giovanni died in 1999 but this pillar of the local community and *maestro di sci* was forever commemorated by the dedication of a small *piazza* in the centre of town to his name.

His family have continued the tradition of hard work; in December 2001 they became the lessees of a bed and breakfast just a short distance from the hotel, Garni dei Fiori, and in December 2006 they also opened a restaurant, Il Ristorante da Alfiero, which continues and extends the tradition of gastronomic meals. I have enjoyed several meals in the new restaurant but the most memorable has to be: *Le Cappelle di funghi porcini cotti alla griglia con insalatine novelle* as a starter, followed by *Le Fettuccelle strette padellate con code di gamberi, zuchette novelle e sapori fresche del Mediterranea* with *Le Nocette di filetto di vitella al profumo di erbe di montagna e trifola ai funghi porcini.* This was translated as grilled mushrooms with salad; homemade fettuccelle noodles with shrimps, courgettes and Mediterranean aromas; veal fillet noisettes with mountain herbs and mushrooms. A translation that did not reflect the exquisite nature of this repast in the same way that the Italian description did.

Wallowing in the luxury of having no place to be and nothing to do I procrastinated showering and dressing before descending to the breakfast room to eat. Giuseppe, the breakfast *maestro* was there and greeted me with his infectious grin. He pulled back the sleeve of his maroon jacket and tapped his watch; "*in ritardo*" he said. "*In vacance*" I retorted and slid into my usual place at the far end of the room where I could watch all the comings and goings and re-tune my ears to the beautiful Italian language. Friendly and courteous but above all a great teacher of Italian grammar Giuseppe ran breakfast with amazing efficiency. He was always on duty by six thirty in the morning so that by the time the guests started arriving everything was ready and the buffet beautifully set out.

* * *

I do remember one time though when Giuseppe was not there at the appointed time. I had arrived in the breakfast room as usual at about seven o'clock to find everything shrouded in darkness and eerily silent. Even the small service area behind its heavy wooden door was without illumination. The buffet tables were decorated with empty plates and I could just make out through the gloom empty glass bowls that were usually full of ripe, fresh fruit. There was no sign of life at all. Yet Marino had greeted me as normal when I strolled through reception. Surely he would have been aware if something was amiss?

As I turned to alert Marino to this mystery Sandro appeared in the doorway and after casting a surprised glance around the dark, empty room, sprang into action. Marino was sent scurrying off to wake the tardy Giuseppe. Within minutes Sandro had everything set out and had even found time to make me my usual camomile tea which was delivered with many mutterings about Marino's failure to notice the absence of Giuseppe. Sandro had a talent for dark mutterings and there were occasions when I had to stifle my laughter, particularly when his impish eyes darted a glance in my direction. When the first guests arrived a few minutes later everything appeared normal and the only indication that anything was out of the ordinary was the sheepish grin Giuseppe cast in my direction when he finally sidled into the room.

* * *

From my vantage point I watched this first meal of the day unfold before me. As each person took their seat a waiter appeared and asked what they would like to drink – tea, café latte, espresso, cappuccino, hot chocolate, herbal tea, the list was seemingly endless. There was a quiet murmuring of conversation from the early risers as guests drifted in, exchanged greetings and then discussed the weather and plans for the day. Soon the trickle of guests became a flood and waiters hitherto preparing for lunch and dinner were summoned to cope. The murmur swelled to a crescendo, waiters scurried to and fro with trays of hot drinks, impassionedly complying with all requests, hot milk for a dog, cold water for a baby, espresso followed immediately by a cappuccino, a particular type of cheese that was not on the buffet. Always smiling, always willing.

Returning to my room I found it had already been cleaned. Through the breakfast room window I had seen some of the young chambermaids arriving, long loose hair obscuring the earphones of their blaring MP3s, laughing and chattering as they made their way downstairs to don overalls and tie back luxuriant locks. This small army of willing and cheerful chambermaids was already on the move through the hotel, cleaning rooms, wiping every carpet with a damp cloth, polishing the large mirrors in reception. The rooms were not just cleaned but left immaculately tidy; bottles were lined up according to size in the bathroom. In the bedroom, stray clothes had been hung neatly on the back of a chair, in fact the rooms were occasionally considered to be too tidy by some clients. In the evening there was a turn down service and a poem and a chocolate were left on each bedside table. This small gift used to be left on the pillow but an inebriated guest, a member of one of my groups, once fell asleep on his chocolate and it melted and matted his hair. He woke in a panic convinced his head was bleeding. The pillowcase never recovered! Bedclothes were placed neatly on the turned down triangle of the duvet and again any stray belongings were captured and tidied away. Often, as I was about to leave my room I would return to hang clothes in the wardrobe and remove objects from the bed in the theory it would be easier to find them if I tidied them away myself.

During my leisurely breakfast I had consulted the walking map and decided to walk along the Giro di Campiglio and then take the path to Lago di Valagola and possibly from there to the top of Doss del Sabion, a peak above Pinzolo, the next town down the mountain. Instinctively following safe walking practices I told Monica, on reception, where I was walking that day. Monica was a lovely lady with no English at all but great empathy and we got along really well. As we spoke I recalled my meeting with the hotel dog and as an afterthought suggested that I might take her with me. This suggestion was greeted with huge enthusiasm because, apparently, she was never taken out for long walks. There was much rushing to and fro searching for lead, dog and owner. The latter eventually arrived, introduced me to the dog, Tabata, presented me with the lead, dog now attached, and off we went. I marched enthusiastically along the path and the dog trailed along behind me with a doleful expression more suggestive of a visit to the vet than a long walk in the mountains. Tabata had not acknowledged me at all, merely acquiesced to my taking her lead with barely a backward glance.

Immediately after leaving the hotel and crossing the bridge over the stream we took a right turn onto the *giro*. This starting point did not look very inviting, piles of grey shale were dotted with clumps of wild flowers and the path itself was barely distinguishable. However after a few metres we were entering the wood and the path reflected this as it was now well defined and covered with shingle. This path made its way across a small bridge over a very narrow stream, over a road and then back into the woods below. We continued along the Giro di Campiglio and then turned onto the path that went to the waterfalls at Vallesinella. This pretty route was stippled with the sunlight that penetrated the spacious beech trees and cushioned with many layers of fallen leaves. After a while we were presented with a choice, left to le Cascate di Mezzo or straight on to Lago di Valagola. We continued straight on and I was now in unknown territory.

It was a perfect day, the sun a brilliant yellow orb in an azure blue sky. The woodland paths were speckled with wild flowers of every hue imaginable and occasionally I caught a glimpse of a red squirrel racing up a tree but even that did not arouse any interest in my canine companion. And so we carried on for several kilometres although Tabata had now reverted to walking ahead of me as she began to realise this was a more serious walk than the usual brief canter up and down the road with a member of staff. As we covered the ground she started to pull lustily eventually dragging me down a steep slope. She was a big dog capable, as I discovered later when she took a liking to my ham and cheese sandwich, of putting her paws on my shoulders. In the interests of my own well-being I decided to let her off the lead as we were well away from any roads.

Witnessing her rapid disappearance into the trees ahead it suddenly occurred to me that I might have made a big mistake. The dog was Italian and I was English. I had no idea how to call her back and I was pretty sure she was not bilingual. I plodded along the path wondering if I would ever see the animal again and making up wild excuses to explain my return with just a lead and no dog. She pulled me over and as I fell to the ground I had to let go of the lead and she ran off? Not too convincing. I would somehow have to explain why I still had the lead in my hand. What about I went round one side of a tree, the dog went round the other side of the tree, the clip on the lead got caught, came undone and the dog escaped. Not very convincing but it would have to do. The final resort of course would just be to throw the lead away but always brought up to avoid 'waste' I didn't think I could bring myself to do that.

Next, I had to pinpoint my position on the map in order to exactly describe the place where this phenomenon had occurred. Ahead of me I could see a clearing in the trees, maybe I could identify this clearing on my map. I sat down on a nearby log and gazed around me. Across the open space a family where picnicking. Italians love their family picnics and I could easily identify three generations. They acknowledged my presence with a smile and I bitterly regretted the fact that all I could do was greet them in their own language and wished I could say, "Have you seen a red setter type dog go past?"

As I watched, one of the toddlers in the group strayed a bit too far away for the comfort of its parents who immediately shouted "*vieni qui*". That sounded like a useful phrase for lost dogs. I got up and started to walk along the path again. When I was out of earshot and would not embarrass myself with my non-existent Italian accent I started yelling "*vieni qui Tabata*". Nothing. I traipsed along, deep in thought, at some point I would have to return to the hotel dogless but at what point? I decided to continue walking towards the lake and make a decision when I got there.

Suddenly there was a flash of amber in the trees and miraculously there was Tabata standing in front of me. Just too far away to catch hold of her. She looked at me briefly and then she was off again. Back into the trees and soon out of sight. This became the pattern of our walk. Every so often there would be rustling either in front of me or behind me and Tabata would appear on the path, cast a brief glimpse at me and then disappear again. She never got close enough for me to grab hold of her and snap the lead back on.

On one occasion Tabata must have decided she needed some amusement and she thundered along the path from behind, hit me squarely in the back of the knees causing me to sit down suddenly and then disappeared again. I hurled a few very English insults at her retreating backside as I scrambled to my feet. Fortunately she did not repeat this trick again on this walk and in the future I was always ready to move when I heard her lolloping along behind me.

Three hours later I reached the lake. It was stunning, deep blue water reflected the dramatic peaks of the Dolomites rising majestically above me in a profoundly blue sky. I walked a little way around the lake and sat down to have my picnic lunch on a large rock conveniently placed right by the cool, clear water. The peace and serenity of this beautiful place washed over me and I lent back to feel the warmth of the sun on my face. Bliss. My quiet moment was brutally shattered by sounds of splashing and panting as Tabata appeared, floundering in the water and intent on making a meal of my packed lunch. At least it was an opportunity to get hold of her and clip her lead on again. After a bit of a battle I succeeded in attaching the leash and tied her up to a nearby tree intending to return to my reverie and enjoy what was left of my lunch.

No chance. Tabata could produce the howl of a hyena when things were not going her way and she proceeded to treat me to her best rendition causing walkers nearby to glance across to check out who was maltreating her. I moved closer and we sat in an uneasy silence as I ate my lunch and Tabata wore her best "nobody ever feeds me" expression. Too close and she launched herself at me trying to snatch a morsel of food. Too far away and the ears flattened and the mouth opened ready to emit truly terrible noises.

Once I had finished eating I was presented with a back view and all my attempts to make friends were rebutted. It did give me a chance to have a good look at her. Although my first impression had been that she was a red setter her coat was not red but a beautiful chestnut amber. It was also not sleek but curly and in some places the curls went in different directions giving her coat a sort of whirlpool effect. Her long shaggy ears I had already discovered were capable of many expressions from hang dog to happy dog. The latter I had briefly glimpsed as she wolfed down half my cheese and ham roll. She was a big dog but very slim. I suspected after seeing her set off through the trees as though on a hunt that she may also have lurcher in her.

Setting off again we completed our circuit of the lake and then started to walk back to the hotel. I decided to return along a different path and despite my resolution not to let Tabata off the lead again I felt that in the interests of not having my arm pulled out of its socket I needed to allow her a little more freedom. She hared off up the path and soon I was entirely on my own in the shade of the trees. I was feeling more confident now and rather than hoping she would return I was expecting her to return and she did so at regular intervals, just to check I was still there. When I told the family later that she had been off the lead they were amazed to hear that she had actually come back to me. Apparently she generally did not return to the person walking her but made her way back to the hotel in her own time. As we got closer to the hotel I began to try and catch her during her brief appearances and then, just I had despaired of ever doing so, she stood motionless on the path long enough for me to catch up with her and put her lead on again. Our return to the hotel was triumphant. The dog was restored to her position outside the hotel and I was glowing with the pleasure of having had a fantastic walk. I spent the evening poring over my map of the local walks planning where to go the following day.

Next day when I collected Tabata I expected some sort of recognition and joy at the thought of another excursion. Nothing. She was huddled in a corner, apparently asleep, but half opened one eye when I approached her. I untied her lead and she responded by dragging herself to her feet and plodding along behind me her head so low I thought she would graze her nose on the tarmac of the car park. Today we were off to investigate the ruins of an old First World War fort perched high up above the road. It was a fabulous walk to get there. Initially crossing the road immediately in front of the hotel we set off anti-clockwise along the Giro di Campiglio. A few hundred metres along this track we turned on to a path that ascended through the woods and then arrived in an open grassy area just below Malga Ritorto. After crossing the grassy slope and skirting a cattle trough we were presented with three options. I chose to investigate the path to Malga Valchestria first and we climbed up and up then emerged from the shade of the trees and continued along an exposed rocky path towards the old summer farm. The path I found myself on was lovely, very narrow in places and very steep in others but it was an exhilarating challenge. There was plenty of evidence that cows had been grazing in the area and Tabata, who was at liberty again, chose to indulge herself by rolling in the smelliest, softest cow pat she could find. I scolded her thoroughly, telling her she was "*brutta*" but she just held her tail high and kept her distance.

When we arrived at the farm I spotted a cattle trough full of water and enticing her close by with my ham sandwich I was able to grab her and drag her towards this vessel. I hauled her dead weight into the trough and then tried to clean her with my bare hands and an empty water bottle while she struggled to resist. Any other time she would have loved to be in water. At the first opportunity she leapt out of the trough and shook herself furiously so that I was soon soaking wet with 'freckles' of diluted cow dung all over my face, arms, shirt and light coloured trousers.

By now we had been walking for a long time without a break, the little pink paths I had followed on the map having taken much longer to walk along than I had expected. Half way through traversing an open meadow area I flopped down on the grass to eat my one remaining sandwich. Tabata appeared from nowhere and lay down a few feet away. She did show some interest in my food but did not resort to the bullying tactics of yesterday. We stayed there for a long time, the views down the valley were spectacular and it was wonderful to breathe in the pure mountain air. When we set off again Tabata raced ahead, circling, coming in from behind, appearing in front but always there and thereabouts. She was much easier to spot in this open area as the path wound its way through this beautiful alpine pasture profuse with brilliantly coloured wild flowers above which clouds of butterflies hovered. All too soon we were back in the trees again following a narrow, shaded, leaf carpeted path. Tabata stayed closer to me this time but never close enough to lose her liberty before she felt the time was right. Our detours took so much longer than expected that we had to head back towards the hotel without finding the elusive fort. Another day perhaps.

We soon found ourselves back on familiar territory and I knew that there was a clear stream not far in front of us where I could try and bath her again. Despite my heroic efforts she still smelt terrible. Tabata had responded to my first shout of *vieni qui* and actually waited patiently while I fumbled with her lead but she was not so patient when I dragged her into the stream and started to shower her with clean water. When we returned to the hotel and I tied her up again she immediately curled up into a tight unresponsive ball. I felt I had served my purpose and been dismissed. I then went and confessed to Barbara that the dog was not quite as clean as she had been when we set off this morning. As I made my way back to my room I tried to avoid looking at Marino who had just come on duty, as I knew he would be the one who would have to bath the reprobate.

At breakfast the next morning I perused the possibilities for the day ahead, consulted my map and the waiters and it seemed the best option was to go up one of the cabin lifts and walk from the top. I checked out the timetable and the notes about dogs on cabin lifts, half price with a muzzle. No muzzle but they could only refuse to let us use the lift and also there was the Italian disregard for rules which may well work in my favour. This morning when I turned the corner of the hotel Tabata half rose to her feet, flicked her tail and gave me her sardonic smile. She had a way of hooking her top lip up giving the impression of a grin. Recognition at last! I attached her lead and we went to find Goran the shuttle bus driver. As other clients wanted to go into town at the same time we were relegated to the space at the back of the bus where they usually carry the skis in the winter. I perched uncomfortably on the wheel hub and Tabata sat with her back to me, bolt upright, gazing out of the window. This suited me as I was not keen on dogs that jump all over you slobbering and trying to lick your face.

When we arrived at the bottom of the cabin lift I tied Tabata to a railing out of sight of the ticket booth in the hope the lack of a muzzle would not be noticed. I bought our tickets, 1 adult *sola andata* and 1 dog only up and we went through the barrier and waited for the next empty cabin lift. Tabata hesitated slightly before bounding into the cabin lift and immediately jumping onto one of the seats. I tried to drag her down onto the floor while keeping between her and the lift attendant in the hope I would not be called upon to put on the muzzle I did not have. After a while I gave up trying to get the dog on the floor where I felt she belonged but she clearly did not. There was too much to see and I had to agree with her. The scenery was fantastic and as we went higher the flowers became smaller. We also spotted a group of marmots sunning themselves on some rocks. When Tabata spotted them she started to career wildly round the cabin lift barking frantically. I drew her attention to the notice that said do not rock the cabin lift and do not lean out of the window but she continued to do both with unbridled enthusiasm.

Finally we arrived at the very top of Grostè and although I had been up there many times before I had been confined to a short walk to the first ridge to look at the beautiful alpine flowers and the view across the next valley towards Bolzano. Now I had the luxury of consulting the signpost which pointed in four directions; did I want to walk to Lake Tovel (an easy and a difficult way), did I want to head for Rifugio Tuckett or did I want to descend to Vallesinella? When I had looked at the map earlier a path called the Queen's Gardens had caught my eye as it was described as 'an interesting area rich with varied flowers and ancient fossils'. I opted for the latter and we made our way down the slope in front of us and then turned onto the path where it was signposted. We followed this very narrow track with a precipitous drop on one side and steeply ascending slopes on the other giving one a feeling of wobbling along in space. Trying to control Tabata on a path of this nature I felt would be impossible so, as there was no one else around I let her run free. At first she trotted demurely along in front of me. Then she spotted some marmots way below us and went straight over the edge of the path, skittering and bounding down the slope. Not sure what to do I decided to continue along the path but the further along I went the more unsure I became that Tabata would be able to find me. When the path ended abruptly at a small caged enclosure accessed by some steps I duly climbed the steps but did not really understand what I was looking at, it just seemed to be a muddle of grey stones. The fossils maybe?

As I turned to retrace my steps I heard a frantic scrabbling just below me. Then two amber paws appeared on the edge of the path followed by a body as Tabata somehow hauled herself back onto the narrow grey track. I was amazed that she had managed to get back up such a steep slope. She was exhausted and as I turned and continued on my way I had this feeling I had been abandoned. I glanced behind me and all I could see of Tabata were two legs sticking straight out from underneath a low overhanging rock as she lay panting in the shade. I waited until she finally heaved herself to her feet and we set off again. I stepped back to let her go in front of me, a prudent move I felt given the nature of the path. Having regained the main route descending to the valley we made our way to the bottom of Grostè, an easy gravelled track used by vehicles to take supplies and people to the Restaurant Stoppani right at the top. Just before we reached the bottom of the cabin lift we picked up a path that led to the Giro do Campiglio and made our way back to the hotel.

On our return I tied Tabata up in her usual place. Her lead was attached to a length of rope that allowed her to wander around the yard in front of the kitchen. Clearly the animal had been thinking and instead of just flopping down as usual she stood watching me go. I collected my key from reception and made my way to my room. As I passed the entrance to the breakfast room there was Tabata sitting bolt upright in the doorway looking extremely pleased with herself. She had made her way along a passage that led to the kitchen to get to this point and I could tell from the shouts in the background this had not been a popular move with the staff in there trying to prepare for dinner. I rushed up the stairs leaving someone else to deal with the errant animal. One of the joys of walking a dog but not actually owning it!

My next objective was to explore the paths above Vallesinella and we set off, the mutt and I, in companionable silence. We had by now reached a tacit agreement, I walked until she dropped. We had over the last few days established a pattern. Tabata would race to and fro and I would walk along the selected path. Oh yes, there were times when Tabata would make the decision. Uncannily when she reached a junction she would go part way down her chosen path and wait within sight of the junction until I appeared. Once confident that I had seen her and was following the same path she would race off again. Occasionally I flexed my muscles and I would stop at the junction and wait until she came back to me which could sometimes be as long as fifteen minutes while we waged our battle of wills. She would approach, give me a pleading look and then dash off again. I would just wait patiently not moving until she came back and I would then set off down my chosen path. The most troublesome junction was that on the Giro di Campiglio below the hotel where the path straight ahead went to Vallesinella with its stunning waterfalls and one of my favourite walks. The path to the left was a continuation of the Giro into town. Both Tabata and I preferred the walk to the waterfalls but occasionally I would have to go into town and there was no time for a long walk so we could not take our ideal route. It became such an issue that I soon learnt to keep her on the lead until we were past that junction and it was clear to her which way we were going. Her defiance, obstinacy and then downright disobedience made this a necessity but I could not blame her as my own penchant would always be to head for Vallesinella as it was such a fantastic walk.

Today we were both happy as we made our separate ways towards le Cascate di Mezzo. It was mid afternoon and the first time I had followed this route at this time of day. When we came within sight of the waterfall there was a wonderful rainbow dancing in the fine spray, it was stunning. I sat down to contemplate this beautiful sight and for the first time Tabata came and placed her head on my lap and actually stayed still for a while before she became impatient and began mincing around me anxious to be off again. We continued on the usual path but then when we arrived at the Rifugio Vallesinella I decided to walk along the path that Nereo, our local walking guide, had indicated was not a good trail. We set off along the narrow leaf strewn track and it was not long before I appreciated Nereo's words of warning as heavy falls of rain had soaked the leaves on the path and I slipped several times, each time aware of the steep drop to my left. However, I soon became accustomed to the conditions and began to enjoy the walk particularly when the path came out into the open and we had a clear view of le Cascate di Mezzo way below us.

We passed a signpost to Spinale and it was irresistible. Off we went, marching along, climbing higher and higher as our way got narrower and narrower. Occasionally my head for heights abandoned me completely and this was one such instance. I had to go down on my hands and knees and crawl along. Tabata obviously thought this was a game and returned immediately and started trying to play by frolicking around me, pushing her head into my face and then retreating a few feet and going down onto her front paws and barking excitedly. I had to keep pushing her out of the way as I clung perilously to the side of the mountain.

When at last we reached the top and I regained my feet I found myself waist deep in shrubs and had no idea where the dog was unless she was close enough for me to see the branches of the shrubs waving as she brushed past them. Descending from our lofty position was not easy. I had forgotten how steep the path was and, as it was a gravel covered track, the small stones often shot away from under my walking boots nearly depositing me on the ground. The last time I had done this walk had been when I naively suggested to a group that we walk to the top of Spinale; after all the walking map described it as easy but did not mention that the path climbed steeply uphill all the way. Still a relatively inexperienced walker I had neglected to check the contours on the walking map but just standing at the bottom of this peak and looking straight up at the summit should have warned me that we were embarking on a very steep ascent. We puffed and panted all the way to the top. However, we triumphed and felt very proud of ourselves but it did teach me that easy in terms of walking in the mountains does not always equate to our English version of easy. Once Tabata and I were safely at the bottom I managed to recapture her, in fact I had to drag her off the roof of an old tin hut in which she clearly thought something interesting was lurking. This was not easy as I was only five foot four and she was a big, strong dog. I had to stand on tiptoe to get hold of her! Finally I succeeded and we completed our walk without further incident.

Subsequently I discovered that the path I had taken was called *il sentiero dell'orso*, the path of the bear, as this was a favourite route for some of the brown bears indigenous in the region. Fortunately we did not meet one that day but one mild January, Jurka, a famous bear in the area, came out of hibernation and surprised and delighted skiers on the slopes of Spinale by strolling along a path above the ski runs with her three cubs. Unfortunately Jurka's escapades continued and it was felt she was flirting with civilisation too closely so she was captured and taken to a conservation centre at San Romedio in the hope that she would settle down in captivity. This sparked an emotional debate among the local people as many felt Jurka should be given her freedom in a more appropriate habitat.

Despite my plans to spend a day exploring the locality by public bus when the blue sky of the next morning heralded another perfect day, I decided that another exploration on foot was in order and we set off in the hotel shuttle bus to Campo Carlo Magno. Reputedly Charles the Great once camped there with his troops on his way to Rome for his coronation as the Holy Roman Emperor. This claim has been disputed but it was pretty certain that if the great man himself did not pass this way then some of his troops did. This early, temporary settlement had blossomed into a small tourist centre with several large hotels, a few shops and a lovely church. I strolled along the road towards the path I was going to take stopping to observe some players on the golf course below me, green and luxuriant now but in the winter it became the nursery slopes for the ski area. After turning off this main road we made our way through a small parking area and then began a long ascent through the woods following a rocky, root strewn path that in places resembled a dry river bed. When we came out of the woods the path levelled out and there were wonderful views below us and across the valley. One final steep ascent along another narrow path and then some stone steps and the lake unfolded gloriously in front of us.

At first when we were walking through trees close to houses I had felt it would be inappropriate to allow Tabata to roam free. Not an opinion shared by my canine companion who behaved outrageously and dragged me along mercilessly. Finally, I gave in and let her off the lead. She dashed ahead and it was a long time before I saw her again. When I did she had already discovered the lake and I discovered her attraction to water. When I finally joined her by the lakeside she was having a great time running in and out of the water and then shaking herself when she got back on dry land. This did not endear her to the people picnicking nearby so I set off determinedly intending to walk to the far side of the lake and hoped that she would follow me which eventually she did. We found a lovely grassy area where I could sit and enjoy the view and Tabata could run in and out of the water without offending anyone. When Tabata finally settled down, exhausted, on the grass beside me I noticed that she heralded the approach of walkers with a low, menacing growl. I realised this was the first time I had heard her growl in our short acquaintance. Was she protecting me? Or maybe she had realised that now she was free of the confines of the hotel she could voice her own opinions.

After our sojourn by the lake I was feeling adventurous and decided to explore another one of the 'pink' paths on the map. Unlike the 'coloured' paths which have names and descriptions the pink paths were not described and all you could be certain of was that they would lead somewhere. The quality and difficulty of these paths was not mentioned but unless they had sections with small crosses in them which indicated *via ferrate* (steel cables or iron ladders where paths were virtually non existent) they should be alright for a walker. We set off, dog and I, the former keeping a healthy distance ahead to avoid the loss of her liberty. I immediately found myself tackling a steep climb up to the ridge above. Despite the narrowness of the path it was relatively easy to make the ascent as the path zig-zagged up the mountainside and the views were amazing. After an hour of scrambling over rocky sections I could see the Pradalago cabin lift ahead and a decision had to be made. Did I take the cabin lift down to the town or did I walk? It was downhill all the way so could be tough on the knees but then again I would rather walk than ride. We walked and soon found ourselves by another lake, the delightful Lago Nambino, where I managed to capture the dog when, in an unguarded moment she stopped dead on the path in front of me nearly causing me to fall over her. I was able to grab her collar while steadying myself. No time to linger as it was now late afternoon and we still had quite a way to go.

We followed a path that was signposted Madonna di Campiglio and wound its way along the valley floor. As it appeared that we were in the middle of nowhere a demure Tabata had convinced me with her soft brown eyes that another bout of liberty was in order and I gave in and released her. It was not until I heard a cacophony of barking in the forest ahead that I realised I had made the wrong decision. I had forgotten that this was where the husky dogs were kept, chained to their wooden kennels scattered amongst the trees. Tabata was right in the middle of them and immune to my pleadings to come back to me. I grew hot with embarrassment as passers by stared at me and the empty lead in my hand, their canine companions trotting self-righteously beside them. Finally after I had paced up and down the road several times Tabata emerged from the depths a wide grin on her soppy face. Grimly I re-attached her lead and we marched along in silence. I resisted all her pleadings to be liberated again and dragged her down into the town along a path that zig-zagged down the black run Miramonti. Despite the steepness of the slope the way the path was cut made it very manageable I just did not really like the feeling of the ground dropping vertically away at my side. Tabata threw caution to the wind and just raced along despite the confinement imposed by her lead. If she missed her footing and stumbled over the edge she kept going down in a flurry of dust and shingle until she regained her balance or stretched the long lead to its limit. I was convinced she would either pull me over or knock me off the path altogether but I think she realised that would put a stop to the walks so she gave me as wide a berth as she could.

This was the first time I had been into the centre of town in the early evening of a summer's day at the height of the season. Bustling, colourful Italians thronged the streets shouting greetings to each other, enjoying an espresso in one of the pavement cafés, window shopping and dog walking. Ah, this could be a problem. I had no idea how Tabata would react to other dogs on leads passing by us. Fortunately she clearly thought that barking back was beneath her and just marched disdainfully by. However, when I tied her up outside a shop while I popped in to have a look round, well that was a different matter and I soon discovered that this lone dog could sound like a whole pack of braying hounds. I had to curtail my visit and rush back outside. She was surrounded by a semi-circle of sympathetic Italians all murmuring softly to her. She did quieten down when she saw me but such was her lack of enthusiasm that I was sure they doubted that I had any right to untie her and march her off down the street. Correction, allow her to drag me off along the road! By the time we had reached the hotel both I and the dog were exhausted and after a quick dinner I retired to bed and fell immediately into a deep sleep, no time to plan tomorrow's activities.

My final day on my own and our final walk together. This time when I rounded the corner to collect Tabata I was greeted with enthusiasm and she strained towards me wagging her tail and rising on her hind legs and pawing the air. We took the shuttle bus to the bottom of the Grostè cabin lift and from there followed a path through the trees that then ascended to the Rifugio Malga Montagnoli. A turning off this path led to Malga Mondifrà and an area I did not know at all. Any plans to stop for a coffee at the *malga* were quickly destroyed when, as we approached the farm two fierce dogs came flying out of the building snapping and snarling. They were closely followed by their owner who was also snapping and snarling and indicated quite clearly that I and my four legged companion were not welcome there. I veered off the path and keeping well away from the buildings ascended the ridge in front of me and once over the top began a gentle descent down the other side.

It was pure heaven, fabulous views and no one in sight, or so I thought. Seconds later two men and an Old English Sheepdog appeared on the horizon. The dog was off the lead and was bounding towards us before the two men realised we were there. By now I knew that the greeting from other dog owners when their pet was loose was a shout of *"maschio o femmina?"* and sure enough that was the greeting. *"Femmina"* I responded. *"Maschio"* was their answer and there were smiles all round, we were not likely to witness a dog fight. However, the two Italians had obviously decided I spoke their language and started talking at a speed that an Italian would have had difficulty following. I took a deep breath and drew on my small knowledge of their beautiful language. "I am English and I don't speak Italian, the dog is Italian but she doesn't speak," I stuttered. They understood and roared with laughter as they continued on their way. I felt a warm glow inside as not only had I communicated in a language other than my mother tongue I had also made a joke in that language.

We had a wonderful last day together; Tabata behaved quite well and came back when summoned. As we were walking on a path that was not used much it was very peaceful and she could chase imaginary rabbits and squirrels without causing any problems. Our circular walk took us back onto the path that led onto the Giro di Campiglio and from there back to the hotel. Tabata was securely attached to the lead by the time we passed the little tin hut that had aroused so much interest yesterday but she still tried to drag me over to it for further investigations. As I had a group arriving the following day and I needed to get back in time to go through my lists and prepare for my Information Meeting, so I was anxious to avoid any of her re-routing exercises.

Fortunately this was not to be the last week I spent on my own in the Hotel Lorenzetti and during the following year I habitually spent time there on my own in the summer. On one such occasion I experienced the national fiesta that was Ferrogosta. This takes place on the fifteenth of August every year and it seemed the entire population of Italy was on holiday that day, with the exception of the tourist industry of course. I was up at my usual early hour that morning and found the hotel all of a quiver. After Christmas, Easter and New Year, this festival, which celebrates the ascension of the Virgin Mary to heaven to join her son Jesus, was one of the most celebrated holidays in Italy. When I drifted into the kitchen to bid Marino, the night porter and also scrambled egg and bacon chef, a cheery good morning I was surprised to see one of the chefs already busy making pastry and it was only 06:30. Breakfast was a frenzy of waiters running around setting tables and preparing for the festivities of the day. Even Paolo's usual calm was ruffled and he repeated the name of a wine to Antonio, a shy, diffident waiter, three times, each time slightly clearer and slightly louder in a manner that gave Antonio no opportunity to stammer an excuse or ask a question.

After a quick breakfast I returned to my room to find the chambermaids already scampering along the corridors, lists in hand, trolleys laden with every possible item the guests may require including large bottles of water, small bottles of toiletries and plastic laundry bags. I did not hang around long and was soon outside in the fresh air and on my way into town with Tabata.

When I returned for lunch the festivities had started in earnest. A party of fifty were lunching in the hotel today and it was all hands on deck. Pietro the receptionist was pouring aperitifs and Goran the shuttle bus driver was clearing away empty plates and putting clean tablecloths on the drinks and nibbles table. I had a quick, simple lunch and watched in fascination as regular guests arrived to find their tables had been hijacked by the large party. Sandro, in between barking commands at the waiters, was smoothing the way, apologising for the disruption in their routine and showing them to a different table. All accompanied by promises that tomorrow everything would be as normal again. There was a special menu for both lunch and dinner and a general air of festivity which was strange to me as it was the middle of the summer. Throughout the summer it seemed the hotel had been working towards this high season crescendo and I had sensed the building of tension among the staff as working hours got longer and free days became fewer. As soon as this special day ended, in the early hours of the morning, the very fabric of the hotel seemed to breathe a sigh of relief and the next morning guests started to pack up and leave. A mass exodus occurred the following weekend when all the roads in Italy seemed to be jammed with traffic. In the vicinity of the hotel there was a general end of season feeling as the plants in the wooden window boxes of holiday apartments were removed and wooden shutters closed tight. I knew that it would not be long until all the large holiday apartment blocks would be empty. As Madonna di Campiglio was a seasonal resort with a small permanent population the ebb and flow of visitors was very obvious. Staff started to leave in proportion to the departure of guests as the season neared its end. Departing waiters and waitresses would throng around the local bus stop and I joined them one early morning on my way to Verona Airport to collect my group.

As the Italians were moving out the English were moving in to enjoy the last warm days of the summer. After just a week of pleasing myself it was difficult to imagine being restricted to a programme of activities again. However, once I was settled on the bus I began to look forward to meeting new people and having company at dinner every evening as well as wondering what new mishaps and adventures were about to occur.

Chapter Five – One of the Group

"We will meet in reception at ten o'clock this morning to walk into the town. Please wear shoes suitable for walking on a path through the woods and bring a lightweight jacket or jumper as it will be cold at the top of the mountain when we go up in the cabin lift." Sometimes it felt as though I must have addressed my group in a foreign language. The result of these instructions which I thought were quite simple, was that half the group were sitting outside on the veranda around the corner where I could not see them, three people were wearing smart shoes with heels, definitely not suitable for traipsing over tree roots and small rocks and four people were without any clothing other than the skimpy sun tops they were wearing. Never mind! I had only given the instructions three times after all! Finally the group were all gathered together, shoes had been changed, jackets collected and peace reigned. I opened my mouth to suggest we set off when suddenly the air was rent with a blood-curdling howl.

The world stood still, was someone being murdered? Wide eyes turned in the direction from which this unearthly sound had come. I looked at my astonished clients. Clearly I was expected to take some action. Hesitantly, slowly, I crept round the corner unsure what I would find beyond the shadows. I should have known. The culprit, as soon as she caught sight of me grinned inanely from flattened ear to flattened ear and dropped low on the ground, the tip of her tail waving in an excited frenzy. "Tabata!" I scolded severely.

Immediately I realised I was being unfair. She was only a dog after all. Following a week of doggy bliss, walking on the mountains every day she was not going to understand why she had suddenly been abandoned and was once again permanently tied up outside the hotel. I spoke to her gently, trying to explain that I would take her out later but as soon as I started to walk away she began to bark excitedly. As I moved further away and indicated to the group that we should leave now, the barking turned to frantic yapping and whining when she saw us departing without her. I had to ignore her and carry on, I just hoped she would settle down soon but I could hear her in the distance for a long time after we had left. I learned later that she had been inconsolable and had spent the morning in the underground garage!

Naturally I felt very guilty so, having walked with the group all day, on my return I went to see if I could take Tabata out for a short walk. I wondered if she would revert to disdain and indifference following my 'desertion' earlier. When I entered reception she was sleeping on the floor in the office behind the desk but as soon as I spoke she came bounding out to greet me, throwing herself at me and yapping and barking joyously, clearly expecting that we would set off immediately for a walk. She was so excited she could not contain herself and threw herself at me enthusiastically. As I turned to avoid her flailing paws they landed instead on the reception desk and she swept every single one of the numerous leaflets neatly arranged along its entire length to the floor. The expression on the face of Pietro, the receptionist was inscrutable as he assured me it was no problem and he would pick the leaflets up. Nevertheless I did try to retrieve them but it was difficult with a large, lively dog bouncing off my body every time I bent down to gather them up. Pietro came to the rescue and insisted again that he would pick them all up, which he did, replacing them meticulously where they had resided previously. Dog and I slunk out of the area my face red with embarrassment and Tabata weaving between my legs begging me to take her out straightaway. All I could do was grip her lead tightly and follow her out of the door.

Tabata had never been trained to walk on a lead and by now it was too late although I did try various techniques to curb her continual pulling. I bought a special harness that was supposed to work wonders with dogs that constantly pulled and indeed on the first occasion I used it she was more sedate. However, it was not long before she became used to the contraption exerting pressure on her chest rather than around her neck and she was back to her old habits. I think she fancied herself as a husky dog towing a sled behind her!

Next I tried a device that went around her nose. I was instructed to introduce this to her gradually so we would set off and after a while I would stop and put the halter around her neck and across her nose. She hated it and as soon as it was in place she would put her head down and remove it with her front paw. I persisted and finally got it in place. But Tabata had decided we were going nowhere while she was harnessed in this manner and she leapt up and down on the spot like a bucking bronco. I had to concede defeat and although I tried once more I decided it was just too exhausting and I would have to admit that Tabata was one of the 10 per cent that did not respond to this training technique. So it was back to the chain and lead, the only way I could handle this strong dog but it was a compromise that she accepted. Against a normal collar she would pull so strongly that her tongue went black which was an alarming experience.

Aware of my struggles Tabata's owner proudly presented me with an extending lead in the hope that this would solve the problem. It just extended and extended until it reached its limit. As Tabata pulled all the time there was never an opportunity to retract the lead and on the few occasions it was possible to do this the 'stop' button was not strong enough to keep the lead, a thin rope, at the desired length so she would just keep going until the rope ran out. I had to wrap the thin rope round my hand to keep the lead at a reasonable length and even with gloves on this was a very painful experience and I soon abandoned it entirely.

* * *

That first week that I was working was exhausting as I would be out all day with the group and then, before changing for dinner I would take Tabata on 'our circuit' for an hour. Our circuit started with a very small section of the Giro di Campiglio, first climbing up through the woods beside the small river across the main road opposite the hotel. At the top of this short ascent, instead of turning right to cross the road and continue along the *giro* we would turn left and walk up the road itself. The views from here were stunning: a panorama of the Brenta Dolomites spread before us, their pink and grey peaks rising magnificently into the azure blue sky. Below the bare rock of the peaks the slopes were clad in dense dark green forest. The mountain sloped down to our left in a tangle of trees, shrubs and long grass dense with a multitude of wild flowers. The blades of grass swayed gently in the breeze then dipped suddenly under the weight of a landing grasshopper. Grasshoppers whirred and chirruped around us; there had been an explosion in the population of grasshoppers and they were everywhere, jumping and flying both amongst the vegetation beside us and on the road around us, settling on my trousers and clinging to Tabata's rich red coat.

Suddenly two white butterflies spiralled up into the shimmering air spinning and fluttering around each other. Maybe they were performing some sort of ritual dance as they wove their pattern above us. I stopped to watch them, fascinated. Then, just as suddenly as they appeared they parted company and disappeared in opposite directions. Seconds later two more butterflies whorled upwards and repeated the process before they too separated and vanished.

We ambled along, dog and I, in silent contemplation of nature's splendours. For me it was a chance to wind down and review the events of the day before planning the activities for tomorrow. Tabata weaved to and fro across the road investigating interesting smells and occasionally lifting her head and pricking her ears to gaze intensely into the greenery. Sometimes she picked up a scent, a rabbit or a squirrel maybe but more likely that of a domestic cat from one of the apartments around us. When that happened, nose to the ground she strained at the leash as she tried to set off in hot pursuit. This always seemed to happen when my thoughts were far away and the sudden tug on the lead alerted me to the fact that swift action was required if I was not going to tumble down the slope behind her.

The road took us towards the Gran Residence Panorama but just before we arrived at this imposing apartment building we turned immediately to our right and walked up the bank and joined the path above us. A lovely path lined with long grass on one side and a wall of trees and shrubs on the other. Wild raspberries grew in profusion here and I was often rewarded by the sight of a red juicy fruit just begging to be eaten. Smaller than their cultivated cousins these fruits tasted exquisite.

A short way along this path was a bench, hewn out of a tree, an irresistible invitation to sit and ponder while drinking in the pure, clear air and marvelling at the spectacular scenery encircling us. The tranquillity was tangible and restorative. Tabata nosed around for succulent blades of grass to eat, an aid to good digestion I believed. She then lay down in the shade under the bench quite happy to relax with me as just being outside and with company gave her pleasure. Sometimes she would sit bolt upright on the ground beside me and then lean gently against me which gave me a warm feeling inside, similar to the sensation generated when a small child takes your hand. We would often rest for quite a while but Tabata was always alert to my slightest movement and would be up and ready to go as soon as I stirred.

Setting off again we meandered along the open path, the lead for once slack between us, before entering a forest of pine trees. The path stretched ahead, roots protruded, rocks sprawled and pine cones were scattered so some concentration was required. Occasional patches of sunshine splashed on the ground before us. On either side of us brown pine needles carpeted the slopes which were interspersed with the glossy dark green leaves of creeping plants and the bright colours of occasional flowers. There was no one around and, lulled into a false sense of security and a pleading expression in my companion's eyes I decided to allow her some freedom and slipped the chain off her neck. She was away, charging along the path ahead of me, crashing down the slope through the trees, re-appearing behind me. Then she raced up through the trees above me before materialising on the path ahead, a face peering round one of the bends. Was I still on the same path? Yes, okay, off again at full speed. Tail wagging furiously and, I imagined, a big smile on her shaggy face.

As we continued on our way I could hear in the distance the rush of water and rounding a bend I saw a wooden bridge spanning the path ahead of me. I suspected that at this point it would be a good idea to confine my charge to her lead but she was there just in front of me, looking back, her face a picture of innocence so I decided to let her gambol some more. I crossed the bridge and stopped to gaze up and down the small river that flounced and bounced over large grey boulders on its way to the valley below us. This waterfall was constantly changing, either a sluggish, slow meandering through crystal clear pools dormant amongst the stones or a fast and furious gushing of tons of milky rainwater.

On the other side of the bridge was a beautiful shrine carved in wood and usually decorated with flowers. It was not unusual in Italy to find shrines beside the paths and roadsides. These beautiful memorials to an event or a person were always neat and tidy and generally decorated with flowers, either fresh or artificial, and occasionally a burning candle. All the cemeteries were the same, graves carefully tended by friends and relatives and adorned with a photograph and flowers. I used to wonder where the beautiful artificial flowers came from until my first exploration of the market in Trento where I found stall after stall of very realistic, manufactured blooms and sprays.

Not far from the bridge I came across a small section of grey stones littering the path that was virtually non-existent having been partially swept away by the rubble of a landslide. Above me I could see a jagged edge of soil, roots and grass. Below a jumble of boulders trailing through a slash in the trees created when their neighbours were swept aside by the momentum of the debris crashing down. A reminder that nature was sometimes a force to be reckoned with and that respect was due at all times. Tabata was waiting for me on the other side of the damaged path, an unusual occurrence when she was at liberty and I wondered if she too had instinctively felt the force of nature at this juncture.

Of course landslides were not an unusual occurrence in this mountainous region and this sight reminded me of the time when I had collected a group form the airport at Verona and we were making our way up the mountain. It was a late transfer and as we were going to have dinner as soon as we got there I called the hotel to inform them of our estimated time of arrival. Doreano who was on duty in reception told me that there had been a landslide just beyond Pinzolo and that therefore our time of arrival was currently unknown. My haphazard acquisition of an Italian vocabulary had resulted in an extraordinarily wide range of words and I immediately recognised the word for landslide. Returning from an excursion to Trento one day we had encountered a stationary line of traffic and an ominous lack of oncoming vehicles. We had stopped and soon realised that the drivers ahead were all out of their cars and standing around talking, no sense of urgency or impatience. Bruno, our driver, informed me that there had been a small landslide and we would have to wait until the road had been cleared. Bruno was very helpful regarding my quest to learn his language and made sure that I knew what he was talking about. We had settled down to wait until we could continue on our way and in an amazingly short time everything was back to normal.

On this second occasion however it seemed the landslide was much more serious and no one could be sure how long it would take to clear. I informed Aldo, our driver, that there was a problem ahead but he did not seem convinced, I suspect that he thought I had got the wrong terminology. However, he called his wife to see if she had any news and she was able to confirm what I had told him. It was not long before we arrived at the point where the road was closed and we could see faces, a curious shade of yellow in the sulphur street lighting, as drivers were informed of the problem and urged to turn back, park up and wait. As Aldo was talking to one of the firemen controlling the traffic the beaming face of Stefano appeared in our headlights. He had been there for some time it seemed thwarted in his attempt to get to the Hotel Lorenzetti to entertain the guests with his musical talent. It was now too late so he was going back home, as fortunately he lived the right side of the landslide. We had no choice but to wait and Aldo indicated that he was going to turn the bus round and park near a bar so that we would have somewhere to wait in comfort.

There was a great spirit of bonhomie in the packed bar and when my group appeared there was a lot of shuffling around to make space for us to sit down together. It had been a long day and several people ordered sandwiches and hot drinks. We had been told it would be about two hours before we could continue. In fact it was two hours to the minute when Aldo appeared and announced that we should get back on the bus to be ready to leave as soon as the road re-opened. I herded the group back down the road to the bus and we were soon all aboard. Vehicles had appeared from every side road and car park and it all looked very chaotic yet within a few minutes everyone was on their way in an orderly line. Clearly they all knew exactly who should be in front of who and had neatly slotted into place and away we went. When we arrived at the hotel we went straight into dinner, even at this late hour there was a magnificent buffet awaiting us.

* * *

My thoughts returned to the present as I wended my way through widely spaced trees on a carpet of brown leaves. Tabata raced along ahead of me and then dashed up the slope, circled in a big loop before re-appearing behind me and careering along the path at great speed. I stepped aside having learnt my lesson very early in our acquaintance. Tabata would not go round me when she was at full gallop so if I heard her approaching at speed I would quickly step to the mountain side of the path allowing her to race by without obstruction. Approaching a bend that coincided with a narrowing of the path I slowed down and so did Tabata who was now trotting along behind me. As we rounded the corner we came face to face with a female *capriolo* (roe deer) and her offspring. Her startled face with its huge dark eyes would be forever captured in my memory. The silence as we stood looking at each other was tangible and seemed everlasting but in fact was almost instantly destroyed by the scrabbling and yelping of Tabata in full pursuit. The racket was unbelievable, the doe was shouting a warning to her calf and Tabata was baying as loudly as a full pack of hunting hounds. Seconds later I was enveloped in silence again and I had no idea where the three animals had gone.

I was certain that they would not have followed the marked path as they had simply crashed through the trees and undergrowth. Unsure what to do I continued along the path in roughly the same direction that they had taken but the deepening quietness and unanswered calls and whistles suggested I was definitely on the wrong track. I re-traced my steps and walked past the point of our initial encounter and then started to make my way back towards the hotel. I had only gone a few yards when I heard a rustling above me and looked up just in time to see the doe bouncing away from me through the trees. How long had she been there watching? Was her young one with her? I could not tell as the undergrowth in this area was very thick. I decided to try and follow in the direction she had taken in the hope it would lead me to the errant Tabata. We had now been separated for three quarters of an hour, the longest she had ever been on a frolic of her own. I searched for ages, both along the path we had been following and the path above that led to Malga Ritorto but there was still no sign of Tabata anywhere.

Time to abandon the search I decided and return to the hotel alone to face the music. No doubt I would be greeted with lots of "I told you so's" as my habit of letting the dog run free had caused consternation among some of the staff not to mention Tabata's owners. However, just after I regained the Giro di Campiglio I heard a high-pitched squealing. My immediate thought was that the baby deer was in trouble. My heart racing I hurried along the path in the direction of that heart-rending sound. I was both dreading what I was going to find but also aware that I was compelled to investigate. As the noise got louder my apprehension grew, it sounded as though something, (Tabata?) was ripping the baby deer limb from limb.

Confused by the echoing sound it switched to a direction from above me and when I looked up I could hardly believe my eyes. There right above me I could see half of Tabata, her tail end in fact which was wagging furiously. The rest of her was down a hole and it was Tabata who was emitting those terrible screams.

I shouted and whistled at her but she ignored me completely. I doubted she could hear anything anyway with her head so far underground. Eventually I had to admit defeat and scrambled up the slope which was not easy as it involved wading through the discarded leaves of many autumns. When I reached her I grabbed two handfuls of fur and tried to persuade her to reverse out of the hole. Nothing happened and there was no abatement of the noise and no acknowledgement of my presence. I shouted in English as I had no Italian words suitable for such an occasion but the dog continued to scream. I hope no one was around otherwise I might be reported to the Italian equivalent of the RSPCA.

I paused to get my breath and ponder my predicament. Clearly I had to find a way to drag the frantic animal out of the hole. There was nothing else for it, bracing myself against a large tree root I grabbed hold of her wildly flailing tail with both hands and pulled as hard as I could. At first nothing happened so I re-doubled my efforts and ... success, Tabata came out of the hole in a rush but before I could grab her scruff and put her lead on, with one withering look in my direction she went straight back down the hole again! Okay, a new strategy was required. I took my rucksack off my back and placed it on the ground ready to block the entrance. I grabbed the tail firmly and pulled without mercy until Tabata popped out of the hole again. This time I was ready for her and I jammed the rucksack in front of the hole, grabbed Tabata's scruff and managed to unite dog and lead before she could push the rucksack away and stick her head down the hole for a third time. Having retrieved my rucksack I was now intent on putting as much distance as possible between us and the hole. It was a real battle dragging the reluctant animal down the steep slope and keeping my footing in the slippery leaves. If I fell over it would be back to square one! I was greatly relieved to have Tabata back on the lead and resolved never to let her off again in this vicinity.

Inevitably I became over-confident in the matter of letting Tabata off the lead and my real downfall was a cat sunning itself on the balcony of an apartment in the Gran Residence Panorama block. Deep in thought and having only just seen Tabata right in front of me I did not ensnare her in time and the realisation that she had run off with purposeful intent was swift and certain. Crashing down the bank, short cutting onto the road below, yelling and whistling I tried to recall the truant before she was out of earshot. Too late, the escape was totally successful and having searched for an hour I made my way back to the hotel empty collar in hand. I felt so guilty that when she had not brought herself back an hour later I went out to look for her again.

Goran, the shuttle bus driver, tipped me off about Tabata's 'boyfriend', Barney, who lived in the Hotel Hermitage, below the Hotel Lorenzetti. I set off and was hesitating in the hotel car park, unsure which way to go when I met Rosina, Signora Silvana's mother. Rosina pointed out a very useful short cut through the woods behind the hotel. I made my way down to the road below and walked along calling and whistling until I reached the Hotel Hermitage. No sign of Tabata, and Barney a handsome Saint Bernard, was sitting innocently outside. I asked in reception if Tabata had been seen in the vicinity but received a negative response so I had to make my way disconsolately back to my hotel. There was no opportunity to search further afield as it was time to join the group for dinner. I was still worrying about the possibility of Tabata spending the night on the tiles when Goran made a detour through the bar to tell me that the Hotel Hermitage had called to say she had turned up there and he had just been and picked her up. At least she was back and we could go out again the next day.

"I'm really sorry," Monica leaned across the desk in reception, her eyes moist with sympathy and understanding, "but *il Direttore* says you cannot take Tabata for a walk today." She covered my hand warmly. I was astounded. I had bounded down the stairs full of joy at the thought of a two-hour walk in the sunshine and now my expectations were dashed. We were grounded! I knew that protesting would make matters worse. *Il Direttore* was very Italian and Italians did not have the same attitude to dogs as the English. Italians consider dogs to be nice accessories or useful but they do not talk to them and make them part of the family the same way that English people do. I was well aware that my friendship with Tabata was considered by most people in the resort as eccentric at best. They had no idea what it was like for me doing the job I did and how lonely it could be sometimes. What a relief it was to get away for two hours a day and talk over the events of the week with someone who would listen sympathetically, never argue …

I stomped childishly back up the stairs. Monica had explained that *il Direttore's* view was that Tabata was using me to escape. It was true that whenever she got the opportunity to slip out of the hotel she took it and had on occasion been out all night. It was well known that she went to visit Barney. Tabata and Barney were great pals and would go off exploring whenever Tabata could get away. Sometimes Barney would appear in the hotel car park and wait patiently in case Tabata was free to join him but he would be shooed away by Goran as some of the guests found his presence quite intimidating, particularly those with small, pampered canines. It was his size that made him so as his temperament was very gentle.

I quickly recovered when I realised that after a frantic week I suddenly had time to enjoy the facilities of the Well Being Centre. A welcome addition to the hotel, this was a place I loved to visit in the early evening when it was deserted as by then everyone had retreated to their rooms to dress up for dinner. As this process generally took me less than ten minutes I was happy to pit my wits against the contra-flow and then wallow lazily in the Jacuzzi enjoying the magnificent vista of the mountains outside. Occasionally I would wrap a luxurious deep pile towelling robe around me and stretch out on one of the sun beds somnolent in the warm atmosphere and let my thoughts wander where they wanted.

When a new group arrived in the hotel if we had time that first day I would take them on a tour of the hotel including the Well Being Centre so they would know where to go for a refreshing swim or one of the many massages on offer. I became a bit wary of this activity after I took a group down there and when I pushed open the large glass door and stepped into the relaxation area from which access was gained to the Turkish bath and the sauna, I found myself staring at a naked body. Before I could stop them the eager group behind me had pushed me forward and entered the room. The gentleman concerned was completely unabashed but I was covered in confusion and waving wildly in the direction of the relevant doors I stammered a brief explanation before ushering everybody to the safer ground of the small gymnasium. My embarrassment was deepened because I had recognised and instinctively greeted the person concerned who was part of the group. A previous visitor to the hotel, he had taken advantage of our early arrival and slipped out of his clothes and into the sauna!

While I wallowed in luxury Tabata had taken matters into her own paws and had engineered an escape. She could sense when the main door had been left open and if she had not been securely tied to something, which was often the case, she could move so fast there was not a chance of stopping her before she was out of the door and speeding purposefully down the road. As I strolled through reception relaxed and happy on my way back to my room Monica informed me that Tabata had *"scapata"*. I received this news with the nonchalance of someone who was completely blameless and continued on my way. I thought no more about it until late the next morning when I found I had a few hours to spare as the group had all gone into town to shop and have lunch. I decided to enquire if Tabata had served her time and could come out to play again. I was concerned when I discovered that she was still absent without leave and had been out all night. Several sightings yesterday evening and this morning had resulted in unsuccessful attempts to capture the delinquent. I offered to go searching for her, collected the lead and set off, heading for the Hotel Hermitage. When I arrived there Barney was lying in his customary position outside the hotel but there was no sign of Tabata. I walked on past the hotel and explored a few paths nearby but there was still no evidence of the absentee.

Then it dawned on me that if she was around she would be near Barney so I re-traced my steps and once I was very close to the hotel I perched on a fence to survey my surroundings. Barney watched me for a while and then rose ponderously to his feet and came over to join me. As I stroked his thick soft fur I noticed that he was staring intently at something in the field below us. Following his gaze all I could see was a small wooden building, like a Wendy House, complete with flower filled wooden window boxes, but nothing else. Then I noticed some movement in the vicinity and peering closely at the building I could just make out a head that had appeared round the corner. Tabata's coat was nearly the same colour as the varnished wood so she had merged nicely into her background. I watched and waited. Soon her whole body appeared and she seemed uncertain what to do next. I called softly to her hoping to encourage her to join us. She looked up but stayed still just watching me and occasionally flicking her tail. I called her again and then jumped off the fence and went a little way towards her whistling and calling and patting my legs encouragingly. She remained stationary and suspicious and then after a while began to slink towards me. I dare not move in case she took fright and ran away again. Barney remained beside me not moving a muscle, just staring intently ahead. When Tabata was close enough I resisted the temptation to reach out and grab her and kept encouraging her to come closer. When she did so I stroked her and talked to her before slipping her collar and lead on. Tabata now decided we must be going for a long walk and when I tried to turn onto the path that went back to our hotel she resisted furiously, sitting down and refusing to move. I was equally determined that we were going straight back. I kept tugging and pulling and finally my will prevailed and I managed to drag her all the way back to the hotel where I handed her over triumphantly to her owner.

That first week, during which I was walking both the group and then the dog and as very little time was left to deal with my paperwork, I started rising really early and going down to the reception area to catch up with my emails. I would not say a word to anyone, as there was no one around I just sat quietly working on my laptop. Sometimes there would be a stirring in the office behind reception and I would suddenly get the feeling that I was being observed and looking up would see Tabata's face peering round the far corner of the desk. I only had to smile and her whole body would emerge and she would trot across the carpet just the end of her tail flicking hesitantly, her ears now pressed against her face and a lopsided grin hovering around her jaws. She knew she was not really allowed to leave her regular spot under the desk in the office but how could I resist her? I knew if I made her go back it would not be long before she re-appeared again. How she knew I was there was a mystery to me. After she had had a bit of fuss she would then lie down on the floor beside me, usually at full stretch, close her eyes and go to sleep. There were regular comings and goings at this hour of the morning, deliveries being made, waiters arriving and each time the door opened there would be a blast of icy air around us and Tabata's tail would thump on the floor but she rarely lifted her head or even opened her eyes. She appeared relaxed and content but if the door was ever left propped open in that split second she would grab the chance to slip outside and enjoy a few hours of freedom.

Just before the second group arrived I had an inspiration. I knew that Goran, our shuttle bus driver, was quite fond of Tabata although he hid it behind a gruff exterior and would always greet her as *Befana* (witch) but with him as an ally regarding the transportation of the dog I thought I could find a compromise. The weekly programme included two half-day walks which technically finished at lunchtime even though most people elected to walk back to the hotel afterwards. I considered these walks were extramural activities so I suggested to Goran that when he came to collect the non-walkers he could stow Tabata in the back of the shuttle bus and then she could walk back with me. I tentatively introduced this idea to the group and they were quite enthusiastic. I promised that Tabata would be on the lead and would stay at the back with me. I also mentioned that I was not officially obliged to do more than the half day included walks. This compromise was a great success although it increased our scope for misadventures.

The first time Tabata arrived to join the group I could see her anxious face peering out of the back of the shuttle bus when Goran drove past us to reverse and then return to collect his passengers. Tabata was so excited it was difficult to untie her lead and get her out of the back! Finally I manage to extract her and we were ready to go. This was the group's first encounter with Tabata and they fussed around her. Tabata was not at all interested wanting instead to get going on the walk and rudely pulled me away from them.

Initially the walk back to the hotel took us through a farmyard where two shaggy dogs of interesting and indeterminate hereditary, a cross between dog and wolf maybe, strained at the extremities of their chains barking at full volume. Tabata ignored this cacophony being much more interested in seeking out and chasing the hens that were pecking around us. Three puppies like furry round balls decided to join in the fun and ran around making yapping sorties at both their parents and Tabata. The latter ignored them all in her intense search for poultry to chase. Nosing around in the long grass she put up a quarry that flew straight up into her face startling both her and me. Tabata regained her composure before I did and tried to gallop across the yard after her squawking quarry until I finally managed to get her under control. Each time we did that walk she tried to drag me across the farmyard hoping to flush out a stray chicken for a bit of fun. My groups found this very amusing, particularly if I suddenly disappeared in mid-conversation.

Once clear of the farm we joined a wide gravel track and began our descent into the valley below. We cut across an open area peppered with large grassy knolls which impeded our progress but were very useful as perches for picnickers. By the time I had stopped at least twenty times for Tabata to investigate interesting smells I was some way behind the group and I was surprised to skirt an overhanging tree and find them all waiting in a clearing in front of me. Nereo did not usually wait for me but this time I could see concern written all over his face but not for me.

One truly never knows what is going to happen next in my job and I soon discovered that one of the group had leapt on top of a grassy knoll and started shouting " I'm the king of the castle!" While capering around he slipped and fell, badly spraining his ankle. It was obvious from his white face and grim expression that he would not be able to even hobble back up the path to the *rifugio* we had left ten minutes earlier. We were in the middle of nowhere. As I had promised the group as we set off, Tabata was secured to a nearby tree trunk and I would worry about her later. Just as Nereo and I were pondering how to get our injured person back to Malga Ritorto from where the shuttle bus could collect him a battered red Fiat came bouncing across the grass full of pots, pans and other kitchen equipment. Driver and spouse were crammed in the front. We hailed them and they stopped. Nereo quickly explained our predicament and without any hesitation the wife had jumped out of the vehicle and indicated that my client should take her place so that her husband could transport him back up the track. There was no question of me going with him unless I clambered on to the roof so I called the hotel, explained what had happened and requested that the shuttle bus come to collect him. Once he was safely on his way I retrieved a rather puzzled dog and we continued on our way.

After passing a small, shuttered stone building, we turned left at a cattle trough and entered the woods picking our way across tree roots to avoid the soft muddy bog created by the trampling of cows that grazed there every day during the summer months, nibbling the grass by the path and foraging in the trees accompanied by a constant clanging of cow bells. These lovely cows with healthy glossy coats were the Rendena breed of cows descended from some pure bred Swiss cows imported to the region in 1712 and now considered one of the most renowned breeds for milk production and endurance. As we picked our way through puddles of brown water and patches of slippery mud, Tabata was in her element because I was concentrating so hard on not falling over or getting my boots dirty that I paid scant attention to the route she was taking, and was horrified when I paused to decide which stone to balance on next to find that she had acquired a long filthy black sock on each leg. I also realised that three pairs of eyes were staring at us curiously. Only cows I told myself although the long slightly curled horns were a bit of a worry. Urging Tabata to keep going I set off again. There was no doubt that the cows were now more than simply curious and were edging towards us in a sort of pincer movement. Tabata, sensing danger, was quivering behind me, tail between her legs. I tried outstaring them but when this failed opted to run as fast as I could as this now seemed the most prudent alternative. Setting off at great speed, throwing caution to the wind I stumbled through the mud and water to the safety of a large dry rock. The cows having lumbered through the mud after us had now stopped short of my perch. I was pleased to see the group just ahead of us but not prepared to admit that I had just been scared out of my wits by three cows!

When we reached the hotel a short time later I immediately telephoned my client to see if he needed to go to hospital to have his ankle X-rayed but after a restorative cup of tea and a rest, apart from a sore ankle he seemed to have recovered from his accident.

Sometimes Tabata would manage to ingratiate herself with the group right at the beginning of their stay. She had several ploys that she used to achieve this objective and one of them was to creep into the bar if she knew I was there and then lie at my feet alert to my every move. She would know from the shoes I was wearing if I was likely to be going for a walk in the immediate future. Naturally any of the group who happened to be with me would ask who she belonged to and once it was discovered that I walked her every day the inevitable progression was an invitation for her to join us on the included walks as well. This was fine when we walked to Lago Nambino as there was not much scope for trouble along that path. However, the first time Tabata walked to the waterfalls at Vallesinella was also the last time she did that walk with one of my groups. Her outrageous behaviour on that occasion meant that I was always able to resist pleas of clients in the future that she be allowed to accompany us.

Everything had gone very smoothly for the first part of the walk and I even allowed Tabata a bit of freedom en route but I had to recapture her very quickly after she splashed through a stream and then shook herself so that the members of the group standing closest to her received an unwelcome shower. When we arrived at Rifugio Cascate di Mezzo I secured her lead to a table well away from some people who were already sitting at the large wooden tables enjoying a coffee and some home made cake. I joined the queue inside to get a cup of coffee and when I finally emerged I saw Tabata, paws on the bench seat of the table delivering a full lick to the face of a German lady seated at the same table. I scolded her soundly and then removed her to another area. I went back and joined some of the group apologising to the lady concerned as I made my way past her. During the ensuing conversation I discovered that Tabata's transgression had gone far beyond an affectionate greeting. When the lady had sat down with her coffee and cake Tabata had emerged from under the table and wolfed down the cake before its purchaser knew what was happening. By now the group of Germans had left parting with a cheery farewell so I guessed there were no hard feelings but had I been aware of this dreadful transgression I would have replaced the slice of cake.

Lulled into a false sense of security by Tabata's distance from any other customers I was taken aback when I heard her start yapping loudly and looked up just in time to see the heavy wooden table start to move across the terrace as Tabata tried to chase two very small kittens that had just appeared on the slope above her. It was too much for the owner of the *rifugio* (and the kittens) who made his feelings very clear and all but gave us our marching orders. I suspected that had I not been with Nereo we would have been on our way rather smartly. I decided not to risk a third mishap and untied her and walked a short distance along the path to wait until the group had finished their coffee and was ready to set off again. Tabata spent the whole time at full stretch yapping and whining trying to give chase to the kittens that continued to play with total disregard for her presence.

Once we were on our way again Tabata settled down and behaved quite well strolling along at the back with me. Everything was fine until we started the ascent up the side of le Cascate Alte. Then she decided she would rather be at the front than the back and tried to work her way forward. Clearly the slower pace did not suit her and I struggled to keep her in check. It must have been quite alarming for the people in front of us because Tabata does pant nearly all the time when she is walking but when she is constantly pulling she sounds as though she is being strangled. "It's not me it's the dog" I would chirrup lamely as Tabata dragged me over a short steep ascent where, having very short legs I was obliged to use both hands as well, not easy with a dog attached to one of them. Finally we reached the top and began our descent to the Rifugio Vallesinella where we were lunching.

As we always ate outside and we were served at the table I was able to tie Tabata up beside me and keep a stern eye on her. She immediately settled down and went to sleep. Unfortunately I did not notice another dog arrive and take his place with his owners at the table next to us. Tabata did and managed to crawl into a strategically excellent position undetected until she blew her cover by launching a full-blooded attack. I and my companions nearly died of shock, it was so sudden and so unexpected. That was her red card and never again did she do the full waterfall walk with a group.

That same day most of the group chose to walk back and, as they were all good walkers we took the narrow path that went high up the mountain from where we had great views of the valley below and behind us including le Cascate di Mezzo where we had enjoyed a break earlier. Tabata was allowed to go free for a while and I warned the group about her habit of thundering along the path with complete disregard for anyone else who might be using it. Should anyone hear her approaching the cry "dog alert" would go up and we would all immediately hug the mountainside of the path as she flashed by.

This path brought us out on the road by the Garni dei Fiori a small wooden chalet that housed the delightful bed and breakfast establishment owned by the Hotel Lorenzetti. Situated on a quiet road below the Hotel Lorenzetti, simply furnished in pine and slightly off the beaten track it was the perfect place for summer visitors seeking an opportunity to enjoy some peace and quiet and to explore the mountains. I had stayed there several times and particularly remember one Easter when the hotel was full to the brim as most Italians go away for *Pasqua* (Easter Sunday) and *Pasquetta* (Easter Monday). Large family groups arrived to celebrate this holiday, staggering into reception under the weight of a variety of receptacles from up-market carrier bags to bulging ski boot bags. Greetings and good wishes, *"auguri di buona Pasqua,* were exchanged with early arrivals and other guests and blasts of cold air chilled the reception area as this took priority over the unloading of vehicles. Throughout the festivities the hotel restaurant and bar were packed with residents and their visitors. Both these areas and also reception were beautifully decorated with painted eggs. These brightly coloured orbs filled baskets on tables inside and hung from branches outside. Much as I enjoyed being a part of this important festival it was a relief to have somewhere so quiet to escape the elaborate celebrations. I did have my meals in the hotel and enjoyed the special Easter menu and in particular the gold foil clad rabbit that huddled amongst small home made sugared eggs and slices of fresh strawberries dipped in chocolate.

* * *

We stood outside the Garni discussing our options. At this point some of the group wanted to walk into town, some to continue on the path back to the hotel. Others decided they had walked far enough for one day so I went inside to arrange for the shuttle bus to come and collect them. I suggested that the walkers continue and I would catch them up once the shuttle bus had arrived. Tabata watched the group split up and go in different directions and clearly not happy about this she became restless and started whimpering. Once the shuttle was loaded and on its way I set off after the group walking back to the hotel. As soon as we were well into the woods I let Tabata run free. She set off like a greyhound from a starting block and never looked back once. She was gone for ages and the silence was menacing. Finally she came charging back along the path, came right up to me, looked at me and then turned and ran off again but reverted to her usual pattern of scampering backwards and forwards.

When I joined the group in the bar for a welcome cup of tea and a well deserved slice of home made cake they told me that Tabata had chased after them, run past them and stopped on the path ahead of them, 'counted' them and then rushed back past them in the direction from which she had come.

During the weeks there was a group with me whenever I had to go into town to do some shopping I would walk with Tabata. Before I left I would ask if anybody needed anything from the shops. This often resulted in a request to join us. It was useful having a companion as Tabata was still dreadful if she was tied up outside a shop and would bark and bark without taking a breath until I re-appeared, usually empty-handed so embarrassed would I be by her outbursts. At least if someone was with me I could ask them to dog sit for a few minutes. Once I accompanied a client inside a shop to assist in the purchase of an item. While discussing the merits of a variety of leather watch straps with the shop assistant I completely forgot that Tabata had been tied up outside because she had waited in silence for the first time ever. When we left the shop we immediately set off back towards the hotel and it was only when I heard a pathetic whimper from behind me that I looked back and saw her woebegone face, ears at half-mast that I remembered she had come with us. Clearly she never forgot that incident as thereafter she redoubled her efforts if ever I dared to tie her up outside a shop.

Once Tabata had become part of the group inevitably she would join us on the optional walks that I organised during the week when we had a free day. Personally my favourite excursion was to take the cabin lift to the top of Grostè. We would then spend some time there exploring the grey shale lunar type landscape, habitat of amazing alpine varieties of many plants and in particular tiny startling blue forget-me-nots and gentians. Then, after coffee and cake at Stoppani we would make our way back down either via the *rifugio* at the top of Spinale or straight down to Vallesinella. Whichever path we took while at the very top Tabata would be allowed some freedom and would race around ecstatically. I had never seen such a happy creature, her tail seemed to wag her whole body and she chased to and fro unable to decide which scent to follow. Sometimes she would disappear completely and I would have to scan the horizon for a fast moving amber dot. I would whistle and shout and eventually she would return but always in her own time of course. She would trot back towards us, her unusually long tongue lolling out of one side of her mouth, a captivating creature who wormed her way into many people's affections.

Chapter Six – Caught in a Storm

An air of excitement was emanating from the breakfast room as I crossed the reception area. When I entered the room all I could see was a row of backs and soles of shoes. Everyone was kneeling on the patterned bench seats gazing out of the window. There were some oohs and aahs and general laughter. Curious I made my way to the end of the room and stood on tiptoes to peer out of the window to see what was going on.

I should have known. Tabata was performing tricks outside. There was a large wooden trough that had been filled with soil and planted with lovely flowers and then placed beneath the breakfast room window. Tabata had worked out that if she scrambled onto this bed of plants it was an ideal perch from which she could peer inside to see if I was there. This ploy had generated more success than she could have imagined for in the space of a few seconds she had acquired a whole fan club!

My immediate concern was for the plants that were being systematically crushed as she padded up and down, wagging her tail and pleading her case with a soppy grin, half mast ears and wide, soft brown eyes. At my command to get down, sensing the possibility of a walk, she got really excited and went up on her hind legs waving her front paws wildly in my direction. I went outside and removed her from the trough and then led her back towards the kitchen entrance telling her to stay there and that I would be back later. By now I had sufficient Italian to issue commands but I was not sure how effective my accent was or how receptive this recalcitrant animal could be.

By the time I had rejoined the group inside she was back on her perch. The group were enchanted and as soon as they saw me there were choruses of "she can come with us can't she?" It was my free day hence my late arrival in breakfast. My plans to go hiking alone had already changed as several people in the group on finding out that I intended to go walking had asked if they could join me. I had succumbed to their pleas but was firm in my decision to take only those who were good walkers and, of course, Tabata. We had arranged to meet some other members of the group at a restaurant on the mountain for lunch. They would get there in the hotel shuttle bus.

This was not to be the first time this wily dog succeeded in charming my clients in this manner as witnessed by the subsequent destruction of the plants in the box. However many times she was told to get off the flowers she remained unrepentant and undeterred. I had often thought it was strange that no one thought of relocating either the dog or the flowers. Eventually, when there was nothing left but earth and strands of greenery, the wooden trough disappeared altogether. The old piece of rope that had secured her to the fencing outside the kitchen was replaced by a brand new leash that I had purchased from a pet shop in Riva del Garda and reduced the area she could cover. Tabata then had to resort to new strategies to attract attention one of which was to pace up and down keeping an eye on the corner around which an unsuspecting guest may stroll. When someone did appear she would fold herself up and crawl round in small circles, tail tip wagging furiously and ears flat to her head, her features composed in her version of a smile. Her other strategy, barking and howling resulted in incarceration in the garage so she had soon abandoned that one. When she was loose in the hotel she generally lay under the desk in the office behind reception but at the sound of an English voice, any English voice, she would immediately spring into action and race round the large wooden desk in reception to investigate the possibility that there may be a chance of a walk.

On this occasion a triumphant Tabata led the way, plumed tail held high, when we set off on that lovely sunny morning to walk from the hotel to Cascina Zeledria probably the most popular mountain restaurant in the area. Crossing the road directly outside the hotel we left this busy main thoroughfare straightaway and climbed up a path through a wood, slowly at first to give our legs and lungs a chance to get acclimatised to the altitude. Full of energy Tabata leapt up the path ahead of me and was not impressed when I had to restrain her enthusiasm and make her drop back so I could take my place as backmarker behind the group. After puffing up this path for five minutes, not assisted by Tabata who always lost her urge to drag me along when faced with any sort of an incline, we emerged onto the road above the hotel. Here we crossed the bridge over the small river that had rushed past us as we ascended.

We paused to enjoy the sight of clear foam flecked water crashing down, bouncing around the large grey rocks that had been rolled down from the top in the great floods of water generated every year when the snow melted. To our left the tarmac road was closed off, the red and white tape that had been wound around the trees and across the road fluttered in the breeze. A warning shout made us freeze in our tracks and looking up we could see several large, whole tree trunks swinging gently above us as they were lowered to the ground a few yards down the road. It was not unusual on summer walks to come across such a restriction on a path. Beyond this barrier trees were being felled, chain saws hummed furiously in the background and temporary pulleys groaned as they delivered the timber to the nearest road. Here it could be stacked and labelled ready for collection in large lorries. A short distance along the road we could see huge piles of tree trunks ready to be collected for transportation to a destination clearly sprayed in paint on the bark. Branches were chopped up to be used as logs and by the end of the summer most buildings had a fresh supply heaped outside ready for the winter. We stayed there for a while to enjoy this spectacle and to catch our breath. I had learnt that frequent breaks made the walks more attainable for those who had never walked in the mountains before and I tried to time our stops to coincide with good views, of which there were many, or interesting buildings. Occasionally, as today, we were also rewarded with a snapshot of the life the local people had led before tourism became their main source of income. When everyone was rested and the logs were safely on the ground we set off again.

On the other side of the stream the path once more meandered into the woods and continued its circular route around the town below. Every walk initiated from our hotel began on the Giro di Campiglio probably the most useful and the most well trodden way in Madonna di Campiglio. Its popularity was reflected in the high standard of maintenance and soon after the path was relinquished from the grip of winter, cheerful workmen would trim back wayward vegetation straying across this shale covered corridor and repair broken fencing, rotting board walks and precarious bridges. This connecting passage was easily accessible from the Hotel Lorenzetti as it crossed the main road right by the hotel. It was defined by distinctive green and white flashes of paint on trees and rocks and smart wooden posts strategically placed to mark the way and lead walkers way above the town. Once up there it was really peaceful as the roaring traffic on the main road became a distant hum. This was a useful route into town as well as a link with a lot of other interesting paths. Today we ignored any detours back down to the main road and the town as we continued through the deciduous wood passing verges speckled with a wide variety of colourful wild flowers that gleamed like precious stones in the rich, lush, dark green grass. Red squirrels sometimes made a dash across the path in front of us and tiny brown wrens could be seen flitting about in the branches of the trees on either side. The tranquillity was tangible and restorative. Benches en route were often occupied by locals devouring the daily news from their papers. A curious nation I soon discovered that my Italian acquaintances knew more about England than I did and they were disappointed when I could not furnish more details of our Royal Family, and *Carlo* in particular, than they had already gleaned from the daily journals and the television.

Our route took us higher and higher and occasional breaks in the dense foliage revealed the panorama of the whole town below us clustered around the lake at its heart. The trees around us completely muffled the sound of traffic on the road below and now we could hear the occasional bird breaking into song. The banks were littered with plentiful and beautiful wild flowers but different varieties from those we had seen earlier. Spotted leaf orchids were very common here, their blooms pinpricks of lilac scattered amongst the thick foliage that crept along both sides of the path. Pale blue campanula nodded gently in the slight breeze and one could imagine tiny peals sounding from nature's perfectly shaped bell. Startling yellow buttercups, dandelions and ragwort carpeted the gentle slopes to our right. Neat, low bilberry bushes and straggling wild strawberry plants and raspberry canes scrambled up the slopes to our left. Frequent stops were made to exclaim, examine and consult my flower book. Lips and fingertips became stained bright red from impromptu tasting.

We strolled along until the path opened out to give us excellent views of the town below and from where we were standing we could see the bright blue and yellow Cinque Laghi cable car swaying very slightly in its dock, waiting for the next batch of people wishing to ride up to the peak above. This was the last summer this cable car would be in operation because, as part of the continual programme to improve the lift system it would be dismantled the following year. It would be replaced by a cabin lift system like the one on Spinale whose white cabins we could see gliding up the slopes across the valley. The lift system is the responsibility of the *Società Funivie* which was founded by Fritz Osterreicher (son of Franz Josef Osterreicher) and thirty two of his associates in the summer of 1947. In January 1948 they opened the first chair lift which went to the top of Spinale. More chair lifts were constructed in the years that followed and the main chair lifts were subsequently replaced with cable cars and cabin lifts transporting visitors to the top of Cinque Laghi, Pradalago, Grostè and Spinale and opening up the mountains to walkers and skiers of all abilities.

From our vantage point we could also see across to the pretty grey granite church that was built on a slight incline behind the Grand Hotel Des Alpes. Easily identifiable was the main square and the white sun umbrellas outside the Suisse Bar with people scurrying to and fro. In this seasonal resort most of the buildings before us were hotels and apartment blocks. During the nineteen sixties the town experienced an uncontrolled building boom as visitors flocked to the area to ski in the winter and walk in the summer. Every available space was used and as many windows as possible faced towards the famous view of the Brenta mountains so from above one had the impression of a field of sunflowers each bloom straining towards the sun in the east. A distant governing council in Pinzolo meant the development was haphazard and not always attractive and roads became impassable due to heavy traffic that inevitably came with rapidly increasing numbers of visitors. Now the traffic problem has been solved by the construction of a tunnel that bypassed the town. New, more attractive buildings have replaced many of the old ones that had served their purpose and once again the primary building material was wood, generally the deciduous larch tree that was found in abundance locally. Beautiful new copper roofs gleamed above these fresh wooden structures.

Pausing to admire the church I took the opportunity to tell my companions about the origins of the town below us including the history of the church. Many years ago this valley that was now occupied by the prosperous resort of Madonna di Campiglio was simply a very poor, infertile and rock strewn region. Its only resource was timber from the large forests and woods that clothed the slopes of the mountains. Then the only people attracted to the area were itinerant workers in the summer who cut the timber, grazed their cattle and hunted wild animals. This sheltered glade or *campiculus*, the word from which the town reputedly gained its name, was the only route between the more fertile valleys of Val di Non and Val di Sol above and Val Rendena below. Frequent passage of travellers inevitable leads to settlement in an area. The first records of a permanent establishment here related to a small hostelry that was founded at the end of the twelfth century and offered assistance to the poor as well as sustenance and shelter for travellers between northern and southern Europe. Believed to have been founded by one Raimondo to expurgate his sins in honour of the Virgin Mary, it was recorded that this hostel was very wealthy as it received numerous donations from the 'faithful'. By the fourteenth century it had become one of the most important sanctuaries in Trentino, the region in which this district was based. It occupied several buildings that included a monastery and a church. A remarkable reversal of fortunes meant that by 1515 this worthy institution housed only two nuns, Simona and Antonia. It was rumoured that due to the criminal activities of Simona it was safer to sleep outside the walls of the sanctuary rather then seeking shelter inside. Subsequently the keys were returned to its owners, the Cathedral of Trento and its life as a monastery ceased. However the church continued to be used as a place of worship, especially during the summer months when the congregation included those who came to the valley both to work on the land and in the saw mills along the Sarca river and to hunt in the forests. In particular during August they celebrated the festival of the Assumption of the Blessed Virgin Mary. Pilgrims also came to attend services conducted under the auspices of a clergyman whose appointment to supervise pastoral activities was sanctioned by the Bishop of Trento in 1706.

In 1836 the now empty buildings were rented by Giacomo Batiste and partially restored to be used as stables and a tavern for people who came to the valley to cut timber during the summer months. The church continued as a place of worship for this temporary population. The son of Giacomo Batiste, Giovanni Righi Batiste, had inherited from his father a passion for this place and after thirty years of negotiations with the ecclesiastical authority managed to purchase the land and property for the princely sum of forty thousand *fiorini*. This visionary opened his Stabilimento Alpino in 1872, the first hotel in the area. He also attempted to set up a spa but this dream was destroyed due to the close proximity of other similar enterprises already well established.

Despite his enthusiasm and interesting ideas for developing the area as a tourist attraction Righi's downfall seems to have revolved around his determination to construct the first road between Madonna di Campiglio and the other towns in Val Rendena. This fourteen-kilometre road that represented the first modern connection between Madonna di Campiglio and the rest of the world was, reputedly, constructed in just two years, between 1872 and 1874, and financed solely by Righi himself. Legend suggests that he used 'pots of gold' he discovered on his land that had been secreted away by travellers and vagabonds alike. In reality it seems that he attempted to raise funds from interested parties in the area and when that failed he used armed guards to control the passage and extract a toll from travellers on his road. It is recorded that this resulted in some unsavoury incidents during the autumn of 1876 requiring the intervention of the public authority in nearby Tione. It is probably no coincidence that six months later, in 1877, his Alpine Plant burnt down.

Righi died in 1882 at the age of fifty-two and left so many debts that his wife was forced to sell the land and in 1886 it was acquired by Franz Josef Oesterreicher who proposed to the Bishop of Trent that he build a new church, more beautiful than the old one, at his own expense. At the end of August 1894 foundations were laid on a site close to the original church and on 16 August 1895 the church was inaugurated. A few days later the old church was demolished. Franz Josef Oesterreicher died in 1909 and was buried in the new church, the church of Santa Maria Antica, as was his wish. The Oesterreicher family remained in Madonna di Campiglio until 1955 when their property was gradually acquired by entrepreneurs from areas such as Lombardy and the whole aspect of the town changed. The boom of the sixties as tourism took hold of the area produced a flurry of building that fashioned the resort that exists now. Righi's contribution to this prosperity has been recognised by a memorial, a bronze bust, near Piazza Righi, the main square.

Continuing on our way we re-entered the trees for a while and then emerged into the open again but this time we were crossing the bottom of Miramonti, a black run in the ski season. Here I took a diversion from the Giro and we started a slow ascent of one of the easy ski slopes. Workmen were busy widening this ski run ready for the next winter and after shouting a cheery greeting they considerately paused in their work to ensure that none of us got scooped up by their JCB as we picked our way through the ruts and round the piles of earth. We then crossed the river again, this time traversed by a very wide bridge because, during the winter, skiers hurtled across it at great speed on their way to the bottom of the slope we had just ascended. Strolling along chatting amiably with my companions I was taken completely unaware when Tabata decided she was thirsty and made a sudden diversion straight down the river bank towards the crystal clear water beneath which each burnished pebble was brilliantly defined. I had no option but to follow her and soon found myself teetering at the water's edge but fortunately managed not to topple into the icy depths. Her thirst assuaged I was allowed to rejoin the group who were ambling along ahead of us. Tabata's enthusiasm remained unabated and she dragged me along behind her as she wove her way to and fro from side to side investigating interesting scents. My admonitions to walk on one side or the other were totally ignored, indeed her waywardness was positively encouraged by our fellow walkers.

We were now in a big clearing and we could hear shouts and whistles from the volleyball court and football pitches where youngsters were having a great time pursuing these activities. This area was a popular venue for summer schools and one would often see large groups of children out walking, the enthusiastic ramblers striding along at the front and the less keen drooping along at the back. In that respect it was often possible to make the same distinction between their leaders. We paused and watched for a while and I pointed out the town's most popular nightclub in the winter season, Zangola. Well away from inhabited areas I believed this was a favourite venue for disco dancing but did not erupt into life until the early hours of the morning, a fact I was never likely to test personally.

We strolled across the meadow grass under a blue cloudless sky, the sun warmed our backs and induced a general sense of well being. Tabata had calmed down finally and trotted along beside me at a very sedate pace. If anyone lagged behind she glanced anxiously back as we were all part of the flock she was herding today. One of the group offered to take Tabata for a while and although I warned him that she had a tendency to pull all the time he assured me they would be fine. I was consulting the book of flowers and having a discussion with someone when I heard a crashing through the undergrowth and looked up just in time to see Jon disappearing into the trees at quite a speed. I followed them and could see Tabata ahead of him, straining at the leash, tail wagging manically as she chased a red squirrel that had just crossed their path. I called out to Jon and he responded, breathlessly, that everything was fine!

A few minutes later dog and Jon re-appeared on the path beside us and all was well for a while until Tabata decided there was something worthy of her investigation in the trees on the other side of the wide grassy track and dragged her companion across the path in front of us and they disappeared again. By now we were helpless with laughter as it was clear who was in control here and it was not the six foot tall, well-built Jon. We continued and dog and escort tacked to and fro in front of us until I decided it was time to put him out of his misery and retrieve the rebellious canine.

Soon afterwards Tabata was presented with a new challenge. A small herd of goats was nibbling the grass ahead of us. Tiny ones with glossy dark tan coats lifted their heads and stared curiously at us as we approached. One large nanny with a long grey beard and wiry coat gave us a quick glance and then turned back and it appeared she must have given a signal to her companions as simultaneously they all scrambled up the bank and, huddling together, moved as one ahead of us. We enjoyed this spectacle commenting that they must think we were the goatherds come to round them up for milking. Cameras were produced out of rucksacks and digital images were recorded. The goats were very obliging and when we stopped they stopped. Meanwhile Tabata strived vainly against the restraint of her leash not sure whether she should be herding humans or goats.

We moved on, the goats continued ahead of us. We tried keeping well over to one side of the path and sneaking past them but they still managed to keep just ahead of us. We formed a single file and attempted to creep round them that way but they still outwitted us. Finally we reached a point where our paths separated and we plunged back into the trees to our right while the goats continued straight down the mountain. This path was very indistinct and was one I had discovered a few years ago as someone had tacked a small wooden sign to a tree with 'Zeledria' carved on it. After a few minutes of ducking under low tree branches, avoiding fresh cow pats and skirting small bushes we were back in the open and making our way up another slope that formed part of a gradually descending ski run in the winter. This was a lovely wide open incline and we had great views across the valley to the majestic peaks opposite.

"Nearly there now," I said to the group. I had told them it would be a two-hour walk barring any misadventures. From our current position it would appear that we were in the middle of nowhere but I knew that in a few minutes, when I swung off to the right and crossed a large meadow we would soon be rewarded with the sight of the roof of the building where we would be having lunch. We picked our way across mounds of grass and small rocks embedded in the ground. There were some boggy areas here but they were easily identified by the dark brown moist soil and we soon reached our objective and joined our companions who had been transported there in the hotel shuttle bus.

Cascina Zeledria, a small chalet type building, straddled a downhill slope against a stunning backdrop of the mountains on the far side of the basin. Opposite the restaurant were the buildings of the *malga*, a summer farm, consisting of a barn and a dairy. Both were still in use although the barn was currently empty as its occupants were munching on the succulent grass around us. These *malgas* opened up the summer months to house large herds of dairy cows that grazed the lush alpine meadows, their bells clanging melodiously through the pure thin air. Each evening they were rounded up and taken back to the barn to be milked. The milk was then used to make butter and cheese. A large copper container hanging outside the small shop that sold this fresh produce reminded me that several local *malgas* would accept early morning visitors. On payment of a small fee, visitors could watch the cheese making process. What better way to start the day? I had visited one such farm and I had been fascinated by the experience. Nothing went to waste and once the ricotta cheese had been made from the whey the curds were separated to make butter or the local spressa cheese, a process that started in a similar copper container suspended over an open fire. Any liquid that remained after the cheese had been scooped out, fashioned into large round pats and wrapped in thin muslin cloth was poured down a pipe which conveyed it straight to the pigs in their sty a few metres away. The whole experience was enhanced by a second breakfast of fresh butter, milk, cheese, bread and white wine. At the end of the summer the herds of cows were ceremoniously 'walked' down the roads to their winter quarters in the villages lower down the valley.

We all settled at the wooden tables outside the restaurant and Tabata was secured to a wooden post well away from the eating area. As we were in full view of her she did not protest too much, just a regular soft whimper reminded us that she felt she should be allowed to join us at the table. When she fell completely silent I was rather concerned until closer inspection revealed that she was munching on a large bone that one of the chefs had found for her. By now there were hardly any empty spaces as the Cascina Zeledria was one of the most popular eating places in the area and as it was accessible by road there was a constant stream of cars that soon filled the small car park. Many of the occupants would go walking first before returning to enjoy the cascina's excellent traditional cuisine.

'*Piastra*' or hot rock was the speciality of the house and aromas of meat cooking on the hot granite slabs drifted around us exciting our taste buds. We could see the large platters of thinly sliced raw meat and vegetables on tables nearby ready to be cooked on the hot salted stones. We would have loved to try this delicacy but as we would be having another fabulous five course meal this evening in the Hotel Lorenzetti we did not want to over-indulge now. Instead we settled for the specials of the day, bean soup, pasta with a venison sauce or roast rabbit. As none of the waiters spoke English, which to me was one of the attractions of the area, I had a busy time flitting from table to table assisting with the ordering and explaining the constituents of local dishes such as *strangelopreti,* small dumplings shaped like priests' hats and made from spinach and potato or *canederli* which were larger dumplings made from bread and parsley and served in a meat broth or covered with melted butter and parsley. Both dishes were very substantial and traditional fare of farmers and forestry workers.

Not only was I able to describe the constituent ingredients of *canerderli* I could also tell them how it was made as it had featured in one of the recipes that had been left by my bed one evening. For once I had found the time to read this daily offering and had been amused by the English translation of the following Italian recipe and cooking instructions:

CANEDERLI DI SPECK TIROLESI
Ingredienti
150 g. di rosette rafferme o pane per canederli (da acquistare (dal fornaio).
100 g. di pancetta non troppo magra (o speck)
1 piccola cipolla
4 cucchiai di prezzemolo tritato
2 uova piccole
1 cucchiaino di burro ammorbidito
sale, maggiorana secca

1 Tagliate i panini a cubetti delle dimensioni di 1 cm circa e metteteli in una terrina.
2 Tagliate a dadini la pancetta (o lo speck) e fateli friggere a calore medio. Sbucciate la cipolla, tagliatela a dadolini, unitela alla pancetta e fatela dorare, poi aggiungete il prezzemolo tritato. Unite questi ingredienti ai dadini di pane.
3 Frullate le uova e il latte e versateli sopra i dadini di pane. Aggiungete la farina e il burro, aromatizzate con sale e maggiorana. Mescolate bene, lasciate riposare per mezz'ora circa.
4 Portate a ebollizione in una pentola capace abbondante acqua salata, poi riducete di calore. Provate a cuocere una piccola pallina e, in caso di necessità, aggiungete all'impasto ancora un po' di farina o di latte e regolate di sapore.
5 Con le mani inumidite formate 6 canederli, fateli scivolare nell'acqua bollente e cuoceteli per 15 minuti circa.

TYROLEAN SPECK CANEDERLI
Ingredients
150 g. hard 'rosette' bread or bread for canederli (from bakery).
100 g. bacon, not too thin (or speck)
1 small onion
4 teaspoons of grinded parsley
2 small eggs
1 teaspoon of soft butter,
salt, dry marjoram

1 Slice the bread in small cubes 1 cm in size and put them in a terrine.
2 Slice the bacon (or speck) in small dices and fry them at medium heat. Peel the onion, slice it in cubes, mix it with the bacon and sizzle it golden, then add the parsley. Mix these ingredients with the bread cubes.

3 Scramble the eggs in the blender with the milk, and then pour on top of the bread cubes. Add the flour and the butter, scent with salt and marjoram. Stir it well, let it rest for about a half hour.
4 Boil in a big pot with plenty of salted water, then reduce the heat. Try cooking a small ball, and if necessary add some flour or milk to the dough and adjust according to taste.
5 With your hands wet make 6 canederli, let them slide into the boiling water and cook them for approximately 15 minutes

Our meal soon arrived brought by very friendly waiters resplendent in their snowy white shirts and distinctive full length dark green aprons. Their smart appearance reflected the pride they took in the service of good food to their patrons. Sitting there bathed in the summer sun I glanced up at the windows of the first floor. My groups had often chosen to eat inside in the winter months while skiing, in order to enjoy the splendid views across the valley and shelter from the cold outside. I recalled one midday meal when there was a large group of us all seated together on one long table upstairs. Next to us was another long table full of Italians who were celebrating a birthday. The birthday boy happened to be sitting with his back to a lady in my group and when she realised what was happening she turned round and offered him a birthday kiss. Not to be outdone I marshalled the rest of the ladies in the group and we took it in turns to salute his birthday in the same manner. This gesture was much appreciated by the Italians and there was a lot of laughter and banter and also some singing. The atmosphere was electric. As we were about to leave large trays loaded with glasses of champagne appeared and we were invited to join in the toast. We happily saluted our host's good health before returning to the slopes. On another occasion we had not been surprised when a gentleman at one of the tables stood up and burst into song as this was not an unusual occurrence in Italy but we were delighted when we realised that the performer was a professional opera singer with a fabulous voice that echoed hauntingly around us.

My thoughts were jolted back to the present because as we finished eating the clouds started to roll in and we could hear ominous rumbles in the background. The hotel shuttle bus was summoned to collect those not wishing to walk back, all but four of us and one dog. Goran soon arrived to take the first group back down the mountain. Never one to miss an opportunity to enjoy an espresso and catch up on the news from the locals, while the first load of passengers scrambled aboard the minibus Goran disappeared inside the Cascina. He re-appeared a few minutes later and with a cheery wave set off down the mountain again.

Despite the ominous sky we still decided to walk back and hoped we would get back before it began to rain. Of course it could miss us altogether as it was not unusual to have rain in one area and sun in another just a few hundred metres away. We set off across the meadow, taking a short cut to join the track that would take us down to the main road that passed through the town. I had decided that if the weather was bad when we got to the road we could call the hotel and ask them to send the shuttle bus to collect us. Tabata was in her element, straining at the end of her new extended lead and sticking her nose down every hole we encountered. Any pleadings from me to stop pulling were simply greeted by a flick of her shaggy tail. When we gained the road by the Grostè cabin lift I saw the hotel shuttle bus coming down the road and waved at them to stop thinking that any of those walking with me who were concerned about the weather could get a lift back in the bus. All the occupants, including Goran the driver, waved back frantically and sped past assuming we were just waving in greeting. Goran always assumed my preference was to walk rather than ride in his conveyance.

More rumbles of thunder and a few drops of rain made me change my plans again and we set off down a beautiful track that wove through a small gorge. Small caves dotted the sheer grey rock face to both sides of us on this shortest route back into town. This very pretty route was called Grotte and in the winter was one of my favourite ski runs, as it narrowly descended through these dramatic craggy formations. I was about to point out some of these caves when I felt a few heavy raindrops land on my bare arms. As they started to come down thicker and faster all thoughts of enjoying the scenery vanished from our minds and we hastened along the path as quickly as possible.

The rain got heavier and heavier so I suggested to everyone that we shelter for a while under some tall, closely packed pine trees in the hope the shower would soon be over. I peered out of our meagre shelter to get my bearings and decide which direction to take. Thunder rumbled around us and I could see white flickers of lightning through the dense foliage. I remembered there were some new buildings quite close to us as I had watched them being constructed during the last two summers. We decided to make a run for it and were soon rewarded by the sight of a chalet with balconies jutting out from the first floor under which we could shelter. There was plenty of room for the four us and one dog and once we had gained our shelter we sighed with relief as we arranged ourselves in a line along the elongated narrow dry patch, our backs pressed against the exterior wall. This building did not appear to be occupied yet but the surrounding residences did show signs of habitation and opposite we could see a young man rushing to and fro collecting stray belongings from the small garden area outside the property. We whispered jokingly that maybe he would invite us inside to shelter in the warm and sip a cup of comforting tea. But then, taking in our rather bedraggled appearance never mind one soggy dog we chuckled and resigned ourselves to an open-air vigil.

Lightning was now flashing all around us and forking down to the ground so close to us that the air around us shimmered with brilliance. Tabata pricked her ears and peered through the gloom in front of us uncertain what she was seeing. I thought she may start barking especially when the lightning was followed by a deafening crash of thunder right above us. She did not react to the noise at all, just turned away, sat down and then stretched herself out along the dry slabs behind my feet with her back resting against the wall of the chalet. Muzzle on paws she seemed resigned to a long wait.

It was now raining even more heavily, great shards of water bounced on the ground in front of us and then rose straight up into the air again. It seemed we were behind a curtain of constantly streaming water. The sloping road of dust and stones in front of us soon became a torrent of brown muddy water a cream scum eddying on the surface. When we had taken shelter the pavement we were standing on was completely dry and edged with a four-inch curb. Now the water was rising at an alarming rate and our dry patch was getting smaller as it started to lap over the edge and creep towards our feet. Instinctively we moved nearer to each other and watched, fascinated as the water continued to swirl past and creep closer to us. Great bolts of light and resounding rolls of thunder still danced and roared around us – exhilarating each individual as we stared in fascination through the gloom. It was a strange moment of togetherness against the elements of nature.

Seconds later the clouds lifted and parted and the storm appeared to have passed over us. Although the rain had abated somewhat it was still very heavy so we decided to wait a little longer before making a dash for the town just below us. We all breathed a sigh of relief confident that we would soon be back in the hotel, safe and dry, and elated by our experience. But within seconds the sky had blackened again and the storm rolled back, above us and around us returning with more huge flashes of incredibly bright, white light and loud crashes of thunder one of which seemed to rock the very building itself. This last violent peal was closely followed by the sound of wailing sirens from several emergency vehicles as they raced down the road and through the town below us. Clearly a thunderbolt had struck something in the built up area. We had no option but to stay where we were as the rain came back with renewed vigour and the torrent which had died down now started to rise again getting even closer and threatening our feet with a good soaking. Tabata remained unperturbed, still flat out behind me. We peered out from our refuge. Now it seemed these spears of water would never stop and the lightning and thunder would ebb and flow furiously around us forever.

During our patient vigil a ghostly figure materialised through the cascade of water. It was one of the lift workers and we all shuffled along to make room for him to share our tract of dryness. He certainly gave meaning to the phrase soaked to the skin; his thick waterproof jacket was dripping with water. His working boots glistened with moisture and his face gave him the appearance of having just stepped out of a shower. At least we had reached shelter in time to avoid such complete wetness. A quick phone call to his colleague on his mobile and a few minutes later he was picked up by a small white lorry that soon vanished from sight through the veil of rain that still persisted. I knew vehicles could get to the place where we were sheltering although I suspected we had come down a private road, and I was sure that if it became necessary I could explain to Goran exactly where we were. However my companions seemed happy to wait until the storm abated. We were dry and we felt safe in the shelter of the chalet.

It was also very exciting watching the forks of intense yellow light streaking across the black, cloud laden sky and hearing the thunder rolling all around us. We had hours before dinner anyway! The deluge continued for some time in full spate and then, finally, there was a lull and we grabbed the opportunity to set off down a path that would take us into the centre of town within a few minutes. Fortunately as soon as the rain eased off the flash flood on the road disappeared and we were able to pick our way through the dark brown muddy puddles and head downhill towards the centre. I was alerted to the fact that we had rushed past a sign that indicated it was a private road but I felt in the circumstances we could be forgiven the intrusion. My objective was in sight, a narrow path through the trees that would bring us out just above the church from where it would take us just a few minutes to reach safety and shelter in the main square.

As we carefully negotiated the slippery path that a few minutes earlier had been a torrent of water my mobile started vibrating in my pocket and then burst into tune. It was the hotel checking we were okay. It seemed that I would have been unable to contact them by telephone as the thunderbolt had affected the lines. I took the opportunity to tell them where we were so that Goran could pick us up as soon as we arrived in the centre of town. We were all dripping wet and fantasising about hot showers followed by tea and scrumptious home made cakes in the warmth of the hotel bar.

It was not long before we spotted the welcome sight of the white hotel shuttle bus speeding to our rescue. We had enjoyed our adventure but we were also glad the end was in sight. While my companions scrambled into the van I opened the back door to put Tabata there so we could avoid her wet fur and muddy paws. She was in mid air when I heard the warning shouts from Goran and, looking down, I realised that I had just loaded her into the back with boxes of grocery supplies for the hotel! I dragged her back out again and we clambered inside the shuttle bus where I perched on one of the seats and pushed a now dejected Tabata down onto the floor in front of me. She took this with very bad grace as she does like to look out of the window, but she did remain there without any more fuss throughout the short journey.

Back at the hotel we all dripped to our rooms to change and then hang sodden jackets in the drying room. Tabata was taken away to dry off although she would much rather have stayed with us. I suspected that she too would be placed amongst the laundry in the drying room. On this occasion I was very glad that my room was in the depths of the hotel and close to the laundry as it meant I could call in on my way back upstairs to hand over my wet gear. When I had left to go to the airport to collect the current group I had a rooming list that indicated that I would be remaining in the same room I had occupied the previous week. That had been a great relief as it meant I would not have to do some frantic late night packing. However when I returned from the airport with the new group I could tell from the sheepish expression on the face of Pietro, the receptionist, that changes had occurred during my absence.

Once all the keys, including 'mine', had been handed to the guests, I was told I had been moved to room two and we set off to find it. Beyond the carpeted area I was shown into a room that must have been one of the rooms of the original bed and breakfast. Pietro had opened the door to reveal very simple quarters with pine bed, wardrobe and a television balanced precariously on one of three very small pine units. The room was dark and musty and when I tried to open the windows, found they were obstructed by the wooden shutters against which a pile of old wooden planks was haphazardly propped. These went crashing loudly to the ground. As soon as the shutters and the window were open I could hear the musical rushing of the stream outside which completely blotted out the sound of the washing machines in the laundry to my left and the hum of the walk-in fridges to my right. Far from the madding crowd and maddening clients I had soon settled into my new surroundings.

It was a while before I was confident of finding my way back to my room through the labyrinth of narrow corridors, obstacle course of chambermaids' trolleys, obsolete wardrobes now used as store cupboards, crates of water and chests of drawers all of which seemed to be strewn with freshly laundered white jackets for the kitchen staff. Sometimes a box of fresh herbs would be perched on top of the general muddle and I would wonder if they would ever find their way to the kitchen one floor above. The floors were paved with tiles and the click of hurrying feet often echoed around them in the early morning and late night. Amazingly the room fairy still found her way to my room and left poems or recipes and a chocolate every evening.

* * *

Within minutes we had all congregated in the hotel bar for tea and cakes. A wide variety of teas and, of course being in Italy, coffees were available as well as an irresistible selection of cakes on the old fashioned wooden trolley in the corner and all beautifully served by the bar man resplendent in his black jacket and black bow tie. Most of us selected the homemade apple strudel which was exquisite, bursting with pine nuts, and it really did melt in the mouth. On Thursdays the guests were invited to try the cakes for free, a delightful gesture and one that not many of its guests could refuse.

Warm, dry and safe we sat back in our armchairs and watched the storm continuing to rage outside. The clouds had rolled right down into the valley and totally obscured the mountains around us producing a completely grey ethereal landscape. Past experience told me that tomorrow would be fresh and bright. A clean page for a new adventure.

Chapter Seven – Lost on the Mountain

"Do you like to walk?" This unexpected question interrupted my thoughts. I had been gazing up at the tree-clad slopes that rose above the buildings across the road while trying to remember some fascinating facts about Italian grammar. I looked at my companion next to me on the seat in the bus shelter. Amneris was very attractive with rich dark shining hair, and soft brown eyes. I loved to walk I told her and her response was to suggest that next week we walk and talk after our lesson. There were murmurs of agreement from other people standing nearby waiting for the bus. Amneris and I had been conversing in Italian and the people around us had also been joining in. It was great practice for me but I was finding it difficult to keep pace with the five-way conversation. Everyone talked at once, answering before the speaker had finished. Probably because in

Italian the verb comes at the beginning of a sentence and therefore the listeners assume they know what will follow.

I readily agreed to the suggestion. I was very anxious to learn Italian but I was not finding it easy. I did not have a gift for languages and that had soon become apparent when I started studying French at school. Indeed my pronunciation was so appalling that I nearly earned myself a detention when my teacher thought I had uttered an expletive rather than the feminine personal pronoun. We had been taught languages the old fashioned way, battling with the grammar for dreary lesson after dreary lesson. I did at least manage to pass the exam. My attempts to learn German were even more pitiful, as we were taught by a very excitable Polish lad, and I spent more time outside the classroom than I did inside it. The teacher did not take kindly to my propensity to talk to my neighbours or read novels under my desk. I would do anything rather than study a subject that did not interest me at all. My sojourns outside the classroom were spent keeping an eye out for the headmistress who was forever patrolling the premises. I did not want to end up in her study trying to justify reading Ten Sixty-Six and All That when I should have been concentrating on declensions of German verbs. Inevitably I did end up in her study several times with the result that it was agreed that I could abandon all attempts to conquer any more languages.

Now, here I was in Italy readily submitting myself to the rigours of learning a language. My quest to learn Italian had started when I was allocated Madonna di Campiglio for a third time because by now I really wanted to converse directly with the owner, Signora Silvana. Stuttering that everything was "*va bene*", that is, okay, was no longer sufficient and I wanted to speak to her without an interpreter about any problems there might be with my groups or simply to tell her what we had been doing that day. The quest became more urgent when I became acquainted with Tabata, the dog, who clearly was never going to respond to commands in English.

As I could not sign up for evening classes self teaching seemed to be the answer. And there were so many packages that included recorded lessons supported by textbooks and promises that listening to the CD for ten minutes a day would soon result in the ability to get by. It did not take me long to learn a few simple phrases which I happily practised on my Italian friends and then branched out experimenting in local shops and bars. Of course what the books do not tell you is how to deal with the response. Speak to an Italian in his own language and he will respond at length and at great speed. I also soon discovered that an immediate response was expected and a nod of agreement or a simple yes would not suffice.

My next step was to book an Italian course in Verona, which I found somewhere on the Internet and after exchanging a few emails I was enrolled and hotel accommodation had been found for me in the centre of the town. It was all coming together very well. I would spend a week in Verona and then travel to the airport to meet the first of several groups that I would be looking after in Madonna di Campiglio that summer.

"You have always wanted to do the Verona Opera trip haven't you?" My boss was suddenly alongside me as I gathered up my photocopying ready for my next trip. I agreed that I had. In fact I remembered that I had made quite a fuss about it as I had never been to the opera in Verona and was longing to do so. It seemed that the person who had been allocated the trip was now unable to travel so I agreed to take her place. As Linda's elegant back swept away from me I realised we had not mentioned dates. "When is it departing?" I called after her. Tomorrow, flight at six in the morning was her response.

I had only just returned from my first sojourn in Madonna di Campiglio where I had been for five weeks and my washing was still an untidy heap on my kitchen floor. As my next trip should have been my week in Verona departing on Sunday, followed by a further three weeks in Madonna di Campiglio I had a lot of preparation and packing to do before then. I followed Linda back to her desk where she was already working on my tour leader pack for the trip. She told me that I could go home now and start getting ready to leave tomorrow. Clearly there was to be no discussion so I resigned myself to an afternoon of washing, ironing and packing. I would have to leave home at two the next morning so I would probably not get any sleep at all. However, I was excited about finally getting to see the opera in Verona, reputedly a unique event.

I was not disappointed as opera, performed in the open air inside the Arena in Verona, is a thrilling experience regardless of whether or not you enjoy this art form. For our first visit, a performance of Nabucco, we had reserved seats and time to enjoy a leisurely dinner before joining the crowds streaming into the Arena. The atmosphere was amazing, the buzz of anticipation was tangible and when the lights went down and everyone lit their tiny candles the pin pricks of light dancing all around us was an unforgettable sight. Nabucco was a splendid production and I will never forget the sight of the entire cast in hooded robes singing the Song of the Hebrew Slaves. Soft voices swelled gradually to a glorious crescendo. The enthusiastic reception of the audience ensured that this wonderful rendition was repeated before the second act continued.

Our second opera was Aida and some of the group decided to upgrade their tickets for a proper seat again. Several of us, well, I had no choice, decided to view the opera from the famous steps and to take a picnic. We had been told that one should enter the Arena as soon as the doors opened at seven o'clock in order to stake a claim to some steps with a good view. We followed this advice and having assembled a picnic from produce bought at the local supermarket and decanted bottles of local wine into empty plastic water bottles we duly queued until we could enter the huge arena and select our steps. By the time the doors were open there were long queues and the rush to get inside up the steep flights of steeps was totally mad!

It was well worth the effort. Cushions were available to rent for the evening which eased the pain of sitting on a stone step for nearly eight hours. Of course, before the performance started one was free to stand up and wander around but as the Arena filled up this became increasingly difficult. We had soon consumed our picnic supper and then sat sipping our wine from paper cups and watched as more and more people arrived and filled spaces that seemingly had not existed before they threaded their way along the crowded gradients. At least we could enjoy an ice cream dessert from one of the many vendors regularly picking their way through the seated masses. The opera did not end until after midnight and then everyone spilled out into the night, filling the Piazza Bra (yes, it really is called that) with people and chatter. I was concerned that we may not meet up with the others in this melee of humanity but in fact we soon found the meeting place and made our way to the bus a short distance away from the square.

Fired with enthusiasm for the opera I decided that I would go again while I was staying in Verona the following week, after all my hotel was just around the corner from the Piazza Bra so it would not be difficult to get back there late at night. I had not been able to find my hotel on the two occasions we had had free time in Verona and when I returned two days later I soon realised why. It was tucked away in a small courtyard and only a small sign above the bell gave the name of the establishment. From the outside it looked like a youth hostel and inside was not much of an improvement. To enter one had to ring the bell and wait as bolts were scraped back and identity established before the big iron encrusted door was opened wide enough to permit entry.

As the group had left early that morning I arrived at the hotel at midday which was clearly inconvenient and I was told to go away and come back in two hours. My suitcase was rather large as I had packed for five weeks and I did not want to drag it round Verona for two hours. The concierge was equally determined that he did not want to take responsibility for it. Finally I was able to convince him that I would not hold him responsible if it went missing, pointing out that it was securely locked anyway. Once he had succumbed to my pleas we crammed the case into a broom cupboard and I set off to explore my immediate surroundings.

Strolling down the street opposite the hotel I was delighted to find that after a few minutes it opened out into the Piazza Bra, a short distance from all the famous landmarks of the town and home of the famous Arena. Incredibly my hotel was next door to the Old Castle which overlooked the River Adige. As I wandered around I decided that I was happy to sacrifice comfort for such a convenient location.

After a snack lunch sitting in the sun outside one of the many restaurants that lined the Piazza Erbe I made my way back to my hotel. Again I had to establish my identity as there had been a change of shift and finally I was free to drag my heavy case up three flights of stairs to my room on the top floor. No lift of course, and I felt very silly for having asked. I was having misgivings about what I would find behind the locked door and wondering if I could cope for a whole week in a room without air conditioning in a city where the temperature was permanently hovering around thirty degrees centigrade.

Inserting the large iron key in the lock I let myself in. The room was tiny, a single bed, a little desk by the one small window, a wardrobe and a sliding door giving access to the shower and toilet. Overwhelmed by the stifling heat my spirits plummeted. The window was shut tight and it took a while to push it open but finally I managed it and stuck my head out to get some fresh air. Below me the small courtyard was coming to life after the obligatory siesta. Turning back to survey the serviceable room behind me I was pleased to see that there was at least a ceiling fan. Once that was whirling above my head and I had cooled down I sorted out the room before going out to search of an evening meal. As I walked through the lobby I was hailed, in French, by the porter who was demanding that I leave my key with him. Obediently handing the key over I took the opportunity to ask the concierge where breakfast would be served the next morning. He gave me an astonished look and then indicated the street outside. Clearly breakfast was not on this hotel's agenda and for the next few days my morning began with a *cappuccino* and a *cornetto* (croissant) seated at a table on the pavement outside one of the local bars. Indeed, by the third day my breakfast would be brought to me as soon as I sat down. I was beginning to feel really Italian!

Dinner that first evening, and every evening thereafter, was taken in an excellent self-service café called Café Brek in Piazza Bra. Here I could purchase a very nice meal at a reasonable price and then sit outside and enjoy the ebb and flow of the opera buffs. There were two tides that swelled around the Arena, early arrivals who had purchased tickets for the *gradinate* (steps) and those lucky ones who could afford to sit in comfortable seats and stroll into the Arena a few minutes before the performance started. I lingered outside, undisturbed, for as long as I wanted. Extraordinarily one could not hear a single note of music from the Arena. I even did a complete circuit one evening convinced that there must be a musical 'leak' somewhere but I never found one.

* * *

My week in Verona passed in a flurry of classes, sightseeing, shopping, two operas and one ballet. It seemed like no time before I was bumping my huge suitcase down the stairs and hauling it on to a bright orange bus on my way to the train station where I caught the regular shuttle to the airport. On arrival at the airport I soon found my coach driver, Bruno, who greeted me like an old friend and willingly took my luggage off to stow it in the bus. I did not have to wait long until the flight arrived and we were soon speeding along the motorway and then winding our way up the mountain towards the place I was now beginning to think of as my second home. Three more wonderful weeks stretched ahead of me. My excitement transmitted itself to the group when we had a short break at the Miravale Bar overlooking the beautiful Lake Toblino not far from the town of Trento. I was determined that during my stay I would practise the Italian I had learnt in Verona and, amazingly, when I conversed with the local people they actually seemed to understand me.

Determined to improve my Italian the following summer when I would be there for five weeks and therefore entitled to one day off each of those weeks I asked Barbara, Signora Silvana's daughter, if she could find me a local tutor. I was overjoyed when, on my arrival, she gave me the telephone number of Amneris who lived twenty minutes down the road on the local bus in Pinzolo. After chatting on the telephone we arranged to meet in Pinzolo at the end of that week for my first lesson. That first lesson took place in a grassy area seated on a wooden bench at a picnic table sandwiched between the river and the main road and shaded by some trees. After an hour we crossed the road to a local bar for a coffee. We sat outside this hostelry for the second hour of my lesson. Constant interruptions from motorcyclists roaring up the mountain soon convinced us that this was not the ideal spot for lessons.

The following week Amneris was able to find a room we could use in her local library. We were due to meet in the afternoon so I had lunch in the hotel bar and here I met Nereo our walking guide and also a cousin of the Lorenzetti family. Nereo rarely drove past the hotel on his way to and from his home in Pinzolo without calling in for a drink. We exchanged greetings and I told Nereo I was going to Pinzolo that afternoon. Immediately he offered to drive me there, an offer that was gratefully received as taking the local bus would not leave me much time to find the library. When we arrived in Pinzolo Nereo insisted that I stop at his *garni* (bed and breakfast) for a *café* or *espresso* with himself and his wife Anna. Such a genuine invitation was hard to refuse so I soon found myself seated in the small dining room, a small cup of strong coffee in front of me, struggling to make conversation. I had soon discovered that Italians love to chat over a coffee. On our airport transfers when we stopped for a break my driver, usually Aldo, would offer me a coffee and never accepted when I responded "*offro io*" (it's on me). Despite the proximity of his establishment to my 'schoolroom' Nereo insisted on driving me there and left me in front of a building that appeared to be closed. I was right on time but there was no sign of my tutor. I sat down on a convenient wall to wait and wonder if I was in the right place.

"*Ecco mi qua*" Amneris cheerily announced her arrival a few minutes later. She produce a large ring of keys and after unlocking three padlocks on the massive iron gate guarding the entrance to the library she opened the main door and we made our way to the room we were using. We spent two hours in a classroom environment with no distractions. We then wandered back through the town to the bus stop and made our plans for the following week when we would use the same room again.

That third week I arrived in Pinzolo wearing my walking boots in anticipation of a good tramp across the mountains. Amneris glanced at them but did not comment. I started to worry. Had I misunderstood our conversation at the bus stop last week? Amneris was wearing casual slip-ons that looked more suitable for dancing than walking. Maybe she had forgotten about our walk or I really had got it wrong. However with just ten minutes of the lesson left Amneris started gathering all her papers together and said we should go now. I trotted after her, waited while she dealt with the triple locks on the entrance gate and then clambered into the passenger seat of her battered old Fiat waiting patiently outside. Everyone in this area seemed to drive a battered old Fiat, most of them maroon like the one in which we were now hurtling along the main street. We made our way at great speed up the road out of town and towards the next village, Sant' Antonio di Mavignolo.

Just outside this village we swung left onto a road that took us through Val Nambrone and after following this road for about ten minutes I spotted a *rifugio* ahead of us. Lunch I thought. Good, I was beginning to feel quite hungry and the little *rifugio* looked very welcoming with its bright umbrellas shading the tables and chairs outside the immaculate wooden structure. We whizzed past and continued along the road which soon became much narrower and the black tarmac deteriorated into grey shingle. We bounced our way higher and higher up the mountain with Amneris occasionally slewing the little car to one side to give way to larger, sleeker and faster models. These manoeuvres were accompanied by muttered comments about interlopers from Rome and Milan. As we climbed I could see the valley stretching out below us, it was breathtaking, although I was beginning to feel as though I was on a big dipper as the pace of our ascent continued unabated. I gazed in awe at our surroundings. The rock here in the Adamello Presanella range of mountains was granite and although more durable than the Dolomite stone of the Brenta range it was also more unstable so there was no skiing in this area but there were some great walks. The peaks rose above us, large rounded grey boulders interspersed with lush green vegetation which was getting sparser as we rose higher and higher and the sheer drop on my side of the car fell away more and more steeply. Where would our journey end I wondered. Right there it seemed as the car stopped abruptly in front of a locked gate. *"Mama mia,"* exclaimed Amneris and jumped out of the car and gave this barrier a few futile shakes. She then got back in the car and announced that our walk would start now and the engine was abruptly switched off.

I clambered out and gazed around me. I felt light headed and elated the air was so clear and thin up here and the silence profound. We seemed to be in the middle of nowhere, no sign of habitation apart from the offending locked gate. Amneris was now rooting in the boot of the car and after a few minutes produced a pair of old fashioned plimsolls that she pulled on to her feet confirming my first impression that this was to be an easy walk. Indeed, as I continued to gaze appreciatively at my surroundings I spotted a building that could be a *rifugio* just below us. I felt slightly disappointed, as I had been looking forward to a challenge but also relieved as it meant lunch would be happening quite soon. I could not see any other route as ahead and to the right of us was just a mountain so we had to be heading down the path that was winding down the slope to our left.

We set off, Amneris bounding along in front of me but in the opposite direction to the *rifugio* I had been looking at, in fact straight up the mountain that blocked our way! I plodded along behind. We went higher and higher and our 'path' got narrower and more boulder strewn. I then realised that we were not actually following a proper path but Amneris was taking a track that she obviously knew well. After an hour of my companion's relentless pace I had to ask her if we could have a break. We had been ascending the whole time and I was getting very tired and hungry. I felt like a small child as I sat there bleating, "Is it much further?"

"Not far," Amneris replied, adding that when we got to the top we would be able to see the *rifugio*. Off we went again, still climbing. The scenery was spectacular, and so very different from the mountains around Madonna di Campiglio that it was a real joy to be there, despite my protesting legs.

We climbed right to the top of the peak in front of us, I was glad when we got there as it signalled lunch to me. At the top we gazed around us. It was incredible, now we were right in the middle of the Adamella Presanella range, truly awesome mountains, some capped with small glaciers. Amneris drew my attention to a small dot half way up another peak across the valley from where we were standing, the Rifugio Segantini, our objective. Then she bounded off again before I could voice my opinion. My opinion being that it was miles away and we had to descend the mountain we had just climbed and then climb another one! I was really hungry by now and had drunk all my water. Amneris did not even have a rucksack or indeed anything at all with her. When she had changed her shoes she had just put a purse in her pocket and a light jacket round her waist.

Now that we were going downhill the path was easier and I relaxed and began to enjoy myself. So far all the walks I had done had been with my groups and had not been challenging but this was something else and it made me realise how much fitness I had lost. We were soon at the bottom and started climbing again, this time on a marked path and not an Amneris special, a trek straight across country, which was much easier. The paths in the area are very well constructed and generally allowed walkers to zigzag up the steep ascents but using the Amneris technique of going directly from zig to zag we soon reached the Rifugio Segantini. My mouth began to water and my hollow stomach growled in anticipation.

I was a bit disconcerted therefore when Amneris skirted the *rifugio* and set off determinedly in the opposite direction. She was going so fast I had the impression she was on a mission. She was. When I caught up with her she was standing in front of a shrine cut into the rock. Inside this memorial there were photographs of climbers who had died in these mountains. By the photographs there were inscriptions and flowers. Amneris pointed out a photograph of two men, her father and her fiancée who had both perished in an accident up there. They had been climbing and were roped together when Amneris' father had a heart attack and they both fell. It was a poignant moment especially as Amneris had not been there for over two years due to working abroad. Our decision to go walking today had given her the opportunity she craved. One forgets that the mountains, majestic and beautiful as they are can also be a hard taskmaster and a cruel host.

Finally we made our way inside the *rifugio* and I was able to still my hunger pangs with a large dish of traditional barley soup accompanied by chunks of fresh bread and assuage my thirst with a bowl of barley coffee, my first experience of these local specialities. We lingered for some time after eating while Amneris renewed her acquaintance with the owners of the *rifugio*. Now refreshed and rested I was anxious to get going again as I was due to meet my group this evening and did not want to be late. However, I need not have worried as the descent was much more gentle than the ascent and followed a completely different route around the mountain rather than over it. After what seemed a very short time we rounded a corner and a small valley stretched out in front of us at the end of which I could see the Fiat abandoned by the locked gate. We skipped down the path; Amneris was now very relaxed and chatty and pointed out landmarks familiar to her since childhood walks with her beloved father. In no time we were back in the car and careering down the road. Amneris insisted on driving me all the way back to the hotel so I was in plenty of time to join my group for dinner.

The following week we changed our routine as we had decided to walk again after the lesson but this time we would tackle the Brenta range above Madonna di Campiglio. We had agreed to walk to the Rifugio Tuckett as this was one of the few walks I had not done in this area. Amneris came to the hotel and we conducted the lesson on the veranda outside the bar where the fabulous view was slightly distracting but then so was the thought of walking to the *rifugio* that nestled high in the peaks in front of us. I had asked Signora Silvana if we could have our lesson there today and she and the staff had been very enthusiastic about it, welcoming Amneris and within seconds of our taking our seats outside offering us coffee and inviting Amneris to have breakfast if she so wished.

We struggled to complete two hours of study and finally gave in and decided to set off for the Grosté cabin lift from where we could start our walk. By now I knew that Amneris had a cat of which she was very fond so I guessed she would not object if Tabata came with us. When I broached the subject she was very enthusiastic about the idea and insisted we go off to meet the dog immediately. Amneris was smitten, Tabata was enamoured and I was jealous! This contrary hound who had ignored me for days when I first met her was treacherously leaping all over Amneris and wagging her tail furiously while Amneris crooned *"Tabatina, poverina"* at her. Maybe it was all in the accent after all.

I requested the hotel shuttle bus to take us to the bottom of the Grosté cabin lift but Goran was out taking other hotel guests somewhere. Typically the hotel quickly found an alternative and arranged for Doreano, one of the hotel receptionists to take us in one of their own cars. We were soon on our way. Amneris chatting away in the front seat and me trying to force an excited Tabata to sit on the floor in the back. Doreano was definitely not a member of the Tabata fan club and I could sense his disapproval as the excited animal tried to scramble up onto the back seat to look out of the window.

It was a glorious day, not a cloud in the sky which was a translucent blue. Tabata leapt into the cabin lift like the regular rider she now was. She jumped straight up onto the seat and sat there smugly surveying the scenery around her, occasionally pricking up her ears and gazing intently at a bush she was trying to make into a marmot. She also sometimes stood up on her hind legs and stuck her head out of the open window. I fervently hoped that she would not see anything worth chasing as I knew by now that the thrill of the hunt overrode all her other senses and she was quite capable of scrambling out of the small space and dropping to the ground fifty metres below.

Tabata was so anxious to get out and get going that she managed to wrap us both round the turnstile through which we had to exit at the top of the second stage of the cabin lift. It was so exhilarating to be high above the tree line and surrounded by patches of tiny alpine flowers. As always I was captivated by the profound deep blue of the gentians and the startling pale blue of the tiny forget-me-nots, so we spent some time examining and exclaiming over these exquisite treasures of nature. I often brought my groups up to this place that resembled a grey moonscape and every time a new treasure was revealed: a group of troilius growing in the middle of a small, dark patch of green grass their beautiful golden orbs dancing gently in the light breeze or a bright red orchid, starkly single and proudly erect among the dry, pale stones. Time to move on but I lingered for one last look. Below me I could see the bright blue and white shutters that adorned the Rifugio Graffer which proclaimed it to be a SAT building. These buildings were run under the auspices of the *Società degli Alpinisti Tridentini* and offered not just refreshment and accommodation but were also featured in 'Sounds of the Mountains' programmes organised locally. One day earlier that summer I had walked down to Graffer to listen to an open-air concert that was taking place there. It was wonderful hearing the music floating through the pure clear air, holding spellbound a large and very appreciative audience of walkers.

By now Tabata, having been granted her freedom, was a long way ahead of us and fortunately had chosen to go in the right direction. Sometimes in her ecstasy at being at liberty she would just run and run and I often had to forgo a coffee while waiting for her outside Stoppani, the restaurant at the top. That was a real hardship as I considered their *latte macchiato* (milky coffee) to be the best on the mountain. I always carried a whistle when I was walking with a group but I used it more often to recall this wayward canine than I ever did for a missing guest. Once when I could only just make her out, a small amber dot across the valley I blew my whistle to summon her back. Through my binoculars I saw her lift her head and look in my direction before deliberately setting off again still moving away from me. She did always come back but in her own time and never in any great hurry.

We followed Tabata along the path to Rifugio Tuckett. It was a fantastic path that wound its way upwards as it followed the curves of the mountain. Tabata was even more excited than usual, racing to and fro, down into a crevice to frisk in some snow, up onto the rocks high above us where she posed like a rampant stag. In front of us one minute, behind us the next. Amneris and I marched along sometimes talking but mostly just enjoying the sheer pleasure of being up there. As it was a Saturday there were quite a few walkers around. We met whole families enjoying their day out. Everyone was so friendly and many of them hailed us with the old Roman greeting, *salve*. Less formal than *buongiorno* or *buonasera* depending on the time of day it was a more suitable greeting than the very informal *ciao*. Some even stopped to say hello to Tabata, if she happened to be in the vicinity

As we approached the *rifugio* Tabata suddenly came thundering past us in full blood-curdling howling hunt. She had spotted a cat which had reacted by shooting straight up a pylon. Tabata was soon circling the pylon and barking furiously. Everyone was looking. I chased Tabata around the pylon for a while and Amneris watched us, commenting, helpfully, that we should walk on and Tabata would follow. I loved her optimism, she clearly was not aware of Tabata's obstinacy when it came to flushing out her quarry and I knew she could be there for hours if I did not grab her and force her to come with us. Finally I succeeded and dragged Tabata down the slope towards the *rifugio* a short distance away. Amneris had perched on a rock to enjoy the view and I sat down next to her clinging on to a wildly excited Tabata. We were surrounded by the magnificent peaks of the Brenta Dolomites. Clearly these stunning pinnacles were different from ordinary rocks. Amazing formations had been created by their morphology because incredibly thick layers of rock were supported by layers of less resistant rock including marl and sandstone. The erosion of these softer rocks had undermined the base and huge slabs of rocks had crashed down the mountain evidenced by the silver scree creeping like a static waterfall around their base and then down towards the jagged green edge of the tree line.

Tracing the outlines of some famous peaks in front of me, Campanil Basso, Cima Brenta and Cima Tosa, queen of this group of mountains, I could understand why Déodat de Dolomieu had found the mystery of their origin so compelling. In 1789 this gentleman was journeying from France to Rome, an uneventful journey it seemed at the time but one that ultimately brought him fame and a fortune during his lifetime and the dedication of a whole mountain range in his name after his death. During his journey Dolomieu picked up some rocks and stones in the Valle Isarca as he was fascinated by their vivid colours and he wanted to analyse them. He discovered that these rocks were different from ordinary rocks and were not, as had been assumed, limestone. Rather they were a calcium magnesium carbonate. Subsequently both the mineral and the rock were given his name, Dolomite.

In 1864, some seventy-five years later, two itinerant English geologists called Gilbert and Churchill published a book entitled the Dolomite Mountains which was an account of their exploration of this region hitherto known by a variety of names including the Venetian Alps and the Monte Pallidi (Pale Mountains). Both the book and the name became popular and soon British pioneers such as John Ball and Amelia Edwards arrived in the region to scale the hitherto unconquered heights of this small mountainous region of the Austro-Hapsburg Empire. These first visitors became entranced with the stunning rose tinted peaks that had emerged from the depths of the sea about seventy million years ago. Since then glaciers had advanced down the valley and volcanoes had erupted and in the eras following these events various processes of erosion had resulted in metamorphic rocks. A romantic geological history reflected in the moods of the mountains. Stunning dawns when spots of orange light appeared and spread across the subdued grey rocks which then suddenly sprang into life under the warmth of the rising sun. At the end of the day enthralling sunsets occurred when the coral deposits caught the last fading rays of the sun and held them, glowing a rosy red until darkness surged in.

This natural phenomenon of alpenglow was known as *enrosadira* in the local Ladin language. Ladins are one of the smallest Ethnic minorities in Europe and despite a chequered history still clung tenaciously to their culture, traditions and legends. There are about eighty thousand Ladins sprinkled throughout the mountain valleys of the Dolomites and they speak an incomprehensible ancient language derived from the Celtic Rhaetian dialects of the original inhabitants during the Bronze Age, and Latin. This had resulted from an encounter between northern colonists and Roman legions in the first century BC.

These first pioneers were followed by English and German mountaineers, skiers and trekkers all anxious to explore these beautiful and diverse mountains. Initially local people and deer hunters acted as guides but then in 1872 the *Società degli Alpinisti Tridentini* (SAT) was founded in Madonna di Campiglio for the promotion of activities in the mountains, the provision of shelter and the publication of information. In 1920 SAT became part of the Club Alpino d'Italia (CAI) but has remained autonomous and between the wars restored and repaired war damaged shelters as well as opening up the excellent network of paths for everybody from all walks of life to enjoy.

Rifugio Tuckett and its immediate neighbour Rifugio Sella were now SAT refuges. Sella was built by the Italians between 1904 and 1905 and then in 1906 the Germans built the Tuckett *'passehutte'* in honour of the British climber, Francis Fox Tuckett, a real aficionado of the area. Both these refuges were laid to waste during the First World War and both were restored by SAT in 1920 by which time it also acquired the German *rifugio*. Rifugio Sella has since become part of the Rifugio Tuckett. This fascinating place not only served food and provided accommodation for walkers spending a few days up there but also housed a small museum dedicated to Francis Fox Tuckett. We enjoyed a tasty lunch surrounded by memorabilia of this famous Englishman from Bristol.

After our meal we resumed our walk. This time we were making our way downhill on an easy path with amazing views right across the valley. Tabata was all over the place again although I had remembered the cat incident and kept her on the lead until we were well away from the *rifugio*, I also kept calling her back in case she doubled back to have another attempt at cornering her prey. I really did not want to walk all the way back up there again in the heat to retrieve her.

Our next pause was at the Rifugio Casinei, nestling in a clearing in the trees half way along the path between Tuckett and Vallesinella. Tabata was bounding ahead of us and ignored my shouts to come back to us as she had smelt water and was intent on getting a drink. There was a trough outside the *rifugio* and Tabata jumped straight into it much to the surprise of the people standing around it waiting to fill their water bottles. She was therefore able to cool her paws and simultaneously quench her thirst, a source of amusement to the crowd of people gathered outside the *rifugio*. I dragged her out while Amneris went inside and bought us some drinks. This time we sat outside, Tabata tied up securely beside us trading insults with an Alsatian who was also attached to a sturdy table.

It was just wonderful sitting there. We were back below the tree line and the views were so very different from those of the stark grey scree far above us. Time was now getting on and we would have to move quickly to get back to the hotel in time for me to meet my group for dinner. We set off at a brisk pace. Tabata was liberated soon after we got on our way and was out of view within seconds. Amneris and I were chatting so intently it was some time before I realised I had not heard or seen the dog for quite a while. I stopped to call and whistle her but she did not materialise. I began to worry, it was the longest time she had not appeared at all. Amneris was not concerned and convinced that she had gone far ahead of us and when we got down to the Rifugio Vallesinella would be there waiting for us. Reluctantly I continued. Tabata had not done this walk before so I was not confident she would find her way there and if she had chased an animal through the trees she could be anywhere.

When we arrived at Rifugio Vallesinella there was no sign of Tabata. We asked at the *rifugio* if anyone had seen her. I knew they would have recognised her as she had often been brought there when I had stopped there for lunch with my groups. Tabata would arrive with the hotel shuttle bus and walk back to the hotel with me and any members of the group who wished to continue walking. Nobody had seen Tabata today. I was exhausted but I had no option, I would have to retrace my steps, all the way back up the steep path to Casinei, to see if the dog had gone back there. We started going back down the path, asking other walkers if they had seen her on their way down. After a few negative responses we got a positive sighting, someone had seen her go straight up the slope back towards Casinei. I did remember that shortly after I set her free she had plunged straight over the side of the path and down the slope. The path zigzagged along so it was possible that she had gone straight down and then come straight back up again and been totally unaware of the direction the path and I had taken.

The thought of having to walk all the way back up to Casinei in the heat and after already walking for four hours was almost too much. Amneris was now convinced Tabata would eventually find her way back to the hotel and suggested we continue on our way. I could not share her optimism and, anyway, I felt that Tabata was very much my responsibility. Nothing else for it and I continued on my way back up the path. Amneris followed me for a while and then decided to wait at the bottom in case Tabata made her way down there. She settled herself in the shade while I dragged myself up the path in the full glare of the sun.

It was such hard work plodding back up the path and now time really was of the essence as there was only an hour before I was due to meet the group back at the hotel and here I was marching along in the wrong direction! As I was carrying the lead in my hand it was clear I was looking for something to attach to it and everyone coming down the path had seen my missing link and shouted words of encouragement. The dog was still there waiting for me, she was sitting in the trough, she was having a drink, she was distraught – and I was not distraught, I felt like yelling back. The companion of the man who made this observation was kind enough to add that he thought that the *signora* was also *distratta*. Too right! My legs were aching, I was thirsty but did not dare take even thirty seconds rest to have a drink, and I was hot and fed up.

As I got nearer to Casinei I started whistling and shouting in case Tabata could hear me and would come down to meet me. Finally she did hear me and there was a crashing through the undergrowth above me and Tabata landed on the path right by me. I was so relieved to see her I sat on the path and hugged her! There were shouts from above us. Was she my dog? Was she alright? Now was not the time to begin explaining that she was not my dog but belonged to the Hotel Lorenzetti. Anyway I doubted I could have done that in Italian so I just shouted back *si, si va tutto bene* and hoped that would suffice. I was more interested in having a drink of water before galloping back down the mountain to the road from where the hotel shuttle bus could pick us up. All thoughts of actually walking all the way back to the hotel had now been abandoned.

We set off, dog on lead, and me running down the path. For once I was setting the pace. I soon caught sight of Amneris sitting serenely on a step, exchanging greetings with all the Italians passing by. It really was an extraordinary sight, everyone who had been walking there today was descending at the same time. When

Amneris saw us she came back up to meet us and took control of the now very subdued dog while I used my mobile to call the hotel and request the shuttle bus to collect us from Rifugio Vallesinella.

The shuttle bus had not yet arrived when we reached the *rifugio* so we had time for a very welcome beer. Tabata sat next to me and within seconds was fast asleep leaning against my leg. How I wished I could just curl up and go to sleep and not wake up until tomorrow. But no, I now had just fifteen minutes to get back to the hotel and shower and change ready for my assignation with the group, one I was beginning to regret making. But it was their last night and I did like to make sure I joined them for dinner even though it was my day off. I just doubted my ability to stay awake throughout a five course dinner. The shuttle bus arrived and we jumped in. Tabata stayed awake long enough to pull herself into the back and then fell asleep again.

On arriving back at the hotel I rushed into the bar to tell those already there that I would join them in five minutes. I raced upstairs and threw all my clothes off, jumped in the shower, grabbed my 'last night' red shirt and was ready in five minutes. My room looked like the finale of a jumble sale and I shuddered to think what the chambermaid would make of it when she came in to do the turn down service but there was no time to tidy up.

I decided I would not tell Signora Silvana about the day's adventure, no point in worrying her and anyway the dog was back safe and tired. As I made my way through to the bar to join my group several of the Italians in there greeted me and asked if I had found the missing dog. All the guests in the hotel must have been on the same path as us today and they had all heard about the dog! Yes, I responded she was found and she was fine. No chance then of keeping the owner in the dark. When Signora Silvana came round during dinner I felt I had to spill the beans. She was, as usual, calm and serene and just smiled and said she thought there may have been a problem as I was so late back. She did however express great surprise that Tabata had waited for me at Casinei when normally this restless animal never stayed in one place for more than a few seconds.

It was a struggle keeping my eyes open during dinner and my calf muscles were nagging like a persistent toothache. Finally we finished the meal and after a quick drink in the bar I was able to make my escape. Most people had gone to their rooms to pack by then anyway. At least I did not have to pack as I had another week at the hotel. I just wanted to sleep. I am sure I was asleep before my body landed on the bed.

Astonishingly several years later I was sitting quietly in the hotel's new restaurant enjoying the splendid views of the mountains outside when another guest came over to my table to say hello. This was not unusual as the hotel had many regular clients several of whom I knew quite well. Having exchanged greetings this lady then reminisced about the day Tabata went astray near Casinei. Clearly my rosy, perspiring face as I toiled back up the mountain had made quite an impression.

Church of S. Maria Antica, Madonna di Campiglio

Tabata

Nereo leading the way at Vallesinella

Madonna di Campiglio

Giacomo, Sandro, Paolo and Giuseppe

Marino and Stefano in festive mood

Signora Silvana and granddaughter Emma

Goran and Karin

Lago Spinale

The Hapsburgs come to town

Fresh Snow in the Town Centre

Strolling through an Alpine meadow in the Dolomites

Tabata enjoys the views from the cabin lift

The path to the top of Groste

Raring to go

The Winter Marathon goes through Madonna di Campiglio

On the top of Grostè

A winter wonderland

Chapter Eight – Winter Adventures

Just two thoughts went through my mind as I bounced down the mountain. The first that I had my mobile in my pocket and the second that I knew the number of the path I had just fallen off. Then a third, terrible notion intruded without invitation as I continued to bump and slither down the slope. Had I managed to hang Tabata with her own collar when I plunged spectacularly over the edge? Was she stretched out motionless on the path above me? I need not have worried because when I came to an abrupt halt against a tree trunk Tabata landed right on top of me, clearly still very much alive.

The day had begun like any other on a ski trip. I had spoken to everybody at breakfast and made sure that they all had ski companions. Several people in the group were having ski lessons and had invited me to join them. I really enjoyed doing this as it was a chance to ski with those who spent the week in ski school and also an opportunity to improve my own technique. I loved skiing and had been trying to master the sport for many years but I was never going to be more than a 'competent cruiser'. Indeed, when a ski instructor was asked if I was a good skier he merely responded 'experienced' leaving me in no doubt about my skills. Madonna di Campiglio was the perfect venue for me as the tree-lined slopes offered plenty of good skiing and the occasional challenge on the well-groomed black runs.

The lesson went well. Pio, our instructor, was a very patient man and very good at instilling confidence in the nervous. He had decided today that we were ready to ski the black run, Amazzonia, so off we went. I was doing really well, tucked in at the back of the 'snake' of skiers following our instructor, when I hit a patch of ice and shot off the piste finally coming to rest imprisoned in the fork of a tree. I could hear Pio yelling from the other side of the run *"non togliere I tuoi sci"* (don't take your skis off). I understood that this was due to the danger of a ski escaping and finishing the descent on its own at great risk to other skiers. What Pio had not realised was that with one leg either side of a thin tree trunk taking one ski off was the only option! I loosened my embrace around the tree trunk and managed to release the ski keeping hold of it all the time. I then pushed myself away from the tree and by the time Pio reached me, still shouting, I was standing in deep snow, one ski off and the other three feet under.

Pio insisted the second ski be put back and that I 'ski' back onto the piste. Somehow I managed to obey his instructions and finally skied down to join the rest of the group who had stopped to watch my predicament. I commented on the sternness of our instructor who I had thought might have just lifted me out of the tree encouraging me with words of concern and sympathy. The group informed me that he had simply glanced back up the slope from where all that could be seen of me was a pair of skis sticking out of a tree and announced "she's okay".

We continued our lesson. In between descents I chatted with Pio on the chairlifts. Pio worked as a ski instructor in the winter and also ran a bed and breakfast in Sant' Antonio di Mavignolo a small village a few kilometres down the mountain from Madonna di Campiglio. We had met when he was assigned by the Rainalter *Scuola di Sci* to one of my groups. In those days he was one of the few ski instructors who spoke good English. He had helped me a lot with my Italian over the years as we always spoke Italian when I skied with him and he would 'practise' what he was about to say to the group in Italian and then I would listen to his English explanation and correct it if necessary. Generally our conversations were about the walks I had been doing the previous summer. That day, as we talked and viewed the area from the chair lift it suddenly occurred to me that the current lack of snow may have meant that some of the walks I had done in the summer were possible this winter. He would also scan the area above the slopes in case he spotted some *camosci* (chamois) grazing there. Often groups of them could be seen foraging in the lichen above the tree line at Cinque Laghi and when he spotted some he would proudly point them out to us.

Pio had become a favourite with our groups as those wishing to perfect their technique found his explanations were clear and helpful. Once Pio was satisfied that the correct technique had been learnt he found new challenges and his pupils progressed rapidly and were soon whizzing around the resort behind him. I was fortunate also to have become acquainted with Fabio who offered a more exciting alternative for the younger, more courageous element in my groups. His flowing locks and youthful demeanour belied a deep love of the mountains because, like Pio, he was a truly local man and between them they covered the full spectrum of ski instruction required by my diverse clientele. Both Pio and Fabio were totally honest when it came to appraising my efforts on the slopes and I was only told it was good if it really was good!

After our lesson was over we joined the rest of the group at my favourite restaurant, Rifugio Viviani, just below the Pradalago cabin lift and during the meal I endured a lot of good humoured teasing about the tree hugging episode. I loved the cosy atmosphere of this restaurant where the tables were sociably circular encouraging conversation beneath the large picture windows that looked out over the slopes. The pastel colours of the painted walls were complemented by the chair and table coverings and it was nice to sit down, order from a menu and have one's food brought to the table. My groups always received a friendly welcome when we ate there and they would organise large tables for us so we could all sit together. Sometimes there was fierce competition for tables there and I remembered one week when a large group of English people regularly occupied the table next to ours and habitually wolfed down plates of fried eggs and chips. Such a shame as the menu changed frequently and offered an interesting variety of delicious pasta dishes. My own favourite was their pumpkin ravioli accompanied by a small carafe of a very palatable local red wine. On this occasion several people followed my example and we all became very relaxed. A decision was made at some point to ski back down to the town, get the shuttle bus back to the hotel and spend the afternoon swimming in the heated indoor pool. I excused myself from this activity as a plan was forming in my mind.

On returning to the hotel I put on my moon boots, sturdy boots with a good grip and ideal for walking in the snow. I did not change from my ski suit, a well-padded one that I had acquired recently in Lapland, and went to reception to ask if I could take Tabata for a walk. It was not unusual for me to walk with Tabata into the town in the afternoon so they were happy to go and find her for me. Tabata stayed inside in the winter and although content to walk with me into the town every day she did not get over-excited about the prospect. She appeared, bleary eyed and submitted quietly to the attachment of her lead before we set off. As we emerged into the chilly air she did liven up a bit but when we crossed the road and started walking up the path through the trees she started leaping up and down and yapping hysterically. This was shaping up to be a proper walk!

Generally the snow drifted down on Madonna di Campiglio from mid November but this particular winter it did not appear at all until March. Thanks to sub zero temperatures the snow makers were constantly in operation throughout the season and most of the ski runs were open and covered with good quality snow so the skiing was as good as ever. Travelling up to the top in the ski lifts one was presented with a crazy pattern of white stripes imposed on a green background. A constant temperature of minus ten Centigrade had enabled the resort to make sufficient snow so that by the time we had arrived in January nearly all the runs were open including the linking run to Marileva and Folgarida and we could ski two other resorts as well.

I had tried walking the paths in the winter before when the fast melting snow as spring approached gave one the impression there was very little snow left in the valley. Walking back from town one day with one of the group I thought that as a lot of the snow had already melted the Giro di Campiglio would be clear enough to walk along it. I had not realised that the shelter of the trees maintained the snow on the paths much longer than on the exposed slopes. For the first few hundred metres we were fine and then, when the path dipped, we found ourselves floundering in snow up to our thighs. We emerged on to a clear path again and I decided to continue rather than take the sensible option of re-tracing our steps and walking back along the main road. After a short while we encountered more snow on the path but this time it went on for as far as we could see and it was so deep that all the markings were hidden and I had to rely on my sense of direction, never good at the best of times. We battled on, giggling when we fell over because it took so long to get up again. Finally I spotted a road below us through the trees and suggested we take a short cut down the slope to reach it. More laughter as we descended by various means but mostly sitting down and sliding over the snow. Finally we reached the road and I realised it was not the road to the hotel! I had two choices, left or right. I decided left and this took us down to the main road and fortunately familiar territory. I vowed this would be my last experience of off-road walking in winter.

On this particular occasion however I knew that there would be no snow at all to trouble us and we puffed up through woods and took the road up to Panorama. It was very exhilarating walking in the cold, dry air and we marched along the road enjoying the silence and the views There was no skiing in this part of Madonna so the slopes around me were green with their permanently snow-capped peaks in the background reflecting the sun's golden rays onto the surrounding grey rocks.

At Panorama we took the path that would lead us onto the Giro di Campiglio and back to the hotel. It was great, the paths were clear and we strode along, I even burst into song occasionally, it was so beautiful with the frosty trees on both sides of me and my breath misting the air in front of me. As we were close to some buildings and not far from the road I kept Tabata on the lead and after pulling like a train for a while to register her disapproval she soon settled down and we marched along in complete accord. Occasionally she would glance back maybe to register her gratitude but more likely to entreat me to stop singing!

Suddenly I came to a full stop. It was so cold that the water in one of the small waterfalls that generally tumbled onto the path had frozen solid. I was confronted with a huge patch of ice that carpeted my way ahead for a distance of two metres. I was stymied. I knew I did not have time to re-trace my steps before it got dark. I studied the path and thought that I could see some grass sticking out in the middle of the ice. Okay, so I could jump onto the grass and then off the grass and back on to the path the other side.

I jumped. As I hit the grass I discovered too late that it was not a growing plant but some loose blades that had been thrown into the middle of the ice. My feet slid away from underneath me, I fell flat on my back and then shot straight over the edge of the path and down the sheer drop beside me. As I bounced and rolled down the slope I was grateful that I had not changed out of my Michelin man ski suit as it was protecting me from the rocks and roots that littered the ground beneath me. When I finally came to a halt jammed against a tree trunk I managed to wedge my feet against some roots and grabbed hold of a small sapling. Thank goodness too for ski gloves. Tabata was struggling wildly so I let her off the lead and hoped that when she scrambled back up the bank I could persuade her to wait for me there. She took off up the slope immediately, scrambled up on to the patch of ice, skidded across it and tumbled back down again. She landed next to me again and just sat there looking at with an expression that said I do not like this game at all.

By now I had formed a plan of action and had started to work my way along the slope by finding footholds amongst the roots of large trees and clinging on to the small saplings around me. Tabata decided she would stay with me this time and followed behind impatiently but wisely after her last experience. Finally I judged we were past the icy patch and began to pull myself back up the slope eventually scrambling up onto the path. I captured the dog and we continued as though nothing had happened.

At the end of that week when the group were enjoying their last evening in the hotel inevitably the talk turned to how many falls people had had skiing. Someone pointed out that I had not fallen at all. True, I said, no falls skiing this week. Often in the summer I would pass the spot where I indulged in a bit of free-falling and I still wondered how I managed to survive without a scratch.

After two months with no natural snow it finally arrived one March morning. I woke up to a profound silence that could only mean one thing: it had been snowing heavily overnight. In my enthusiasm to get to the window and check it out I swept the entire contents of my bedside table onto the floor with my duvet. Bounding across the room I was rewarded by the sight of large white mounds, that were once cars, littering the car park at the front of the hotel. Goran was already busy digging out his shuttle bus ready to convey the inevitable early risers to the slopes. Amazingly the main road outside the hotel was clear of snow and as I watched the bright orange ski bus trundled along, snow chains clanking and pulled up in the middle of the road. The driver looked perplexed, there was a parking bay there yesterday but now there was just a wall of snow, pushed there during the night as the snowplough waged its battle against the accumulating drifts. I could see in the headlights of the bus that it was still snowing. Meanwhile the bus driver had decided to turn round and go back from whence he came, causing a minor traffic jam both ways while he executed a perfect ten point turn.

Time to get myself organised as I knew almost the entire group were plotting last night to get the earliest shuttle and as it only took ten people I was expecting to find rival groups huddled in the car park from first light to discourage any competition. When it came to putting my contact lenses in I discovered that due to its tumble from the bedside table one lens was stuck to the lid of its container. Try as I might I could not remove it so after five minutes of gentle persuasion I employed a completely new tactic and tried to suck it off. This was so successful that it flew straight down my throat. No spares with me so I would have to ski wearing just one lens. I looked out of the window again, everything was white anyway, white ground, white snowflakes drifting down against a pale grey sky. Should be fine I thought as in this flat light it would not be possible to see any definition anyway.

There was a rustling of salopettes in the breakfast room this morning, everyone was up early and dressed, ready for the off. A riot was avoided in the car park by persuading the hotel to run two shuttles and cajoling the group into getting off at the first cabin lift, Spinale, just three minutes away. Finally peace reigned and I could creep back inside and enjoy a coffee and a large slice of perfect, moist carrot cake in solitude while waiting for the late starters. I was not too enthusiastic about skiing today because, apart from my reduced vision I was pretty sure that the snow would be so deep on the runs that it would be very hard work whizzing up and down with two large planks of wood on my feet. Oh to be able to enjoy reading a book by the crackling fire in the bar and let others swaddle themselves in layers of vests and fleeces and spend the day shaking snow out of pockets, goggles and hats.

Once everyone had breakfasted and was on their way I joined the last few in the shuttle bus and we headed for the slopes. Emerging from the warmth of the cabin lift my face was whipped by icy particles of snow as I gazed into the dense greyness ahead of me. I could not even see the coffee bar one hundred metres below me. This was going to be fun I groaned inwardly. Fortunately I did not have to work very hard to persuade my companions to make an early coffee stop. We did one short run, bouncing over bumps obscured by flat light and struggling through deep snow on the edges of the runs because skiing down the middle involved avoiding large piles of fluffy snow pushed there by the early starters and a certain recipe for disaster if you attempted to turn in them. Trying to avoid some skiers who had ground to a halt in the middle of the piste, I blithely swung round them only to find my progress immediately halted by knee-deep snow. I was imprisoned and could move neither backwards nor forwards. My companions paused to laugh while I tried to extract my skis and get back onto a skiable surface. It took a while and it was exhausting but I daren't take my skis off as I could see that another skier who had tried to take the same avoiding action had removed his skis and was now prodding around in the snow with his poles trying to retrieve them!

The coffee bar was full of skiers gently steaming, gulping down a hot chocolate or a *bombardino* (a bright yellow concoction of eggnog, whisky and rum that goes straight to the knees) and contemplating the relentless snow and grey skies outside. We arranged to meet for an early and prolonged lunch before setting off again. I suspected some may go straight from coffee to lunch and wished I could do the same but I waited with those having lessons having decided that a ski class was the best place to be today; at least following a ski instructor reduced the risk of failing to see a precipice in the flat light!

***

On one memorable occasion I had a lady called Rosie in my group who insisted on wearing fashionable sunglasses when she was skiing. Despite my often repeated suggestion that she would find it easier to ski with lenses that would give her clearer definition she continued to wear them. Rosie, a fashion slave, also had the latest in hat, gloves and scarf. For some reason all these items were removed every time we ascended in a cabin lift and then we had to wait while they were meticulously replaced. After several repetitions of this ritual the patience of her ski instructor, Marco, had begun to wear thin. As I had joined them for the lesson to try and ease the growing tension I suggested to Marco that he set off with the group and Rosie and I would follow as soon as she was ready. I relayed this plan to Rosie and then skied a short way down the slope and positioned myself so that I could see both Rosie and the group. Marco had not gone far and then he had stopped on the edge of a precipice, the group had followed and they were all lined up neatly beside him looking down into the valley. When Rosie was ready she pushed off towards me; I pointed out the direction we were taking, and we skied down together.

Unfortunately for Rosie her fashion statement sunglasses let her down and she could not distinguish the edge of the run so to her it seemed that the whole area was flat. I heard a whoop as she flew past me towards the group and instead of slowing down as she approached her companions she was actually gathering speed. It seemed her aim was to ski through their orderly line rather than stop beside them! As I watched she ran out of piste and took off. Time stood still and she appeared to be suspended spread-eagled in mid air. Arms and legs akimbo she free fell some twenty metres and landed face down in deep soft snow. Marco skied straight down the vertical slope towards her. My heart was in my mouth, I was convinced a helicopter would be required. I peered down and could see Marco bending over Rosie who lifted her head and spoke to him. Marco, a huge grin spreading across his face, looked up and gave me the thumbs up. Relief flooded through me, so much so that all I could see in my mind was Rosie in full flight. I began to giggle hysterically and moved away from the group who were watching Marco half dragging and half carrying Rosie back up to the piste. I had recovered my composure by the time Rosie re-joined the group. Her demeanour was remarkably calm and having re-adjusted her apparel she announced, to my amazement, that she was ready to continue.

When we met the rest of the group later for lunch Rosie's adventure was the main topic of conversation. Those who had not witnessed the event were convinced that we were exaggerating the whole incident. Rosie herself just smiled and graciously accepted the attention she was receiving. At breakfast the next morning she mentioned that she had a stiff neck and could not imagine why! She continued to ski in her *a la mode* sunglasses which, astoundingly, had survived their misadventure.

***

My thoughts were interrupted by a cheery greeting from Pio, it was difficult to distinguish the instructors today as their faces were all eerily enveloped in peaked hoods and dark lensed goggles. Once everyone had identified their instructor we set off in small groups that soon vanished into the swirling snow laden mist around us. Tucked in at the back of my class after a few turns I started to feel reasonably confident and able to cope with the mild blizzard and a missing contact lens. They do say that it would be possible to ski with your eyes closed (provided the slopes were empty and wide) by just 'feeling' the snow through your boots and skis. We then swung into a black run. This was going to be interesting, a steep slope, covered by mounds of soft snow with snowboarders careering down at great speed! Normally you could hear the boarders scraping along so you knew where they were but in this muffled atmosphere they glided silently up behind you and often the first indication that they were there was the yelp when they turned to avoid you and ended up waist deep in snow pushed to one side by our predecessors. When we were stationary I noticed that there were a lot of snowboarders digging themselves out and those who had ventured into the trees resembled manic snowmen as they reappeared on foot, their snowboards carried aloft.

We stopped for some instruction and were advised that in deep snow it was easier to lean back slightly. This was a novel idea as generally leaning back was totally forbidden because it had the effect of making the skis go faster and without control. I experimented. It worked perfectly and the drag effect of the deep snow meant turning was redundant and I could just go straight down. Pio was not impressed and I was rewarded with five minutes of instruction while the rest of the class proceeded down the mountain executing their turns perfectly. During this discussion he informed me that I turned better to the left than I did to the right. This was not surprising as the right was my 'blind' side. I agreed with everything he said and we set off again and made our way down to the bottom with me feeling my way round bumps and through deep snow and somehow managing to remain upright despite a few alarming wobbles. At the end of the run I told Pio that I had to leave to go to the restaurant to meet the rest of the group and quit with my honour still in tact. No falls so far this week.

We parted company and I set off for the Cascina Zeledria which involved skiing down a track off-piste. Earlier tracks had already been covered by fresh snow and my skis soon disappeared completely so that when I looked down all I could see was my knees furrowing a path through the deep powder which made me laugh. Fortunately the slope was steep enough to keep the momentum going and I soon reached the restaurant where I was not surprised to find half the group had already arrived and were enjoying a hot mulled wine. Eventually everyone else appeared and we had a really enjoyable lunch watching the snow floating down outside.

Once we had finished eating and indulging in coffees and *grappas* we were ready to be towed back up to the piste. This restaurant had its own snow cats to which lengths of rope were attached and each skier held on to a knot while being pulled along by the vehicle. We managed to get twelve of us clinging to two ropes and off we went. I was not sure that even had I noticed the large mound of snow looming up in front of me I could have avoided it. As it happened I did not see it until my skis were firmly embedded in it and I was flying through the air without them but still hanging on to my knot! I had to let go and landed in a heap in front of the person behind me who also had to relinquish his knot and the resulting skittle effect left six of us sprawled in the deep snow. Fortunately the driver stopped and waited patiently while we retrieved skis and poles and re-attached ourselves to his rope. I had seen him abandon the fallen on previous occasions so I was glad that I had regularly tipped him a few euros each time he had pulled my groups back up to the slopes.

After much laughter we regained the slopes without further incident and tackled the run back down to the bottom of the chair. It was fun but hard work as the snow was getting deeper all the time. Several people decided to call it a day and go tobogganing instead. I was persuaded to join them and we made our way back to the hotel to change. At the hotel Pietro convinced me that it would be a good idea if Tabata walked back into town with us. This was not as easy as it sounded because the snowploughs had left six foot high piles of snow on the pavements and pedestrians had to walk down the middle of the road leaping out of the way of cars and shuttle buses. In the centre of town there were mountains of snow that had been pushed up to allow people to promenade around the squares, window shopping and chatting while their children scrambled up to the top of them and descended at great speed with or without plastic trays. Some of the youngsters demonstrated amazing gymnastic talent as they hurtled through the air. The whole atmosphere was very festive and thick snow flakes continued to drift down, shimmering in the pale yellow street lights and flecking hats, faces, scarves and coats with white.

Tobogganing in deep snow was even harder than skiing through it and I was glad I was just a spectator as I watched the others staggering up the hill dragging their bright plastic conveyances behind them. As this slope was also used by skiers and boarders to get back into town lots of them were descending around us, bumping down over mounds and floundering through waist deep snow when they had to take avoiding action to miss the tobogganists and snow ball fighters now gathering on the lower slopes. My companions sat at the top of the slope for a long time, recovering their breath I was told, before careering down in a flurry of snow and landing in a heap at my feet. We giggled hysterically like school children as the process was repeated again and again. I remained smugly upright taking photographs until Tabata decided she wanted to join in and set off up the mountain at great speed, forgetting that she was tethered to my leg. I found myself flat on my back in three feet of snow with an exuberant dog bouncing on my chest and my camera held aloft to keep it safe! Eventually we managed to scramble to our feet and followed the group back into town and into the nearest bar for drinks and snacks, a great end to a wonderful week. Tabata was delighted to be included in the *après ski* entertainment especially as it involved tit bits of crisps, peanuts and *pizza* bites. Thereafter whenever we went past that bar she would try to pull me inside to join the group that she was certain she would find there. In fact with some groups it would develop into a regular habit. We would all ski down together and they would stop off in town and go to either the posing Suisse Bar in the main square or the Franz Josef Stube Bar and I would return to the hotel and collect Tabata and then walk into town to join them for a drink.

One week the slopes seemed to be overrun with small children, careering down the slopes completely fearless, leaning back and defying gravity by remaining solidly upright, long snakes of them behind stern ski instructors. But just occasionally they came to grief and once, when leading my group down the mountain in orderly fashion I spotted a toddler right in front of me: a small heap on the ground skis akimbo. No other adults in sight so I could hardly ignore it. The child was in an extraordinary position, face flat on the snow, arms and legs spread out and skis crossed preventing any movement at all. Unaccustomed as I was to dealing with small children I nevertheless stopped just below it and immediately a small hand was held out. I took it and pulled hard. Nothing happened, the entangled skis impeding all attempts to get it upright. I pulled a little harder and found I had a small empty glove in my hand. I dropped my ski poles in the snow in order to replace the glove and to lift the child up off the ground and then stand it up on the snow. Once the skis made contact the child was in motion and set off down the slope bawling ungratefully! Following along behind I tried to slow it down by grabbing the hood of its jacket. Unfortunately it was detachable and the hood remained in my hand while the child continued to trundle down the mountain. I overtook it, swung across its path and stopped The child managed to slow itself down by skiing straight at me (big mistake to stop downhill of it) and now both sets of skis were entangled. Finally I extricated it again, re-attached the hood and this time held its arm firmly while steering it down to the waiting ski instructor who had watched the scenario unfold from below. My group had also stopped to watch this little drama so I re-joined them and we skied on.

The very next day I was skiing happily behind my group when I came upon another small child face down in the snow in exactly the same position. Only a day older but definitely much wiser concerning such matters I stopped above the child. Discarding my gloves and poles immediately I grabbed it firmly by the back of the jacket, hoisted it to its feet, looked around for the 'responsible adult', dad, standing waiting below us, and then gently shoved it in his direction. As dad was gazing up at us and shouting his thanks the errant child scored a direct hit, head-butting him soundly on the kneecaps with his helmet. A two-foot high rug rat in skis and ski helmet can be quite a dangerous missile! We skied on and left them to untangle themselves.

That same week as I was guiding my group down an easy run a small child whizzed across the slope in front of me and disappeared over the edge in a flurry of powder. His progress was rapidly slowed and then halted by two feet of soft deep snow and all I could see as I flew past was the top of his blue shiny helmet. Did I stop? No, the thought of ploughing through deep snow to retrieve another errant rug rat that was not my responsibility was too much; I skied on and hoped that its owner was aware that his charge had just extended his talents to include off-piste skiing. My conscience pricked enough to look down from the ski lift as we passed over that point on the piste and I was relieved to see that someone had dug it out and all that could be seen now was a new hollow in the snow.

Later that day, having joined some of my group in a ski lesson with Pio I was cruising contentedly along at the back when I was rugby tackled from behind and at speed by an Italian lady who had completely lost control of her skis. I found myself flat on my face, arms stretched out on either side (ski poles still attached) and legs at an impossible angle with my skis still in place. I could not move; I was unable even to lift my head high enough to spit out the snow in my mouth. My attacker had recovered herself and was asking if I was all right. How could I possibly tell? I did know that if my legs remained in this unnatural position for much longer I was going to get stretch marks where no one had ever dreamed it was possible. I told the lady who was obviously not very observant that I could not get up without someone removing at least one ski. She tried to oblige but then I heard a shout from behind. Pio was coming to the rescue! I was puzzled when I heard him tell my aggressor not to remove my skis. Nevertheless I envisaged a pair of strong arms encircling me and lifting me to my feet and, preparing to smile my thanks at my gallant rescuer, I pulled off my snow filled goggles in order to ensure he could appreciate the gratitude glowing in my eyes.

No strong arms just a ski pole whacked on my skis and the question *"dimmi che va tutto bene"* (tell me you are not hurt). I responded that I did not think I was. Right he said, now bend your legs. He must have been kidding, I was doing a great impression of a frog flat on its belly, legs fully extended and bending my knees from that position was just not feasible. I pointed this out but this only encouraged him to assist from behind and he lifted both my skis. This had the effect of bending my knees, the skis were then freed and I was instructed to roll over, put the skis on the slope and stand up. Amazingly I managed to accomplish this in two easy moves. Meanwhile Pio retrieved my goggles, tipped out most of the snow inside them, handed them back and told me to put them on and follow him. It was like skiing under water – I could not see a thing. Somehow I made it to the bottom of the ski lift and while heading back up the mountain managed to empty the rest of the snow out of my goggles, pockets and hat. No fuss from this matter of fact *maestro di sci.*

Following the success of my summer holidays alone in the hotel I decided to take a winter break there on my own. It was wonderful. I could be on a ski lift as soon as it opened early in the morning and then skied hard while the slopes were empty. By midday when the slopes were getting crowded I returned to the hotel, changed and then lunched in the hotel restaurant. This was a chance to observe lunch, a full dress rehearsal for dinner. Everything was just the same but the pace was more leisurely and the staff more relaxed. Some guests were on a full board basis and appeared to move from one meal to the next with sojourns in the bar in between. I would take my place and enjoy the parade of guests through the restaurant. One gentleman walked in with an arrogant swagger, a baseball cap pulled down almost to his nose, dark sunglasses and a newspaper tucked under his arm. Once seated the newspaper was shaken open and he began to read, seemingly oblivious of his lunching companions, his family, who conversed at full volume around him. In the dining room annexe a lady dined alone, her pampered pet stretched out on the bench seat beside her. A large family appeared with their two children, large in size rather than number, and a huge fuss ensued as they tried to attach the baby chair to the edge of the table. Much sighing and gesturing went on until a waiter appeared and gently suggested that they seat the baby at another place where their attempts to attach its seat were not thwarted by a join in the tables.

Lunch was Sandro's stage and he filled it magnificently. He glided from guest to guest, conversing, teasing, choosing their menu and occasionally involving Paolo in a harmless joke for example getting him to make a call to a guest concerning a table reservation a few days later. He knew instinctively when he could take liberties without causing offence. Annalisa and her parents were regular guests in the hotel and often Annalisa stay there on her own. On one such occasion when Annalisa was talking to her mother, Pinuccia, on her mobile, Sandro took the mobile from her to exchange greetings with Pinuccia. All the time he was talking he was patrolling the dining area. When he reached my table he passed the mobile to me and indicated that it was Pinuccia. After our conversation I had to walk across the restaurant to restore the mobile to its owner as by now Sandro was occupied elsewhere, seating a doting couple. The subject of their devotion? A Pekinese dog that used to accompany them everywhere, even into lunch but this time at least it was consigned to the floor. Other perches included the dashboard of the shuttle bus, the windowsill in the lobby area and a chair at their table during breakfast. Perhaps the most amusing event was the production of a pistol that had been tucked in his cummerbund and then flourished at guests his instinct told him would be amused. Just where the pistol came from and why it was being brandished in the restaurant has remained a mystery but it did unite all the diners in a moment of hilarity.

    These lunchtimes were also an opportunity to sit with Signora Silvana's mother Rosina as she had resided in the hotel through the entire winter. My Italian had improved to the extent that I could converse reasonably well and it was delightful hearing Rosina reminisce about her childhood when her father had been the tenant of Malga Ritorto, the very place where we lunched on our summer walks. She would talk nostalgically of the days when they made fresh butter and manually and pressed it into wooden rectangular boxes, the family mark on the lid of this receptacle. Memorabilia of those days decorated the ledges around the dining area along with gleaming copper cooking utensils.

    As I made my way through to the restaurant one lunchtime in March, I was personally presented with a small bouquet of mimosa by Signora Silvana. While walking towards my table I noticed that all the ladies were elegantly attired and they were offering new arrivals their best wishes. I was puzzled as clearly it was a special day but I had no idea why. Then Sandro solved the mystery by informing me that it was the *'festa delle donne'*. This celebration of ladies, took place every year on this day to commemorate an event on the eighth of March, 1908 in New York when the workers of a cotton cloth plant went on strike to protest against poor working conditions. The strike lasted for several days until the owner of the plant became very upset, closed and locked all of the doors and exits and set fire to the building. One hundred and twenty nine women inside the building were burnt to death and after this terrible tragedy the day was celebrated in support of women's rights worldwide.

After lunch I would have the whole afternoon to relax. Alas there was no chance to go on proper walks with Tabata this time as all the paths were deep in snow. However, the roads were clear so every afternoon after returning from the slopes Tabata and I developed the habit of walking into town along the road. I loved seeing the town in the winter when it was illuminated with beautiful white light decorations and full of people meeting and greeting. Ski gear exchanged for evening finery. We would walk right through the town to the Internet Café at the far end and there, amid the clatter and buzz of the pinball machines I would check and compose emails while Tabata slept under the desk at my feet. So confident did I become with this reformed, comparatively well behaved animal that I let my guard down and did not tie her lead to the chair but just dropped it on the floor beside me. I would grab the lead before standing up because as soon as I was on my feet Tabata was off, one leap and she was nearly out of the door.

One day when I was engrossed in composing a long email I was aware that someone came and sat down at the computer next to me but I did not look up. Alerted by a deep throated growl from beneath my desk I did lift my head then but before I could react Tabata had erupted into the space between me and the person next to me. In a flash her paws were on the lady's lap and she was at full stretch, lunging towards her face. With horror I realised that she was after the fur stole draped around the neck of this smartly dressed *signora.* *"Mi scusi, mi scusi"* I kept intoning as I grabbed Tabata by her scruff and pulled her away, apologising profusely. I was so embarrassed I felt compelled to shut down my computer straight away, pay my dues and then drag the reluctant miscreant out into the cold, crisp evening air.

Outside the town was throbbing with people all heading for the floodlit slope, Miramonti, above the main street where the World Freestyle Championships were taking place. I had forgotten all about them but now thanks to my early exit from the Internet Café I had time to take a look. I marched a reluctant Tabata up the piste, ignoring her doleful expression as she plodded along on the snow. She hated walking on hard cold snow but she was not getting any sympathy on this occasion. We walked up to the finish line where I stopped to watch the competitors jumping, spinning and twisting over the moguls. A lot of shuffling was going on beside me. Tabata would sit down briefly and then immediately stand up again, look long and hard in my direction, and then start straining at her leash. When this ploy did not work she would hang her head, roll her eyes and stare dejectedly upwards at me for thirty seconds before starting the whole process all over again. I was absorbed in the skiing and apart from muttering a few Italian words in her direction I ignored her discomfort quite successfully. That was okay until she started to employ the lean hard against my legs strategy. She was a big dog and easily induced numbness in the lower limb by this method. No good, I had to force myself to leave this spectacular display and the magical atmosphere of diffused light on white snow and expectant faces. We walked back into town, the booming voice on the loudspeaker and the excited shouts of the audience getting more distant and faint as we made our way back through the main square, past the brightly lit shops and down the road towards the hotel.

Since people began to take skiing seriously in Madonna di Campiglio it had been the venue for top class events. The first recorded attempts to ski in this area related to some 'crazy' English skiers who, as early as 1910 tried to ski the slopes of Spinale and their attempts were ridiculed in the local press. Several years later the first tow rope lift was built at Campo Carlo Magno followed soon after by the foundation of the first ski school, the Nazionale, in 1935. By then FISI (*Federazione Italiana Sport Invernali*) had already made an official visit to the area alerted by its potential as a venue for skiing and skating competitions. This potential had been brought to their notice through the timely union of one of their members and a local lady. Between 1938 and 1941 Madonna di Campiglio became the centre of the *littorali* of the snow and ice. The *littorali* were undergraduates who competed against champions and experts in various disciplines. Qualifying competitions were held throughout the country to select the best teams and the events took place initially on Monte Spinale and then moved to Patascoss. Then in 1957, in its eighth year, a World Cup slalom race was held here and it remained the venue for this, the oldest Italian event in World Cup skiing until 1998. It took place on the run named 3Tre, 3 for the three events that comprised the original three discipline races, slalom, giant slalom and downhill and Tre for Trentino. A variety of World Championships continue to be held on Miramonti, a black, floodlit run immediately above the town, easily accessible for spectators and the last section of the 3Tre course.

Skiing events were not the only events the town hosted and every year veteran cars gathered in the area for the winter marathon. One memorable day this event coincided with the climax of the Formula One Press Conference and a go-kart race on the frozen lake involving Michael Schumacher. This meant that one hundred and fifty veteran cars were trying to get out of town and hundreds of cars full of spectators were trying to get into town. Complete gridlock. I had descended into the centre of town and then could not get back to the hotel as the shuttle bus was unable to get through to any of the pick up points. I shouldered my skis and set off to walk all the way back to the hotel. Goran, our shuttle bus driver was not too discontented as it gave him a legitimate opportunity to watch his hero Schumacher. During the week he had gone AWOL several times trying to get a photo and had finally succeeded. Goran did stop and offer me a lift when he saw me plodding along the road having finally managed to make his way into town and it was relief to give him my skis although I continued to walk as I was nearly back by that time and did not fancy doing the full tour of the pick up points.

The walk back from town to the hotel was a pleasurable stroll down the main road following the construction of a pavement nearly all the way there, even through a short section of the tunnel that bypassed the town. Of course this would have been much easier if the snow was cleared from this pavement as well as the road but you can't have everything and at least wading through three foot of snow was safer than dodging high speed Italian drivers in their cars and on their motorbikes. Tramping through deep snow could be quite hazardous and there were several occasions when my feet just shot away from me and I crashed down flat on my back. Tabata would wait patiently while I recovered myself and any shopping I may be carrying. At any other time when she felt the lead go slack she would have taken advantage and grabbed her freedom but on these occasions she seemed to prefer to stand still and enjoy the spectacle of me scrambling to my feet, a pitying expression on her face. As our friendship developed I had begun attempting to persuade Tabata to play with me but all my efforts had been disdainfully ignored. Perversely she suddenly decided that me lying on the ground was an invitation to play. Rising up on her hind legs, an expression that said "Yippee, its playtime" she would pounce on me. We would roll in the snow, me yelling at her to "Get off you stupid animal" and trying to push her considerable weight off me in order to struggle back onto my feet. Passers-by would chuckle and croon *"canellino"* (an affectionate name for a dog) at Tabata but no helping hands were offered. Presumably assuming I had volunteered to roll in deep snow with an excited dog.

Most afternoons followed the usual pattern but then one day I decided to investigate one of the paths we used in the summer, to the beautiful waterfall at Vallesinella. The temperature had been constantly below zero and I had long harboured an ambition to see the waterfall completely frozen. I was amazed to find that a track had been 'flattened' through the deep snow and not only were we able to walk along the narrow road that wound its way up there we could also take a path through the woods. It was glorious, the sun glinted on the snow and bounced off the peaks of the Dolomites all around us. When we got to the waterfall it was solid ice – fantastic! The larch trees now bare of leaves enhanced this amazing sight and pale sunlight filtering through the branches glowed on the snow and translucent static ice among the dark rocks.

There we were, miles from anywhere when I heard a menacing growl above me. I glanced up and saw a huge retriever crashing down through the trees and then throw itself at Tabata. My first, ungallant, thought was to drop her lead and let her fend for herself but my second thought was a reminder that if I let her go I would probably never see her again which would not endear me to her owners. I hung on, yelling at her attacker in my best (or maybe my worst) Italian. Eventually the owner of this assailant appeared and after a struggle managed to attach the errant dog to its lead. This did not make a lot of difference as the dog just dragged her where it wanted to go! So the animals remained locked in combat. Finally with the help of a few well aimed blows from both me and the owner we managed to separate them and she dragged her companion away along the path while I waited for ten minutes before setting off myself.

Peace and harmony restored I was strolling along, enjoying the scenery and the tranquillity when the hound of horror appeared menacingly on the path in front of us. His super intelligent owner had let him off the lead and was far ahead of us, I could hear her plaintiff calls in the distance. Tabata cowered bravely behind me while I searched for a missile to launch at the aggressor. Nothing to hand, just tons of snow. After a few minutes fending off the brute its owner came running round the corner screaming abuse at the dog and apologies at me. Finally the dog was attached to its lead again but not its owner and I ended up with a lead in each hand trying to hold the dogs apart! It was some time before the lady was on her way again, her reluctant canine in tow, yelling at me to wait until she was out of sight. This time the plan worked and I completed my walk untroubled by neither man nor beast.

The highlight of any winter season in Madonna di Campiglio has to be Christmas and one Christmas Eve I was able to 'escape' from the group and catch the last lift to the top. This was a great opportunity to indulge in the final run of the day. I waited until the few people gathered at the top had begun their descent and the *carabinieri* had retreated to the shelter of Rifugio Viviani for a drink, gossip and, if any were left, a delicious *tiramisu* before doing their final sweep of the pistes. At last I was alone at the top of Pradalago the slopes of Madonna di Campiglio spread out below and around me. Across the valley I could see the glistening white snow on the Grostè ski area. A vast pale expanse above the tree line which had been, earlier that the day, a mass of brightly clad skiers all enjoying the wide, well groomed runs and the lovely powdery snow. Music had echoed around the peaks from Ristorante Boch, the mid-station restaurant and people had been dancing on the tables. Rarely could I resist a little jig on my skis when passing this lively spot but for rest and refreshment I preferred the quieter Ristorante Stoppani at the very top of the Grostè cabin lift.

Earlier that day in rather high spirits we had paused at Rifugio Graffer, whose lit windows I could just make out far across the valley, as we hurtled down from the top of Grostè, to enjoy a *bombardino,* guaranteed to embolden the most timid of skiers. Some of our group were wearing funny hats and the rest, feeling they should make an attempt to match them had extracted bits and pieces from the table centre and attached them to their ski hats. We would have escaped undetected but the main perpetrator left the empty container on the table and it was obvious what had happened. As we donned our skies ready to depart an extremely angry lady erupted out of the *rifugio* and ran at us yelling and gesticulating. Then, jumping up and down she began to extricate sprigs of holly from woolly hats. We did not need to speak Italian to understand her feelings on the matter. So, trying to suppress my laughter I dutifully collected all the decorations and sombrely returned then to their rightful owner.

Just to the right of Grostè the white stripes that were the runs down from Spinale wound their way through the trees. These were some good challenging reds and already I could see the lights of the piste basher weaving to and fro across the slopes of the black run down the front of this mountain, aptly named Spinale Direttissima. The top half was a great run but the bottom half was more of a challenge. This second section had recently been named for one of the town's most famous visitors, Michael Schumacher. Apart from the Hapsburgs Madonna di Campiglio has been host to many famous visitors. As long ago as the 1920's Giuseppe Cipriani, founder of Harry's Bar in Venice, had trained as a chef in the resort. Great skiers have competed in World Cup events here including Alberto Tomba who has been a regular guest at the Hotel Lorenzetti. Loris Capirossi and Valentino Rossi, Italian heroes of the motorcycle track have also visited and Pinzolo has been used as the regular summer training camp for the Juventus football team.

Profound silence surrounded me and I was reluctant to move, after a busy day guiding people around this was the perfect end. Sighing, I pulled on my gloves, adjusted my pole straps and prepared to ski down. One last look. I could see the peak of Monte Vigo behind me and remembered our early morning runs across there on the interesting red run, Genziana Alta, best done at that time before it got busy with skiers on their way to Marileva and Folgarida. We had had some good skiing exploring these two smaller resorts that included some nice black runs.

Time to go, my skis swished and crackled on the crisp snow as I set off down Pradalago Facile a lovely blue which would take me right down into the town centre. However, when I reached the first junction I swung onto Pradalago Diretta a super run through the trees that required a bit of thought. It was so exhilarating, speeding down alone in the fading light. The sun, a red luminous ball was sinking rapidly through a sky streaked with pink, creating a warm glow reflected in the summits. At the bottom of this run I swept right onto Collegamento Campiglio a connecting blue run that would allow me lovely views of the main square now adorned with a Christmas tree, twinkling lights looped around the tips of its branches. That was the great thing about skiing in this resort, all the main lifts were linked by connecting runs. I was too late to catch the hotel shuttle at the bottom of the run so I would have to walk into the town centre and get it from there. No problem, a chance to join the throngs of promenading Italians all meeting and greeting or sitting outside the popular Suisse Bar in Piazza Righi enjoying a drink.

I stopped immediately above the town and I could see the Christmas lights sprinkled like frost on the buildings below and the big Christmas tree on the slopes opposite like a lookout guarding the many hotels, bars and shops clustered in the valley. The final stretch was performed more quickly and less elegantly than I would have wished but it was difficult to maintain control on ice-crusted snow. I landed with a clatter at the entrance to the Cinque Laghi cable car, now hanging dormant for the night above my head.

I made my way slowly down the icy road into the Piazza Righi. The atmosphere was magical. Beside the large Christmas tree that dominated this small *piazza* was a small craft stall around which children and parents were clamouring to buy last minute gifts and decorations. As it was Christmas Eve shouts of *Buon Natale* echoed round the square, light and warmth spilled out from the open doors of the bars and cafés and voices mingled in a crescendo of greetings and gossip. In Italy one did not exchange Christmas greetings before Christmas.

Time was getting on and I needed to catch the next shuttle to give me a chance to change for drinks before dinner so I made my way down the main road where the street lamps were supplemented by the lustre from the shooting star lights that decorated them. Not long to wait for the shuttle and then I was on my way back to the hotel and could soon pick out the strip lights that outlined the building a permanent glowing invitation to enter and savour the welcoming ambience inside. In the pale light I could make out the splendid back drop of the Brenta Mountains. As I passed the main entrance I paused to look at the nativity scene displayed on the top of an old farm cart. Nostalgia swept over me as I recalled many nativity scenes viewed at home over the years. The crib was empty because the Baby Jesus traditionally arrived in the crib at midnight. A smile stole across my face as I remembered last year when the baby had arrived at midnight but was gone by midday on Christmas Day. Frantic searching by members of staff finally revealed him safe and sound beneath the straw in the crib. One of the youngsters in the hotel had wanted to make sure he kept warm!

Later when I entered the bar I was immediately captured by the Christmas spirit. An open log fire crackled and danced in the grate and bright red poinsettias decorated every surface. I remembered having seen the huge delivery of poinsettias and watching Karin and

Signora Silvana spend all day in front of the fireplace in the bar area re-potting and arranging these startling red plants and then decorating the restaurant and bar with them creating a real traditional Christmas setting. Karin was Goran's Croatian girlfriend and to me a season did not really start until they were back in residence. A slight, pretty girl Karin was constantly cleaning the reception areas. Often her duties were extended to flower arranging and baby-sitting the grandchildren. This evening she passed me on her way to start the turn down service and we exchanged Christmas greetings. People were drifting around exchanging Christmas greetings. All the guests behaved like one big happy family and there was bonhomie and excitement in the air as we took our places in the crowded restaurant anticipating a sumptuous Gala Dinner. Every table was full as the hotel was a popular venue for dinner and never more so than a special occasion such as Christmas.

A special menu was placed at each setting offering a splendid choice. Did one follow the traditional menu or choose from a wide selection for each course? The anticipation was enhanced by the endearing translations "stewed venison bites scented with Teroldego wine, served with soft polenta". In an area renowned for its hams and salamis the anti pasta had to be "*Culatello* ham from *Zibello* and *Strolghino* salami with mushrooms and slivers of parmesan cheese" followed by a house speciality, "risotto with champagne and apples from Val di Non" and a finale of "walnuts mousse with smooth mascarpone and chocolate, crispy waffle with ice cream". Every choice offered a blend of subtle flavours to tempt the palate in portions that satisfied but did not satiate. All accompanied by an excellent local wine from the wide choice available.

During dinner Father Christmas appeared and went round greeting each guest and wishing them *Buon Natale*. If you had been good all year you may even get a present! Then, after dinner there was *panettone* and dessert wine in the bar ... really I couldn't, well, maybe, just a small piece and a drop of Moscato!

These festivities were followed by live music in the bar, chairs were pushed back and people danced, others sat and chatted and towards the end of the evening there was some singing. A real traditional Christmas and always a wonderful finale for the first skiing group of each winter season.

Chapter Nine – The Long and Winding Road

My heart was thudding and I felt like a teenager about to embark on a first date. Indeed all around me colourful, lively youngsters were gathered, chattering non-stop, bringing life to this bleak, soulless place where I had to spend the next two hours. I supposed bus stations worldwide were just like this one in Trento where brightly lit, garishly stocked shops crowded around the sliding doors at the entrance with the ticket booths stretching out behind them. There was a small seating area after the non-functioning ticket barrier and the automatic doors to the bus bays opened and closed continuously as people rushed in and out. These bays displayed a number and the main stops on the route allocated to that number. I decided to find more congenial surroundings for my sojourn and headed for the Parco Dante across the road, an oasis of green grass and shady trees surrounding an imposing statue of Dante Alighieri probably Italy's greatest poet. This monument was inaugurated in October 1896 but the idea was initiated in 1886 when the *Pro Patria* society was founded in Rovereto to install a symbol of Italian nationality that was evidence of their fierce loyalty to Italy, despite being geographically part of the Austro-Hapsburg Empire. An allegiance for which people had been prepared to die.

Here I could relax for a while and try to calm my nerves. It would still be the same, of course it would. But a small part of me wondered if maybe some of the regular staff would not have returned, the food would not be so good. Tabata would have made her final escape never to come back.

When the bus finally pulled into the bus station it was a bright pink, matching the colour of the route, coincidence I am sure as even though routes and vehicles were supposed to match invariably they did not, like the chairs on the ski lifts which never marched up and down the mountain in numerical order. Everybody seemed to be going to Madonna di Campiglio and it took a while to stow all the bags in the boot and jostle for seats inside.

Swinging out of the bus station we briefly glimpsed the beautiful church of Saint Lawrence immediately next door, an original tower, Torre Verde, on the city walls flashed by and then the Adige River flowed below us flanked by the multi-track railway line. On the far side of the river we passed the lovely little church of S. Apollinare built during the fourteenth century and one of the oldest buildings in the city. Then soon afterwards we began winding our way up the lower slopes of the Dolomite Mountains that crept down almost into the town itself. Rising above us were the cables of the busy Sardegna cable car which transported workers to and from the town and this mountain village every day. Perched on the cliff face was the impressive circular monument to one of the regions most famous partisans, Cesare Battisti.

Born in Trento in 1875 Battisti was one of the leading members of the Irredentist movement, an association that was initiated in 1870 around the same time as *Il Risorgimento* when Rome was captured from the Papacy and Italy became a unified nation with Rome as its capital. Despite having been part of the Austro-Hapsburg Empire Trentino had always remained Italian in language and culture and many of the inhabitants supported the *Italia Irredente* which was formed to liberate Italians who lived in 'occupied' regions. As the Austro-Hapsburg Empire was composed of many such areas the Austrians fiercely suppressed this movement. At the start of the Great War Battisti left Austria and went to Italy where he joined the Italian army and fought for the *Alpini*. He was captured in 1916, tried and found guilty of treason having been denied Prisoner of War status. He and two compatriots were hung in the moat of the Castello di Buonconsiglio. Contrary to tradition when the rope broke at the first attempt his death sentence was not commuted but a new rope was sent for. Although condemned as a traitor in Austria Battisti was considered a patriot, hero and martyr in Italy as evidenced by the many streets and *piazze* that have been given his name.

Finally, when Italian troops entered Trento in 1918 signalling the end of the war and the defeat of the Austrians, Trentino was annexed to the Kingdom of Italy. But that was not the end of the story as it was not an ideal relationship and Trentino continued its struggle for autonomy that had began as early as 1848 when Trentino petitioned the Frankfurt Assembly requesting administrative separation from the German Tyrol. A large and very vocal segment of the local population never accepted that political arrangement. Although this aspiration was initially suppressed by fascism, in 1939 Mussolini gave the residents the chance to either accept Italian citizenship and remain or assume German citizenship and emigrate north. The overwhelming majority chose the latter option, leaving this largely rural territory even more under populated than before. As a part of the country Trentino was involved in the hostilities when Italy entered the Second World War in 1940 and the inhabitants of Trento endured a long battle for survival against hunger, food rationing and bombings. Following the armistice in 1943 the Germans became enemies rather than allies and Trentino was placed under their direct control. However when the Second World War ended and German occupation ceased the Italian legislature made Trentino an autonomous region in 1948 and subsequently, in 1972 the final Statute of Autonomy transferred real autonomous power to the Province of Trento.

Our ascent into the mountains steepened and below me the industrial zone of the town stretched out across the valley floor. Tree clad slopes lined the road to our left and as industry gave way to agriculture a patchwork of fields was spread out across the lower slopes below us. All of a sudden we were flying through a long, brightly lit tunnel, the first of many on this route which penetrated the rocky landscape. We emerged to join a newly constructed dual carriageway and raced past a small settlement featuring multi-storey buildings that straddled the incline. A grassy slope dotted with trees rose up above me to the left and to the right thick vegetation obscured my view of the cultivated plain glimpsed occasionally through the greenery. Fields of maize flew by and also a huge field of lettuces of all varieties evidence of the fertility of this area. We continued along the main road, passing under a bridge with painted panels and some beautiful beds of flowers before negotiating a large roundabout. On our right we passed Lago di Massenza connected by a narrow channel to Lago di Toblino. The road took us alongside this beautiful lake allowing us wonderful views of Castello Toblino. Approaching Sarche we began to climb quite steeply alongside a gorge with spectacular views of its craggy sides and the river running below and a glimpse of a solitary fisherman wading in the fast running water, flicking his rod in an attempt to entice any fish passing by to take the bait.

Rounding a hairpin bend I could see the Bar Miravale in front of me and remembered the many stops we had made there on transfers to and from the airport. This small bar appeared to be tiny on the outside and it did have a very small interior but at the back there was a large terrace strewn with tables and chairs where one could enjoy a cool breeze and splendid views of Lago di Toblino and Castello Toblino. A welcome break for my groups who had usually been travelling since very early that morning and a chance for me to get to know their names and check their heights as we always had two lovely little rooms in the attic of the hotel and I had to assess who would be the best 'fit'. When we arrived at the hotel I gave these names to Pietro immediately so that any necessary changes could be made. Of course it would have made more sense to allocate one of these rooms to me as being a mere five foot four inches I was a good 'fit'. However, it was more convenient if I was peripatetic and could charge rooms when necessary for maximum flexibility.

Generally checking in was a smooth operation as Pietro and I had collaborated for many years regarding this exercise. Afterwards I dutifully sat in reception waiting to see if anyone would come back to complain about their room as all the rooms had different characteristics. Some groups arrived, settled in and just got on with the holiday, some would start inspecting each others rooms and it would not be long before there were requests for a room with a view like hers, or a room the same size as his. There was one room that often caused problems, the infamous room twenty-five, a long narrow twin room with no balcony. We did not always have to use this room but when we did the easiest solution would be to give it to the gentleman who was the last to book. I was happy to leave the choice to Pietro. On one occasion, returning from the airport I was concerned to find that we would have to use this room. Pietro glanced at the group and then asked me the name of the man wearing a panama hat. Puzzled I gave him the name and he was allocated room twenty-five. I was not sure it would work but I was wrong and there was not a word of complaint concerning this room the entire week. Over the years rooms have been added and existing rooms enlarged and improved and every room is delightful but the individual character of each is retained. Recently the last remaining rooms of the bed and breakfast days have been transformed into stunning suites with either a Viennese or Tyrolean theme.

Pietro has been the receptionist for many years. A gentle personality he was born in Uruguay and spoke English very well although when I was informed that the hotel now had a receptionist who spoke English I felt obliged to inform them that the English would consider he spoke American! I could always rely on Pietro to support me in a crisis but I am sorry to say that when he had a crisis of his own my attempts to conciliate were not very helpful. I returned on my own one day and Pietro was in reception his face as white as a sheet. I asked him if he was alright and he told me that he had been cleaning in the office and had accidentally sucked up the tiny portable disk that belonged to *il Direttore* with the vacuum cleaner. Goran, who had just passed me outside with an unusually large grin on his face, had been dispatched to check out the rubbish that was collected below stairs by the central vacuum system. On returning from his mission Goran had not told Pietro if it had been successful or not. I could not help but grin myself as I knew Pietro held *il Direttore* very much in awe. I re-assured him and reminded him of the many times Goran had teased me and Pietro had been the calming influence. I was relieved when I walked through a short time later to see that Pietro's countenance was once again serene and he gave me the thumbs up and beamed at me as I passed by his desk.

Pietro was a bit of a 'techi' and would often search the internet looking for new 'toys' and, if they could not be ordered in Italy he would ask if he could order them in the UK and then I would take them to Italy on my next visit to the hotel. Generally the items were quite small and light but on one occasion he had ordered a CD copying machine that was on special offer and he had assured me it was very small. Even out of its polystyrene surround it was the size of a video recorder and I had to carry it separately as hand luggage. Fortunately this was before hand luggage was restricted but it was quite a struggle on public transport with three pieces of hand luggage and one large suitcase. Never again I told him, until the next time, a small car radio!

* * *

I became aware that we were picking up speed as the road flattened out and to my right I could see a green grassy area speckled with the brilliant colours of flowers in beautifully kept beds. We were going through the spa of Terme di Comane which was surrounded by an extensive public park criss-crossed with paths along which people were leisurely strolling. Almost immediately we were in Ponte Arche a small ribbon development of shops and bars and we turned into the bus station where the bus stopped for a while during which time the driver had a break and then re-appeared with a conductor, smartly dressed in blue shirt and tie. We were on our way again continuing through this pretty town past pavement cafés and over a bridge under which the river flowed down from the mountain in a series of shallow weirs, the rushing water swirling round bright patches of green grass. Next we passed a beautiful fountain surrounded by beds of brilliantly coloured flowers, it all looked so interesting from inside the bus. It was one of those places that made you want to jump off the bus and go exploring.

Vividly I recalled that last winter having spent a week on my own in Madonna di Campiglio I then had to make my way to Verona airport to meet a group and travel back to Madonna di Campiglio with them. For some time now I had been looking for an opportunity to go and visit Ponte Arche and have a walk around the pretty town and the lovely public park at Terme di Comane. This seemed like the ideal opportunity so I had arranged to meet the bus at the bus station there.

Expecting that the weather would be warmer in Ponte Arche than it was higher up the mountain where I had been staying I had nevertheless put my silk thermals on under my navy blue 'uniform' trousers. I was so glad I had done so as the icy blast that came round the corner of the bus station building as I descended from the bus took my breath away. My enthusiasm for a long walk was immediately dampened and I made my way to the nearest bar and sat inside warming up over a cup of coffee. I had promised myself an exploration of the public park and I was determined I would at least take a short walk through the lovely gardens I had seen from the bus. I walked a little way along the main street before finding a path that would take me across the wooden roofed bridge and into the park. The hitherto green grass was stiff and white with frost. I marched along huddled inside my red ski jacket, arms folded tightly across my chest for extra warmth. My objective was the large spa building ahead where the curative waters could be taken. Mission accomplished I then crossed back over the river on a modern footbridge and made my way briskly back to the bus station for my rendezvous with the transfer bus. Fortunately I did not have to wait long but by the time Aldo arrived the hairs inside my nostrils had frozen and I presented a woebegone picture when the bus door slid open. Aldo grinned from ear to ear and laughed out loud when I stuttered that I had expected it to be much warmer given the lower altitude. He still had a smile on his face as he pointed out the temperature when we passed an illuminated sign, minus fifteen.

* * *

My excitement was mounting as we continued on our way up the mountain passing through several small towns huddled around large medieval churches. We crossed the River Sarca yet again and the gorge it coursed through still shelved steeply away to our right and sometimes I caught sight of shimmering green waterway beneath us. We came to a junction with a road that crossed this dramatic gorge via a splendid bridge that spanned its seemingly endless narrow depths and then wound its way up the mountain to Lake

Molveno and the resorts around it. The main road continued along the edge of the gorge that soon narrowed into a ravine with trees clinging to the sharp edges of bare rock and a waterfall gushing out and plummeting to the bottom. On the other side the sheer rock face jutted out into the road clad in strong wire meshing to protect travellers from landslides and rock falls.

Another small town was negotiated and then we entered a long, dark tunnel punctuated with flashes of light flooding in through arches at each side. There was a bus stop in one of these arches and if I craned my neck I could just see a roof of a building way down the slope. I wondered how often this isolated stop was actually used. Emerging into the daylight again we cruised along a winding road where the perpendicular drop was protected by a low metal barrier battered into an incongruous shape by careless drivers. Now we were traversing a small plain where the ears of corn in the fields on either side swayed gently in the breeze. Rows of sweet corn stood upright in small battalions like armies marching through a meadow of lush green grass. This corn was used to make the local traditional dish polenta and I remembered my first experience of this in Madonna di Campiglio when a polenta party was held at Patascoss and I walked up there with some of the group. Large buckets of polenta were being stirred with giant size wooden spoons and when it was ready we all lined up for a plate full of this porridge-like substance, meat stew and sauerkraut. Real bulk food but washed down with a very acceptable red table wine. Perched on wooden benches at large wooden trestle tables and surrounded by hundreds of Italians it was quite an experience. Once all the food had been eaten a small group of local musicians began playing and there was singing and dancing. A great way to spend a day in the mountains.

My very first experience of polenta had been in a small mountain village above Trento when the hotel manager, Mario, had walked us down the mountain to a local restaurant where we had all been presented with a plate of polenta and rabbit stew. Mario took great pleasure in video recording the reaction of this first experience of what was once the staple diet of people who lived in this region. My first impressions were not very favourable and as I struggled to eat the rather bland mound of cornmeal 'porridge' it seemed to get larger rather than smaller. As we ate Mario reminisced about the earlier poverty of the region and family celebrations that entailed killing the fatted rabbits that had been raised for the purpose.

*　*　*

Next was Tione, the biggest town we would pass through and notable for its large hospital and bus station. Just thirty minutes to go now. Over the years I had experienced a few adventures involving the hospital and now I remembered that once I had raced down the mountain in a taxi after one of my group who had fractured his hip when he fell while skiing. Usually I was able to travel with an injured client in the ambulance as first they were taken to the local emergency centre to assess the injury. I was known by the staff there as I was a frequent visitor as inevitably with several groups skiing during the winter there were bound to be injuries. On this occasion I was not informed of the accident until it was too late and despite skiing down at break neck speed and rushing to the centre I had just missed him. Anxious to get there as soon as possible I went back to the hotel and asked them to order me a taxi. As I had not eaten any lunch Signora Silvana prepared some filled rolls for me to eat as I hastily changed my clothes and gathered together everything I thought my client might need including a book to read, but I forgot his reading glasses!

At the hospital we had to wait for X-rays to be taken and then a bed to be found on a ward. Once Bill was settled I could think about my return journey to the hotel. Buses back to Madonna di Campiglio were few and far between and the last one was at six o'clock, in ten minutes time. Bidding my client a brief farewell, because I knew that

I had to walk down into the town and then find the bus stop I set off through winding streets heading for the main road below me. When I reached this road I had no idea which direction to take to find the nearest bus stop and so I went left. After a few minutes I realised I was almost out of the town and there was no sign of a bus stop. Turning back I began to run down the road, this was not easy as I was carrying Bill's rather large and heavy ski boots, a bulky package in a large plastic carrier bag. I was feeling very sorry for myself and hesitating by the roadside when there was a screech of brakes and a car stopped right beside me. That was all I needed, some Italian stallions on the pull. Well, it was dark and my long blonde hair could lead them to mistake my age. I glanced down and saw Flavio and Pio grinning up at me from the car interior. They were both ski instructors in Madonna di Campiglio and they had been taking ski classes on the small slope near Tione. I told them why I was there and that I needed to find the bus stop to get the *corriera* back. There was no question of my going back by public transport and within seconds the boots were being stowed away and, despite my protests, Pio was folding his tall body into the small back seat while I slid gratefully into the front.

 I sat back in my seat and chatted happily all the way back up the mountain to the village of Sant' Antonio di Mavignolo where my rescuers lived. I would have been quite happy to get the bus from there but no, Flavio insisted that after he had taken Pio home he would drive me all the way back to the hotel. Over the years Flavio and I have had an up and down relationship. Flavio was the ski school director with whom I locked horns the first time I had worked in the resort regarding a refund for one of my clients. On my return the following winter I was worried I would get a hostile reception. Far from it, a hearty hug and an exuberant kiss on each cheek heralded my hesitant first appearance at the ski school's office. Fiercely loyal to his instructors he would not hear a word of criticism about any of them so I soon learnt to take a more indirect route to tackle problems concerning clients whose expectations exceeded their abilities. We were now good friends and if he saw me skiing even if he had a large group with him he would always stop and exchange greetings Italian style, a kiss on each cheek.

* * *

Iavre and Dare went by in a flash of churches and football pitches and then we were in Vigo Rendena where we passed the salami factory. I recalled the time I had a group doing a gourmet week in the Hotel Lorenzetti and we had travelled down there in the local bus to take a tour of the factory and taste the hams and salami they made there. Salami had never been a favourite of mine and I had no idea how it was made but it was a speciality of the area so it seemed appropriate to find out. The sight of row upon row of mould-encrusted sausages did not endear me to this delicacy especially when I learnt of the variety of flesh that could be used to make it including wild boar. I did sample some and was pleasantly surprised but not completely converted. Our gourmet weeks had only lasted one summer and then *il Direttore* had put an end to them as they interfered too much with the work of his kitchen.

As our ascent got steeper our speed slowed down. Now tall trees obscured the drop on the right and the rock face on the left was still clad with strong metal meshing. Occasionally the trees opened out into a grassy area where wooden tables and benches invited travellers to picnic or simply pass some time in contemplation of the daily news. Emerging from yet another tunnel where a series of arches had allowed natural light to filter into the gloom the ground had flattened out dramatically and was occupied by a pretty lake. On the far side of the water dense trees climbed up the slopes beyond the lake and above this forest the buildings of a small village clambered up the slope or lined the road. Cream, yellow, pink and russet all capped with dark red roofs they clustered around small churches with onion domes reminiscent of their Austrian heritage. These domes were decorated with yellow and green tiles made of wood baked hard until they looked like glass. Now we were passing by more cultivated fields punctuated with the occasional tank of a trout farm, opportunist herons perched on protective fencing.

Approaching Saone we passed a small walled cemetery on the outskirts of the town. Through Pelugo and past a small solitary grey stone church complete with fresco and bell tower on the outskirts. Now coming into Borzago with a *vinoteca* outside which a sign invited passers by to come and taste and buy. All the villages were beautifully kept and clearly their occupants took a great pride in the appearance of their habitat, the lovely buildings all had balconies splendidly clad with ever flowering geraniums.

Entering into Spiazzo I remembered the time when one rainy day we were looking for something to do and I had investigated the possibility of visiting a local *grappa* distillery. I was unable to find any information from the local telephone directory so I found a bottle of gentian *grappa* in the bar and Doreano on reception called the number for me and arranged a visit. We set off down the valley in the local bus. When we arrived we soon found the distillery in this small village and were delighted to discover that it was a true family run cottage industry. Father had not realised that we were English and was immediately thrown into a state of panic, constantly calling his English speaking daughter on his mobile and begging her to come home and assist. Meanwhile we were all getting on famously and had a tour of the distillery and learnt about the use of the locally grown gentian roots to make this spirit. Our tour was followed by a tasting and we were offered both the gentian and juniper *grappa* but in very small measures due to the strength of this clear liquor. We then had a second tasting with a sugar lump added. Mother then decided that black coffee all round was in order and arrived with a tray full at the same time as the daughter appeared and discovered that her English speaking skills were now redundant. Finally we staggered down the road in search of the bus stop only to find that we had just missed the bus and had two hours to wait for the next one. An enterprising member of the group wandered off down the road to the local bakery and purchased a supply of delicious cream cakes which sustained us until the bus arrived and transported us back to the hotel just in time for dinner.

* * *

Now, to my right I could see golfers strolling along the verdant fairways of the Golf Club Rendena and then Giustino loomed up in front of me, another attractive old stone church and bell tower and a large children's playground with a pink elephant slide which had been there as long as I could remember.

Now we were entering Pinzolo and generally when I caught sight of the statue of a knife grinder at the entrance to the main street I would reach for the microphone and spend the last fifteen minutes of the journey giving the group information that most of them would not listen to and the rest would not remember. Today I am alone with my thoughts which can wander at will. This statue was erected in 1969 by the descendents of the knife grinders or *moletas* who had emigrated, mainly to America, in the early part of the twentieth century when life was a struggle in this sparse, rocky, hilly region. For some reason this little town produced an inordinate number of people with this particular skill, many more than were necessary to sharpen the implements required for the timber industry and agriculture. These emigrant families did well and have kept in touch with their roots and some of the second generation have returned to live and work in the area which is now prospering thanks to tourism.

Winding our way through the main street we passed shops, bars and restaurants all bustling with people after the peace of the midday siesta. On my right the cabin lift climbed the mountain to a mid-station from where a chair lift completed the ascent to Doss del

Sabion, the very top. For those in my summer groups who had never been on a chair lift it was a thrilling experience rewarded with wonderful views up and down the valley. To my left, on the outskirts of the town, proudly erect in splendid isolation, we approached the small church of St Viglio. This church dated back to the eleventh century when it was customary to build cemeterial churches outside the town. The original structure was rebuilt and enlarged during the fifteenth century. My seat on the bus was a good viewpoint from which to marvel briefly at the ochre figures of the macabre masterpiece Dance of Death processing across the southern wall.

Over the bridge that crossed the Sarca yet again and immediately we were in Carisolo and passing the junction with the road to Val di Genova which brought memories flooding back of a chaotic and charismatic adventure. Throughout the summer the local association of Alpine guides in Madonna di Campiglio organised three walks every week and these were open to guests in the hotels so I was delighted to discover that a walk in Val di Genova coincided with my holiday week. I was not so delighted to read that I had to take a car. The hotel called them to ask if the car really was a necessity. No it was not as they could find someone to give me a lift. Could the dog come too? Yes but she had to have a muzzle. No problem, I had bought one with me from England.

On the Friday morning Tabata and I were taken into the town centre in the hotel shuttle bus where we met up with the guides. I was surprised to find that Tabata was the only dog doing the walk. The guide asked if anyone had room in their car for me and the dog and a gentleman volunteered to take us. Stefano and his wife Theresa were from Bologna and were a delightful couple. Fortunately they were dog lovers but they had not been able to bring their own dog on holiday with them.

I was concerned when we reached the car to see it looked brand new, expensive and exceptionally clean. Tabata had gone into full moult mode the previous day so I knew there were going to be hairs everywhere. I tried to limit the damage by keeping her on the floor rather than letting her scramble on to the gorgeous leather seats but she squirmed constantly under my restraining hand and just would not settle down. It was amazing how much she could move around in a confined space and an unguarded second on my part and she would be nearly on Stefano's lap or trying to reverse into the front to see Teresa. It was a long journey under these conditions and I was very relieved when twenty minutes later we arrived in Carisolo, the starting point of the walk.

Our instructions were to take the first right turn as soon as we passed the sign for Carisolo and wait for the guide there. The first car did just that and stopped just around the corner. There were twelve cars in the convoy so eleven cars had to stop on the main road. The mountain roads were not very wide and eleven stationary cars could cause chaos within seconds. Traffic soon started building up behind us including the *carabinieri* who just drove round us, and also the local fire engine that sounded its siren to clear the way.

Patiently we waited for our guides who eventually arrived and indicated that we should follow their cars down the road. We all set off again and drove for a long while down a narrow road to the car park at Rifugio Stelle Alpine. Having parked the cars we were then told that we had to take a bus the rest of the way so we paid our €1 (Tabata was allowed to travel free) and we all clambered aboard. I had attached the muzzle to my rucksack but I was not asked to put it on the dog. We made our way to the back of the bus where I hoped we would be inconspicuous even though I knew by now that this word was not in Tabata's vocabulary.

Initially Tabata settled down under the seat but as soon as someone sat down beside me she wriggled out to investigate. I shoved her back under the seat and for a while all was well and I even relaxed enough to take an interest in the passing scenery. I was startled by a muffled yelp from the person in front of me and the young lady who had emitted the sound was looking suspiciously under her seat. Tabata had quietly edged her way forward so her head was under the seat in front of us and her wet nose had come into contact with the lady's bare calf causing her consternation as she had not realised there was a dog in the bus. Tabata was encouraged by the sound and immediately reversed out from under the seat, reared up on her hind legs and tried to cement the friendship by climbing over into the seat in front. In desperation I grabbed her scruff and forced her down on the floor again but, of course, she preferred to remain upright so that she could look out of the window.

When we arrived at Rifugio Bedole I waited until everyone was off the bus before allowing Tabata to drag me off behind her. She sensed that a walk was about to happen and was quivering with anticipation. We were greeted by park wardens as most of the area was part of the Adamello Brenta Parco Naturale. One young girl came up to me to explain that the dog should not go free until we were past the open grass area as there were chickens at liberty around the Rifugio Bedole that was just ahead of us. No problem I said. I had already decided that Tabata was going to remain on the lead anyway due to her lack of consideration when walking with other people. I also had visions of a solitary vigil waiting for the wayward animal while the group all vanished into the distance.

We gathered together to listen to our guide. There were thirty-two of us altogether, all different sizes and walking abilities. First we had a talk about the geology of the area and the glaciers that we could see glistening at the tops of the mountains that surrounded us. These mountains, the Presanella Adamello Mountains were composed of granite rather then the dolomite rock of the Brenta Mountains. This granite was still quarried in the area and occasionally a lorry bearing huge chunks of the rock would lumber past us. The peaks above us had been the scene of fierce fighting during the Great War as the front had passed through Trentino and there was still an abandoned canon embedded in one of the glaciers, a testimony to what was referred to as the 'white war'. The Italians had not only had to fight their Austrian enemies but also the extreme conditions and tens of thousands of soldiers perished in avalanches on this front. Written reports suggested that when an avalanche did occur hostilities were suspended while both sides helped to dig each other out of the snow. To this day the retreating ice fields and glaciers have sometimes revealed reminders of this dreadful time and the remains of several unknown *Kaiserjager* and *Alpini* are interred in the sparse soil of these harsh mountains where nature proved to be the deadliest of enemies.

Explanations finished and questions answered then we set off along the waterfall walk. As soon as we go into the trees the hunt was on, the *porcini* hunt that was, and whereas a few minutes earlier I had been right in the middle of a group of people now suddenly I was entirely on my own which was eerie. But it soon became apparent that they all scattered in different directions to search for this treasure. Several were found and carefully wrapped and stowed in rucksacks. This local delicacy is often seen sliced and spread out to dry in the sun outside local restaurants and houses.

I was the only non-Italian in the group but everyone was very friendly and lots of smiles and greetings were bestowed on me. It was a big group and there was a lot of passing and re-passing as people stopped to take pictures, pick wild fruits, rush up banks checking for mushrooms or just overtake the slower walkers. When we stopped at a waterfall I tied Tabata to a wooden fence and went a short way down the bank of the river to take some photographs. She started to bark furiously even though she could see exactly where I was and immediately attracted a sympathetic crowd. I could sense her glancing at me sideways and I am sure I could see a smirk on her face as the Italians murmured endearments at her. The noise did not abate so I had to abandon my attempts at artistic picture making and return to collect my companion. Every time I tied her up and moved away from her we had to go through the greeting and excited to see me routine and it was a while before I could get past the flailing paws to untie the lead. Eventually all was calm and peaceful again and we set off. I decided to walk at the back this time and stay out of everyone's way.

A very short time later we stopped again, this time for lunch at a lovely *rifugio*. I had barely got into my stride and Tabata was still pulling enthusiastically. I unpacked my small picnic and sat down away from the group because Tabata liked to beg for food whenever the opportunity arose so it seemed the safest option. The rest of the group settled down either at tables to eat a restaurant meal or on the grass and picnic benches to eat their packed meals. Several people found themselves deck chairs and a patch of sunlight and got down to the serious business of sunbathing. One couple settled down close to us. Tabata gave them 'the look' when they opened up their sandwiches and was rewarded when they started throwing her food. At least that gave me a chance to eat my cheese and ham rolls without having to fight her off all the time. By the time she realised I was eating as well it was too late!

Now I had a problem. I wanted to go into the *rifugio* to use the toilet but knew that if I left Tabata outside she would start baying again. It had to be done so off I went while she was still casting pleading eyes at the remaining apple strudel on her new friend's plate. I went inside. There was a queue. I listened apprehensively. Nothing but silence, I thought it was strange but welcome.

Finally it was my turn. Silence still reigned. I expected to find a consoling crowd around Tabata when I got back outside but no, there she was all on her own but sitting very close to my rucksack which I had left with her. Maybe that was the answer, to leave my rucksack so she knew I was coming back. On future walks I began to experiment with great success and it clearly reassured her that I would be back so she did not make a noise. She would often pull the rucksack towards her if she felt it was too far away. A well meaning member of my group once picked it up and moved it out of reach and that was rewarded by a volley of yapping that had me flying out of the *rifugio* where we were eating to find out what had happened. No dog! Then I was hailed by a family picnicking nearby. Tabata was in the thick of them enjoying an unexpected lunch.

After an hour we all gathered together again and then set off along the path to the next waterfall. When we arrived at this waterfall there was a beautiful rainbow dancing in the spray and we spent quite a long time taking pictures. This time I dragged Tabata with me and she actually stood still while I composed and took my photographs. An unusual event.

Our next stop was a lovely little church, this was one of the enchantments of walking in this area, unexpected discoveries of real gems on the way. We spent some time looking at the church and the memorial close by to the partisans of the First World War. In the distance we could see the descending white frothy water of la Cascata di Folgarida. We set off again. When I asked the guide how much further we had to go I was surprised to learn it was just twenty minutes to the car park. By now I had decided to walk at the front and this suited Tabata as well as we could go at our own pace.

As we approached the car park we arrived in a clearing that had *ferro via* type activities for children with several cable walkways strung in the trees. We stopped to observe this increasingly popular pastime. When the guides arrived they joined in, as did some children who had been walking with us and we watched as the adults among them revisited their childhood wobbling along the steel cables and whizzing down the pulley. We all parted company here and Stefano and Teresa came over and asked if we could leave immediately as they had an appointment that evening. No problem. We set off for the car park and then made our way back to Madonna di Campiglio. Tabata actually settled down on the floor in the back so I was able to converse with my new friends. I was slightly disappointed that the walk had not included la Cascata di Lares as I had heard that it was the most beautiful of the seven waterfalls in this valley but we had finished our walk just short of the path that led to it. However the following summer a shuttle bus service was initiated that carried people from the centre of Madonna di Campiglio to Malga Bedole so I was able to visit Laris when I took a group to this valley on the *navetta* and we walked back along Val di Genova visiting the various waterfalls and watering holes on our way.

I had visited the first waterfall, la Cascata di Nardis, on many occasions as I would often take my groups to Carisolo on the local bus and after looking around the small weekly market we would walk to the church of Santo Stefano and from there continue along the road to la Cascata di Nardis, a stunning waterfall. On one of these excursions Tabata had joined us and had finally succumbed to wearing the muzzle which was compulsory for dogs on public buses. As she was with me and did not take kindly to being tied up outside anywhere while I explored the interior I sent the group inside the church and waited for them outside. It was a good opportunity to enjoy the sixteenth century fresco depicting the legend of the passage of Charles the Great through this valley. As I was within sight of the main entrance I was sure the group would find me easily. But when nobody had re-appeared thirty minutes later I began to get worried so I did a complete circuit of the church and there was no sign of anybody. I checked the path up to the mound on which a large wooden cross proudly stood and which was also a good viewpoint over the towns of Carisolo and Pinzolo. Nobody there. Retracing my steps I made my way back to the main entrance and was just ascending the steps when the curator came out and started locking the door. Clearly there was no one inside so I must have missed them.

I was surprised that the whole group had come out and got past me without my seeing them but even more surprised that they had clearly decided to continue the walk without wondering where I was. I knew a path that was a short cut to the road we had been following and decided that if I moved quickly I might get to the junction of this path with the road at the same time as the group. Tabata was delighted to have me running along with her instead of constantly reining her in and we bounded along in harmony.

Tabata and I sat for a while at the junction but no one appeared so, assuming they were ahead of me I continued down the road at a brisk pace towards la Cascata di Nardis. What a sight it was, tons of foaming white water tumbling from a great height over huge, shiny black boulders. I stopped to admire and take some photographs. No sign of my group. I crossed the road to the Ristorante la Cascata di Nardis and ordered a coffee from the cheerful waitress who came out to greet me. It was delightful sitting outside enjoying some refreshment, mesmerised by the thundering water. My coffee appeared and I had spent five minutes watching the reflection of the water, like a never-ending video, in the dark glass of the restaurant window when I heard a call and looking up saw my group coming up the road towards me. What a relief! They all sat down and ordered coffees before explaining what had happened. They had spent very little time in the church and when they emerged went back up the same path we had taken to reach the church from the road above. At the junction with the main road they had realised they must have walked past me so they waited there for thirty minutes. This was enough time for me to get ahead of them! We laughed about the incident and then turned to the serious matter of deciding where to have lunch!

By now we were running out of time so we decided to have some lunch and then get a taxi back to Carisolo rather then walking. As the Ristorante la Cascata di Nardis was packed with people and as there was no room inside I enquired if we could eat outside but was informed that food was only served inside unless we ate at their barbecue. Although tempted by the smells drifting across from there we were discouraged by the long queue. Then I remembered that there was a small *rifugio* a little way further along the road. We set off again and after a few minutes reached the Ristorante Chalet di

Gino, such a charming little place with a few tables under large sun umbrellas outside. We sat on a large wooden bench at a big wooden table and were soon happily engrossed in the menu. Tabata, seizing the opportunity that presented itself while I concentrated on the menu tried to sneak through the gap at the back of the bench and take her place on the seat beside us. Needless to say she was soon relegated to the ground again.

Lunch took much longer than we had intended and everyone decided to take a taxi all the way back to the hotel. The look on the face of the taxi driver was enough to convince me that it would be better if Tabata and I completed our journey on foot and public transport so I parted company with the group at this point. While waiting at the bus stop I re-introduced Tabata to the idea of wearing the muzzle and she was clearly not impressed. By the time the bus arrived she had managed to remove it at least three times. Often the driver would not be concerned particularly if there were not many passengers on board but on this occasion I was told very firmly to put the muzzle on. I promised dog and muzzle would be united as soon as I sat down, paid my fare and pushed Tabata onto the floor under the nearest seat before commencing battle. Finally I got the muzzle in place but I had to hold it there as Tabata was equally determined to remove it at as soon as I let go. Gradually her resistance subsided and sighing deeply she relaxed and lay down although she continued to give me her soulful *why are you making me suffer* expression. Realising I was not going to relent she stretched out on the floor under the seat. When the bus turned a sharp bend, of which there were many, Tabata would slide across the floor and then at the next bend she would slide back again. One particularly sharp corner sent her to the edge of the ledge above the rear passenger exit. Anxiously I peered over the back of my seat and I could see that she had lifted her head to survey her surroundings and was now simpering at the oohs and aahs from the passengers around her.

Fortunately on this occasion I had found my way directly to the main road but on several occasions previously when I had taken a group to see the spectacular la Cascata di Nardis, because I hated retracing my steps, I had tried an alternative path through the woods. But it was not possible get into the centre of Pinzolo very easily as it emerged into the valley a long way from the only bridge over the river and one had to walk back on the wrong side of the river before being able to get onto the main road to catch the bus. My various attempts at short cuts had included struggling across a boggy field, being chased by an irate landowner and being charged by an angry horse. But, despite these escapades I had always managed to get my groups safely back to the hotel and it had given us something to laugh about at dinner that evening.

* * *

A sign announced that we had entered the small village of Sant' Antonio di Mavignolo, the last settlement before my destination. The old road between Madonna di Campiglio and Pinzolo passed through this tiny village and it was now a lovely walk and one I had done many times with the keener walkers in my groups. We generally paused for a break by the pretty little church in this village where one could sit for a while enjoying the fabulous views down the valley. Sometimes we would be tempted to drink a coffee outside the small bar on the main road. I had often sat outside this bar when I was on my way down the mountain on the first bus of the morning as the bus would stop and the driver and conductor would jump off and disappear into the interior to drink an *espresso* and munch a *brioche*.

I also recalled the time a small group of us had decided to extend a walk rather than making our way straight back to the hotel with the others who continued with Nereo, our local guide. We parted company at Clemp and set off in the direction of Valchestria. Our path took us way above the valley and through a lovely Alpine meadow where the long green grass was studded with many varieties of brightly coloured wild flowers and brilliant butterflies filled the air around us. It was a wonderfully exhilarating walk and Tabata, who had been brought up to join us at Malga Ritorto where we had lunched was allowed to go free. She had gambolled ahead of us, her plume of tail upright and wagging with pleasure as she bounded back and forth, returning to check we were still behind her and then racing off to investigate interesting smells above or below the path. The sun shone, the sky was blue and we had plenty of time to enjoy the scenery as we strolled along.

Our objective was an old fort perched high up on a ridge which we eventually spotted below us through the trees. Tabata had raced ahead to investigate these remains and my heart was in my mouth as she trotted across a narrow wall with a steep drop on one side and then, totally unperturbed jumped down and raced off again. From the fort it seemed we could see almost the entire length of the road as it threaded its way through Val Rendena. It was a wonderful vantage point and one could understand why the Austrians had built it there to defend the region during the First World War. To reach the ruin we had had to walk along a very narrow path and it was here that I had discovered that one of the group suffered from vertigo. I grabbed Tabata to prevent her racing past everyone, which she loved to do occasionally, and another lady walked beside him on the drop side of the path. We managed to get him along this section of the path but he was adamant that he was not going back that way!

Fortunately I knew an alternative route even though it did mean going almost into the village of Sant' Antonio di Mavignolo and then climbing back up again on a different path. We were all good walkers so I did not anticipate any problems and we set off again, our spirits still high. But, after a short while the sun was suddenly obscured by an ominous black cloud. Large drops of rain began to fall, at first intermittently and then steadily. We stopped and sheltered in the trees for a while hoping it would pass but it just continued and the sky was now a blanket of steel grey, not a speck of blue to be seen. Waterproofs were retrieved from rucksacks and pulled on, hoods raised and then, heads bowed, we plodded on. I revised my plans and decided to continue down to the main road and catch the local bus back up the mountain from Sant' Antonio di Mavignolo rather than walking all the way back in the rain.

By the time we emerged onto the road we were all dripping wet and Tabata was soaked through, her sodden tail curled between her legs and her ears drooping and flattened against her head. Every so often she would look back at me with frank disapproval written all over her face. Making our way along the road we saw a small white car approaching from the opposite direction. The car stopped and the window was wound down revealing the driver who was Nereo, our walking guide. He told us to jump in and he would take us back to the hotel. The car was very small, pristine white and brand new! I told my companions to get in and said I would make my way back to the hotel either on foot or by bus. I could not bear the thought of making a mess of the clean upholstery with a wet, muddy dog. Nereo was very insistent so I picked Tabata up in my arms once the other three were settled in the car. This was not easy as Tabata was a large dog and did not like confinement. I then scrambled into the back and sat there restraining the restless animal by pinning down all four legs with my arms. Somehow I managed to keep her still but at some cost to my waterproof jacket which was now very muddy as well as very wet.

We were soon back at the hotel and I was able to hand Tabata over to a member of staff. I did offer to dry her with a towel if they could find me one but my offer was refused and she was dragged off to be tethered in the drying room while her fur gently steamed dry. I could tell by the looks being cast my way by both the dog and Marino, who had taken charge of her, that I was definitely not in favour!

After a nice hot shower we hung our wet clothes in the drying room where Tabata was still sulking in the corner and then made our way to the bar and a welcome cup of tea. The rain was still lashing down outside. Nereo was leaving the bar as we entered and cheerily waved aside our repeated thanks for rescuing us. Nereo was happy enough as he had had a legitimate opportunity to enjoy a glass of wine before setting off home again.

* * *

My reverie had lasted until the final kilometre of my journey and I began to scan the road anxiously looking for familiar landmarks so that I could ring the bell before the bus sailed past the hotel. Ah, there it was, the pale green walls of the apartment building next to the bus stop could just be seen through the trees. I jumped up and rang the bell. The boot was opened for me and within seconds I was standing by the roadside surrounded by my luggage. Adorned like a Christmas tree with bags round my neck and across my shoulder I started to drag my suitcase along the road towards the hotel. As I approached I could see Goran busy on the veranda collecting the soft cushions from the chairs. He gave me a cheery wave. Then Giacomo appeared with a tray of drinks for guests catching the last rays of sun outside. He too waved and shouted a greeting. As I was making my way across the car park Pietro came out of the main entrance and insisted on carrying my impossibly heavy suitcase inside for me. News of my return must have spread as Sandro and Paolo arrived in the reception area to greet me and tease me as usual. Shortly afterwards Signora Silvana came and welcomed me enthusiastically. It was so good to be back among my very dear friends and back to rejoin that part of my spirit that would reside here for ever.